Early Praise for *Modern C++ Programming with Test-Driven Development*

Jeff Langr has written another excellent book. This time he brings Test-Driven Development to the world of C++. Jeff's starting example brings us face to face with the stark simplicity of good TDD. He explains why we work that way and then provides key practical details, all the way through test doubles, working with legacy code, threading, and more. This one is a keeper for anyone working with C++!

➤ **Ron Jeffries**
  Co-creator of the Extreme Programming methodology

Jeff Langr has written the best C++ book in years. *Modern C++ Programming with Test-Driven Development* is the perfect mixture of theory and practice. The abstractions are explained with clarity and gusto, but the details are right there when you need them. It's sure to be an instant classic, in C++ and in TDD both.

➤ **Michael D. Hill**
  XP coach and writer

Jeff is an expert software craftsman, and in this book he shares his considerable wisdom about crafting great software. This book is not about testing, though you will learn valuable testing techniques. It is about improving your skills, code, products, and life through test-driving. Whether you're a novice, expert, or in between, Jeff will show you the how and the why of an expert who test-drives better products with C++.

➤ **James W. Grenning**
  Author of *Test-Driven Development for Embedded C*

D1425088

Modern C++ Programming with Test-Driven Development

Code Better, Sleep Better

Jeff Langr

The Pragmatic Bookshelf

Dallas, Texas • Raleigh, North Carolina

Many of the designations used by manufacturers and sellers to distinguish their products are claimed as trademarks. Where those designations appear in this book, and The Pragmatic Programmers, LLC was aware of a trademark claim, the designations have been printed in initial capital letters or in all capitals. The Pragmatic Starter Kit, The Pragmatic Programmer, Pragmatic Programming, Pragmatic Bookshelf, PragProg and the linking *g* device are trademarks of The Pragmatic Programmers, LLC.

Every precaution was taken in the preparation of this book. However, the publisher assumes no responsibility for errors or omissions, or for damages that may result from the use of information (including program listings) contained herein.

Our Pragmatic courses, workshops, and other products can help you and your team create better software and have more fun. For more information, as well as the latest Pragmatic titles, please visit us at *http://pragprog.com.*

The team that produced this book includes:

Michael Swaine (editor)
Potomac Indexing, LLC (indexer)
Kim Wimpsett (copyeditor)
David J Kelly (typesetter)
Janet Furlow (producer)
Juliet Benda (rights)
Ellie Callahan (support)

Printed in the United States of America.
ISBN-13: 978-1-937785-48-2
Printed on acid-free paper.
Book version: P1.0—October 2013

Contents

Foreword

Don't let the title mislead you.

I mean, here is a really, really *good* book about design principles, coding practices, Test-Driven Development, and craftsmanship, and they go and give it a title like *Modern C++ Programming with Test-Driven Development*. Sigh.

Oh, don't get me wrong. This *is* a book about modern C++ programming. I mean, if you are a C++ programmer, you're going to love all the code in this book. It's just filled to the brim with really interesting and well-written C++ code. In fact, I think there may be more code than words. Go ahead, thumb through the book. Do you see a page without code on it? Not many I bet! So if you're looking for a good book to teach you modern practices of C++, by example after example after example, then you've got the right book in your hands!

But this book is about a lot more than just modern C++ programming. A *lot* more. First, this book may be the most complete and accessible exposition on Test-Driven Development that I've seen (and I've seen a lot!). Virtually every TDD issue we've uncovered in the last decade and a half is talked about in these pages, from fragile tests to mocks, from the London school to the Cleveland school, and from Single Assert to Given-When-Then. It's all here, plus a whole lot more. Moreover, it's not some academic compendium of disconnected issues. No, this book walks through the issues in the context of examples and case studies. It shows the problems and the solutions in *code*.

Do you need to be a C++ programmer to understand it? Of course you don't. The C++ code is so clean and is written so well and the concepts are so clear that any Java, C#, C, or even Ruby programmer will have no trouble at all.

And then there are the design principles! For goodness sake, this book is a design tutorial! It takes you on a step-by-step voyage through principle after principle, issue after issue, and technique after technique. From the Single Responsibility Principle to the Dependency Inversion Principle, from the Interface Segregation Principle to the Agile principles of simple design, from

DRY to Tell-Don't-Ask—this book is a gold mine of software design ideas and solutions. And again, these ideas are presented in the context of real problems and real solutions in real code.

And then there are the coding practices and techniques. This book is just chock-full of them, from small methods to pair programming and from coding katas to variable names. Not only is there a ton of code from which to glean all these good practices and techniques, but the author drives each point home with just the right amount of discussion and elaboration.

No, the title of this book is all wrong. It's not a book about C++ programming. It's a book about good software craftsmanship that just happens to use C++ as the language for its examples. The name of this book should really be *Software Craftsmanship: With Examples in Modern C++*.

So if you are a Java programmer, if you are a C# programmer, if you are a Ruby, Python, PHP, VB, or even a COBOL programmer, you want to read this book. Don't let the C++ on the cover scare you. Read the book anyway. And while you are at it, read the code. You won't find it hard to understand. And while you are learning good design principles, coding techniques, craftsmanship, and Test-Driven Development, you might also discover that a little C++ never hurt anybody.

—"Uncle Bob" Martin
Founder, Object Mentor Inc.

Introduction

Despite the current explosion in programming languages, C++ soldiers on. It is the fourth-most popular programming language, per the July 2013 Tiobe index. (You can find the latest index at http://www.tiobe.com/index.php/content/paper-info/tpci/index.html.) The 2011 ISO standard (ISO/IEC 14822:2011, aka C++11) brings features to C++ that may increase its acceptance...or at least soften objections against its use.

C++ remains one of your best choices for building high-performance solutions. If your company's products integrate with hardware, chances are you have a sizeable existing system built in C++. If your company has been around since the 1990s or earlier, chances are you have a long-lived C++ system, and chances are also good that it's not disappearing anytime in the next several years.

Given that you're now working in C++, you might be thinking one of the following things:

- It's 2013. Why am I back in this difficult (but entertaining) language that I thought I'd abandoned years ago? How am I going to survive without shooting myself in the foot?

- I'm a seasoned C++ pro, I know this powerful language like the back of my hand, and I've been developing successfully for years. Why would I need to change how I work?

- Where's my paycheck?

My personal sentiment is that I first worked with C++ around the early 1990s, before the rise of things like templates (and template metaprogramming!), RTTI, STL, and Boost. Since then, I've had a few occasions where I've had to return to the powerful language and have done so with some dismay. Like any language, C++ allows you to shoot yourself in the foot—but with C++, you sometimes don't realize you shot yourself until it's too late. And you're probably missing more toes than folks working with other languages.

If you've been working with C++ for years, you likely have adopted many idioms and practices to help ensure your code remains of high quality. Die-hard C++ veterans are some of the more careful programmers across all languages because surviving in C++ for so long requires meticulous care and attention to the code you craft.

With all this care taken, one might think that the code quality on C++ systems should be high. Yet most C++ systems exhibit the same problems we all see time and time again, usually regardless of language.

- Monstrous source files with thousands of lines
- Member functions with hundreds or thousands of lines of inscrutable code
- Volumes of dead code
- Build times extending into several hours
- High numbers of defects
- Logic too convoluted by quick fixes to be safely managed
- Code duplicated across files, classes, and modules
- Code riddled with long-obsolete coding practices

Is this decay inevitable? No! Test-Driven Development is a tool you can master and wield in order to help stave off system entropy. It may even reinvigorate your passion for programming.

If you're simply seeking a paycheck, there are plenty of C++ jobs out there that will keep you employed. However, C++ is a highly technical and nuanced language. Wielding it carelessly will lead to defects, intermittent failures, and possibly multiday debugging sessions—factors that can put your paycheck at risk. TDD can help.

The effort required to add new functionality on such large, long-lived C++ systems usually disappoints and often is inestimable. Simply understanding a passage of code in order to change a few lines of code can take hours, even days. Productivity is further drained as developers wait hours to determine whether their changes compiled and wait even longer to see whether they integrated well with the remainder of the system.

It doesn't have to be this way. *Test-Driven Development* (TDD), a software design technique devised in the late 1990s, can help you wrestle your C++ system to the ground and keep it under control as you continue adding new features. (Notions of writing tests before code have been around for considerably longer. However, the TDD cycle in its formal, disciplined form was devised by Ward Cunningham and Kent Beck [*Test Driven Development: By Example* [Bec02]].)

The primary intent for this book is to teach you a disciplined approach for the practical application of TDD. You'll learn the following:

- The fundamental mechanics of TDD
- The potential benefits of TDD
- How TDD helps you address design deficiencies as they arise
- The challenges and costs of doing TDD
- How TDD can reduce or even eliminate debugging sessions
- How to sustain TDD over time

But Can It Work for Me on My System?

"What's all this fuss about unit testing? It doesn't seem to be helping me much."

You might have already tried unit testing. Perhaps you are currently struggling with writing unit tests against your legacy system. Maybe it seems like TDD is OK for those rare other souls fortunate enough to be working on a new system. But does it solve your day-to-day problems of working on a long-entrenched, challenging C++ system?

Indeed, TDD is a useful tool but is no silver bullet for dealing with legacy systems. While you can test-drive many of the new features you add to your system, you'll also need to begin chipping away at the years of accumulated cruft. You'll need additional strategies and tactics for a sustained cleanup approach. You'll need to learn about tactical dependency-breaking techniques and safe code change approaches that Michael Feathers presents in the essential book *Working Effectively with Legacy Code [Fea04]*. You'll need to understand how to approach large-scale refactorings without creating large-scale issues. For that, you'll learn about the *Mikado Method [BE12]*. This book will teach such supportive practices and more.

Simply adding unit tests for code you've already written (something I call *Test-After Development* [TAD]) usually has little impact as you struggle with "this is just how the system is." You might invest thousands of person-hours in writing tests with little measurable impact to system quality.

If you allow TDD to help you shape your systems, your designs will by definition be testable. They will also be different—in many ways, better—than if you did not use TDD. The more you understand what a good design should look like, the more TDD will help guide you there.

To aid you in shifting how you think about design, this book emphasizes principles that underlie good code management, such as the SOLID principles of object-oriented design described in *Agile Software Development, Principles, Patterns, and Practices [Mar02]*. I discuss how this sense of good design supports ongoing development and productivity and how TDD can help a mindful developer achieve more consistent and reliable results.

Who This Book Is For

This book is written to help C++ programmers of all skill levels, from novices with a fundamental understanding of the language to old salts steeped in language esoterica. If you've been away from C++ for some time, you'll find that the rapid feedback cycles of TDD will help you rapidly reramp up on the language.

While the goal of this book is to teach TDD, you will find value in this book regardless of your TDD experience. If you are a complete novice to the concept of writing unit tests for your code, I'll take you small step by small step through the basics of TDD. If you are fairly new to TDD, you'll discover a wealth of expert advice throughout the book, all presented in simple fashion with straightforward examples. Even seasoned test-drivers should find some useful nuggets of wisdom, a stronger theoretical basis for the practice, and some new topics for exploration.

If you are a skeptic, you'll explore TDD from several angles. I'll inject my thoughts throughout about why I think TDD works well, and I'll also share experiences about when it didn't work so well and why. The book is not a sales brochure but an eyes-open exploration of a transformative technique.

Readers of all stripes will also find ideas for growing and sustaining TDD on their team. It's easy to get started with TDD, but your team will encounter many challenges along the way. How can you prevent these challenges from derailing your transition effort? How do you prevent such disasters? I present some ideas that I've seen work well in *Growing and Sustaining TDD*.

What You'll Need

To code any of the examples in this book, you'll need a compiler, of course, and a unit testing tool. Some of the examples also require third-party libraries. This section overviews these three elements. You'll want to refer to *Global Setup* for further details around what you'll need.

A Unit Testing Tool

Out of the dozens of available C++ unit testing tools, I chose Google Mock (which sits atop Google Test) for most of the examples in this book. It currently returns the most hits on a web search, but I primarily chose it because it supports Hamcrest notation (a matcher-based assertion form designed to provide highly expressive tests). The information in *Global Setup* will help you come up to speed on Google Mock.

However, this book is neither a comprehensive treatise nor a sales brochure for Google Mock. It is instead a book that teaches the discipline of TDD. You'll learn enough Google Mock to practice TDD effectively.

You'll also use another unit testing tool named CppUTest for some of the examples. You'll find that it's fairly easy to learn another unit testing tool, which should help ease any concerns you might have if you're not using Google Mock or CppUTest.

If you are using a different unit testing tool such as CppUnit or Boost.Test, no worries! These other tools work much like Google Mock in concept and are often similar in implementation. You can easily follow along and do the TDD examples using virtually any of the other C++ unit testing tools available. See *Comparing Unit Testing Tools* for a discussion of what's important in choosing a unit testing tool.

Most examples in this book use Google Mock for mocking and stubbing (see *Test Doubles*). Of course, Google Mock and Google Test work together, but you might also be able to integrate Google Mock successfully with your unit testing tool of choice.

A Compiler

You'll need access to a C++ compiler with support for C++11. The book example code was originally built using gcc and works out of the box on Linux and Mac OS. See *Global Setup* for information about building the example code on Windows. All examples use the STL, an essential part of modern C++ development for many platforms.

Third-Party Libraries

Some of the examples use freely available third-party libraries. Refer to *Global Setup* for the specific list of libraries you'll need to download.

How to Use This Book

I designed the chapters in the book to function as stand-alone as possible. You should be able to pick up a random chapter and work through it without having to fully read any other chapters. I provide ample cross-references throughout to allow you to jump around easily if you're using an ereader.

Each chapter begins with a quick overview and ends with a chapter summary plus a preview of the next chapter. I chose the names of these brief sections to correspond cutely to the initialization and cleanup sections used by many unit test frameworks—"Setup" and "Teardown."

The Source

The book contains numerous code examples. Most of the code presented will reference a specific filename. You can find the complete set of example code for this book at http://pragprog.com/book/lotdd/modern-c-programming-with-test-driven-development and also at my GitHub page, http://github.com/jlangr.

Within the code distribution, examples are grouped by chapter. Within the directory for each chapter, you will find numbered directories, each number effectively referring to a version number (which allows the book to use and show examples of code changing as you progress through each chapter). As an example, the code with caption c2/7/SoundexTest.cpp refers to the file Soundex-Test.cpp located in the seventh revision of the Chapter 2 (c2) code directory.

Book Discussion

Please join the discussion forum at https://groups.google.com/forum/?fromgroups#!forum/modern-cpp-with-tdd. The intent for the forum is to discuss the book as well as doing TDD in C++ in general. I will also post useful information regarding the book.

If You Are New to TDD: What's in the Book

While this book is geared to all, its primary focus is on programmers new to TDD, so its chapters are in a correspondingly sequential order. I highly recommend you work through the exercise in *Test-Driven Development: A First Example*. It will give you a strong feel for many of the ideas behind TDD as you work through a meaty example. Don't just read—type along and make sure your tests pass when they should!

The next two chapters, *Test-Driven Development Foundations* and *Test Construction*, are also essential reading. They cover core ideas about what TDD is (and is not) and how to construct your tests. Make sure you're comfortable with the material in these chapters before learning about mocks (see the *Test Doubles* chapter), a technique essential to building most production systems.

Don't skip the chapter on design and refactoring (*Incremental Design*) just because you think you know what that means. An essential reason to practice TDD is to enable you to evolve your design and keep your code clean continually through refactoring. Most systems exhibit poor design and difficult code, partly because developers aren't willing to refactor enough or don't know how.

You'll learn what's far enough and how to start reaping the potential benefits of a smaller, simpler system.

To wrap up core TDD techniques, *Quality Tests* takes a look at a number of ways to improve your return on investment in TDD. Learning some of these techniques can make the difference between surviving and thriving in TDD.

You'll of course be saddled with the struggles of an existing system that wasn't test-driven. You can get a jump start on some simple techniques to tackle your legacy code by reading *Legacy Challenges*.

Just past the legacy code material, you'll find a chapter dedicated to test-driving multithreaded code. The test-driven approach to TDD may surprise you.

The next chapter, *Additional TDD Concepts and Discussions*, dives deeper into fairly specific areas and concerns. You'll discover some up-to-date ideas around TDD, including some alternate approaches that differ from what you'll find elsewhere in this book.

Finally, you'll want to know what it takes to get TDD going in your team, and you'll of course want to make sure you're able to sustain your investment in TDD. The last chapter, *Growing and Sustaining TDD*, provides some ideas that you will want to incorporate into your shop.

If You Have Some Experience with TDD

You can probably get away with picking up chapters at random, but you'll find a lot of nuggets of hard-earned wisdom strewn throughout the book.

Conventions Used in This Book

Any sizeable code segment will appear separately from the text. When the text refers to code elements, the following conventions are used:

- A *ClassName* will appear in the same font as normal text ("text font") and will be UpperCamelCase.
- A *TestName* will also appear in the text font and be UpperCamelCase.
- All other code elements will appear in a code (nonproportional) font. Examples of these include the following:
  - functionName() (which will show an empty argument list, even if it refers to a function declaring one or more parameters). I will sometimes refer to member functions as *methods*.
  - variableName
  - keyword
  - All other code snippets

To keep things simple and waste fewer pages, code listings will often omit code irrelevant to the current discussion. A comment followed by ellipses represents obscured code. For example, the body of the for loop is replaced in this code snippet:

```
for (int i = 0; i < count; i++) {
    // ...
}
```

About "Us"

I wrote this book to be a dialogue between us. Generally I'm talking to you, as the reader. When I (ideally infrequently) refer to myself, it's usually to describe an experience-based opinion or preference. The implication is that it might not be a widely accepted concept (but it could be a fine idea!).

When it gets down to coding, I'd rather you didn't have to work alone, particularly since you're trying to learn. *We* will work through all of the coding exercises in the book together.

About Me

I've been programming since 1980, my junior year in high school, and professionally since 1982 (I worked at the University of Maryland while pursuing my BS in computer science). I transitioned from programmer to consultant in 2000, when I had the joy of working for Bob Martin and occasionally alongside some great folks at Object Mentor.

I started Langr Software Solutions in 2003 to provide consulting and training solutions related to Agile software development. Much of my work is either pairing with developers doing TDD or teaching it. I insist on alternating between consulting/training and being a "real" programmer on a real development team so that I stay up-to-date and relevant. Since 2002, I have been a full-time programmer in four different companies for significant durations.

I love writing about software development. It's part of how I learn things in depth, but I also enjoy helping others come up to speed on building quality code. This is my fourth book. I wrote *Essential Java Style: Patterns for Implementation [Lan99]* and *Agile Java: Crafting Code With Test-Driven Development [Lan05]*, and I co-wrote *Agile in a Flash [OL11]* with Tim Ottinger. I also contributed a couple chapters to Uncle Bob's *Clean Code: A Handbook of Agile Software Craftsmanship [Mar08]*. I've written more than a hundred articles published at sites other than mine. I write regularly for my own blog (at http://langrsoft.com/jeff) and have written or contributed to more than a hundred blog entries for the Agile in a Flash project at http://agileinaflash.com.

In addition to C++, I've programmed in several other languages extensively: Java, Smalltalk, C, C#, and Pascal, plus one other that shall remain unmentioned. I'm currently learning Erlang and can code enough Python and Ruby to survive. I've played with at least another dozen or so languages to see what they were like (or to support some short-lived effort).

About the C++ Style in This Book

While I have extensive experience on C++ systems of all sizes, ranging from small to extremely large, I don't consider myself a language expert. I've read the important books by Meyers and Sutter, plus a few more. I know how to make C++ work for me and how to make the resulting code expressive and maintainable. I'm aware of most of the esoteric corners of the language but purposefully avoid solutions requiring them. My definition for *clever* in the context of this book is "difficult to maintain." I'll steer you in a better direction.

My C++ style is very object-oriented (no doubt because of a lot of programming in Smalltalk, Java, and C#). I prefer that most code ends up scoped to a class. Most of the examples in this book fall in line with this style. For example, the Soundex code from the first example (see *Test-Driven Development: A First Example*) gets built as a class, but it doesn't need to be. I like it that way, but if it wads yer underwear, do it your way.

TDD can provide value regardless of your C++ style, so don't let my style turn you off to its potential. However, a heavier OO emphasis makes introducing test doubles (see *Test Doubles*) easier when you must break problematic dependencies. If you immerse yourself in TDD, you'll likely find that your style shifts more in this direction over time. It's not a bad thing!

I'm a little lazy. Given the relatively small scope of the examples, I chose to minimize the use of namespaces, though I would certainly incorporate them on any real production code effort.

I also prefer to keep my code as streamlined as possible and thus avoid what I sometimes view as visual clutter. In most implementation files, you'll find `using namespace std;` for this reason, although many consider that bad form. (Keeping your classes and functions small and focused makes this and other guidelines such as "All functions should have only one return" less useful.) No worries; TDD won't prevent you from sticking to your own standards, and neither will I.

A final word on C++: it's a big language. I'm certain there are better ways to code some of the examples in the book, and I would bet that there are library constructs I'm not taking advantage of. The beauty of TDD is that you'll be able to rework an implementation a dozen different ways without fear of breaking something. Regardless, please send me your suggestions for improvement, but only if you're willing to test-drive them!

Acknowledgments

Thanks to my editor, Michael Swaine, and the great folks at PragProg for the guidance and resources needed to create this book.

Thanks, Uncle Bob, for the exuberant foreword!

Many thanks to Dale Stewart, my technical editor, for providing valuable assistance throughout the process, particularly feedback and help on the C++ code throughout the book.

I always ask for brutally honest feedback during the writing process, and Bas Vodde provided exactly that, supplying me with voluminous feedback on the entire book. He was the invisible pair partner I needed to keep the conversation honest.

Special thanks to Joe Miller, who painstakingly converted most of the examples so that they will build and run on Windows.

Many thanks to all the other folks who provided ideas or invaluable feedback: Steve Andrews, Kevin Brothaler, Marshall Clow, Chris Freeman, George Dinwiddie, James Grenning, Michael Hill, Jeff Hoffman, Ron Jeffries, Neil Johnson, Chisun Joung, Dale Keener, Bob Koss, Robert C. Martin, Paul Nelson, Ken Oden, Tim Ottinger, Dave Rooney, Tan Yeong Sheng, Peter Sommerlad, and Zhanyong Wan. My apologies if I missed anyone.

Thank you to those who supplied feedback on the PragProg errata page: Bradford Baker, Jim Barnett, Travis Beatty, Kevin Brown, Brett DiFrischia, Jared Grubb, David Pol, Bo Rydberg, Jon Seidel, Marton Suranyi, Curtis Zimmerman, and many others.

Thanks again to Tim Ottinger, who supplied some of the words in the introduction plus a few ideas for the book. I missed having you as a co-conspirator!

Thank you all for helping make this book better than I could ever hope to make it on my own!

Dedication

This book is dedicated to those who continue to support me in doing what I love, particularly my wife, Kathy.

## CHAPTER 1

Global Setup

1.1 Setup

Getting everything installed and working can be among the more painful tasks in any software endeavor. In this chapter, you'll learn what tools you will need in order to build and execute the examples contained in the book. You'll learn a few relevant tips that may help prevent you from tripping over the same things I did.

This chapter currently includes setup instructions for Linux and Mac OS. If you are a Windows C++ programmer, refer to the information in *Windows*, on page 3, for recommendations.

1.2 The Examples

You can download the source files for the book from http://pragprog.com/titles/lotdd/ source_code. The examples are grouped by chapter.

Much of what you will learn about TDD involves incrementally growing code. As such, the examples you'll see within each chapter present incremental versions of the code. The versions correspond to numbered subdirectories (1, 2, 3, ...) within the directory for the chapter. For example, the first code snippet in *Test-Driven Development: A First Example* is c2/1/SoundexTest.cpp; it shows the first version of the file SoundexTest.cpp. The second version appears as c2/2/SoundexTest.cpp.

You can also find the example code at GitHub (https://github.com/jlangr). At GitHub, you will find a repository for each relevant book chapter. For example, the repository named c2 corresponds to the Soundex example built in the second chapter of the book.

The version number for a given code snippet shown in the book corresponds to a branch within a GitHub repository. For example, you can find code for the listing c5/4/PlaceDescriptionService.cpp in the file PlaceDescriptionService.cpp in the branch named 4 in the c5 repository.

Within each version directory you will find the necessary source, including a main function to run tests and a CMake build script. You will need to install and configure a few tools to run any examples. Some examples require the installation of additional third-party libraries.

You will need a C++11-compliant compiler and make utility in order to build the examples. Most require Google Mock as the unit testing tool. Examples from three chapters use another unit testing tool named CppUTest.

You might want to change the source distribution to support other compilers (or pre-C++11 compilers), incorporate a different build tool, or use a different unit testing tool. Fortunately, most of the example codebases are small, with the exception of the library code used in the *Quality Tests* chapter.

The following table identifies the subdirectory, unit testing tool, and additional third-party libraries required for the examples in each chapter.

Chapter	Directory	Unit Testing Tool	Third-Party Libraries
Test-Driven Development: A First Example	c2	Google Mock	None
Test-Driven Development Foundations	c3	Google Mock	None
Test Construction	c3	Google Mock	None
Test Doubles	c5	Google Mock	cURL, JsonCpp
Incremental Design	c6	Google Mock	Boost (gregorian)
Quality Tests	c7	Google Mock	Boost (gregorian, algorithm, assign)
Legacy Challenges	wav	CppUTest	rlog, Boost (filesystem)
TDD and Threading	c9	CppUTest	None
Additional TDD Concepts and Discussions	tpp	CppUTest	None
Code Kata: Roman Numeral Converter	roman	Google Mock	None

1.3   C++ Compiler

Ubuntu

I originally built the examples in this book on Ubuntu 12.10 using g++ 4.7.2.

Install g++ using the following command:

```
sudo apt-get install build-essential
```

OS X

I successfully built the examples in this book on Mac OS X 10.8.3 (Mountain Lion) using a gcc port. The version of gcc shipped with Xcode at the time of this writing, 4.2, will not successfully compile the C++ examples in this book.

To install the gcc port, you may need to install MacPorts, an infrastructure that allows you to install free software onto your Mac. Refer to http://www.mac-ports.org/install.php for further information.

You will want to first update MacPorts.

```
sudo port selfupdate
```

Install the gcc port using the following command:

```
sudo port install gcc47
```

This command may take a considerable amount of time to execute.

(If you prefer, you can specify the +universal variant at the end of the port command, which will enable compiling binaries for both PowerPC and Intel architectures.)

Once you have successfully installed the gcc port, indicate that its installation should be the default.

```
sudo port select gcc mp-gcc47
```

You may want to add the command to the path name list.

```
hash gcc
```

Windows

On Windows, your best bet for getting the code working *as it appears in this book* (and thus as it appears in the source distribution) is to consider a MinGW or Cygwin port of g++. Other avenues for exploration include the Microsoft Visual C++ Compiler November 2012 CTP and Clang, but at the time of this writing they do not provide sufficient support for the C+11 standard. This subsection will give a brief overview of some of the challenges and suggestions associated with getting the examples to run on Windows.

Visual C++ Compiler November 2012 CTP

You can download a community technology preview (CTP) release of the Visual C++11 compiler.[1] A Visual C++ Team Blog entry[2] describes the release.

A cursory look at using the CTP for this book's examples quickly revealed a few things.

- In-class member initialization does not yet appear to be fully supported.

- Support for C++11 appears to be most deficient in the std library. For example, the collection classes do not yet support uniform initializer lists. There also appears to be no implementation for std::unordered_map.

- Google Mock/Google Test uses variadic templates, which are not yet fully supported. You will receive a compilation error when building Google Mock. You'll need to add an entry to your preprocessor definitions that sets _VARIADIC_MAX to 10 for all affected projects. Refer to http://stackoverflow.com/questions/12558327/google-test-in-visual-studio-2012 for further information on how to get past this problem.

Windows Example Code

As this book approaches final publication, efforts are underway to create working Windows code examples (by eliminating unsupported C++11 elements). You can find the reworked examples as a separate set of repositories at my GitHub page (https://github.com/jlangr), one repository per chapter. Refer to the Google Group discussion forum at https://groups.google.com/forum/?fromgroups#!forum/modern-cpp-with-tdd for further information about Windows examples as they get posted.

The Windows GitHub repositories contain solution (.sln) and project (.vcxproj) files. You should be able to use these files to load example code in Visual Studio Express 2012 for Windows Desktop. You can also use MSBuild to build and run tests for the examples from the command line.

If you want to rework the code examples on your own, it shouldn't be too horrible an experience. Changing to out-of-class initialization should be easy. You can replace std::unordered_map with std::map. And many of the new

---

1.   http://www.microsoft.com/en-us/download/details.aspx?id=35515

2.   http://blogs.msdn.com/b/vcblog/archive/2012/11/02/visual-c-c-11-and-the-future-of-c.aspx

additions to C++11 originated in the boost::tr1 library, so you might be able to directly substitute the Boost implementations.

A Few Windows Tips

I Googled my way through a number of roadblocks in the form of compilation warnings, errors, and other build challenges. Here are a few things I learned along the way:

Error/Challenge	Resolution
C297: 'std:tuple': too many template arguments.	Add preprocessor definition for _VARIADIC_MAX=10. See http://stackoverflow.com/questions/8274588/c2977-stdtuple-too-many-template-arguments-msvc11.
Specified platform toolset (v110) is not installed or invalid.	Set VisualStudioVersion 11.0.
Where is msbuild.exe?	Mine is in c:\Windows\Microsoft.NET\Framework\v4.0.30319.
Warning C4996: 'std::_Copy_impl': Function call with parameters that may be unsafe.	-D_SCL_SECURE_NO_WARNINGS
Console windows closes on completion of running tests with Ctrl-F5.	Set Configuration Properties→Linker→System→SubSystem to Console (/SUBSYSTEM:CONSOLE).
Visual Studio tries to autolink libraries for header-only Boost features.	Add BOOST_ALL_NO_LIB preprocessor directive.

Many of the resolutions for these challenges are already embodied in the project files.

Visual Studio 2013 Previews

Shortly before my final deadline for book changes, Microsoft released preview downloads for Visual Studio 2013, which promises additional compliance with the C++11 standard as well as support for some proposed C++14 features. In the short term, the Windows code at the GitHub site will work under the November 2012 CTP. But you'll soon find updated versions that take even more advantage of C++11 as we (myself and a few great folks helping out) work with them under Visual Studio 2013. I'm hoping you eventually don't find Windows-specific versions at all. Here's to a fully C++11-compliant Windows compiler!

1.4 CMake

For better or worse, I chose CMake in an attempt to support cross-platform builds.

For Ubuntu users, the version used for building the examples is CMake 2.8.9. You can install CMake using the following command:

```
sudo apt-get install cmake
```

For OS X users, the version used for building the examples is CMake 2.8.10.2. You can install CMake using downloads at http://www.cmake.org/cmake/resources/software.html.

When you run CMake against the build scripts provided, you might see the following error:

```
Make Error: your CXX compiler: "CMAKE_CXX_COMPILER-NOTFOUND" was not found.
Please set CMAKE_CXX_COMPILER to a valid compiler path or name.
```

The message indicates that no appropriate compiler was found. You might receive the error if you installed gcc and not g++. On Ubuntu, installing build-essential should solve the problem. On OS X, defining or changing the definition for CXX should solve the problem.

```
export CC=/opt/local/bin/x86_64-apple-darwin12-gcc-4.7.2
export CXX=/opt/local/bin/x86_64-apple-darwin12-g++-mp-4.7
```

1.5 Google Mock

Google Mock, used in many of the book's examples, is a mocking and matcher framework that includes the unit testing tool Google Test. I refer to the two terms interchangeably throughout the book but most of the time refer to Google Mock to keep things simple. You may need to peruse Google's documentation for Google Test in order to understand features that I refer to as belonging to Google Mock.

You will be linking Google Mock into your examples, which means you must first build the Google Mock library. The following instructions may help you get started. You might also choose to refer to the README.txt file supplied with Google Mock for more detailed installation instructions: https://code.google.com/p/googlemock/source/browse/trunk/README.

Installing Google Mock

The official Google Mock site is https://code.google.com/p/googlemock/. You can find downloads at https://code.google.com/p/googlemock/downloads/list. The version used for building the examples is Google Mock 1.6.0.

Unzip the installation zip file (for example, gmock-1.6.0.zip), perhaps in your home directory.

Create an environment variable called GMOCK_HOME that refers to this directory. Here's an example:

```
export GMOCK_HOME=/home/jeff/gmock-1.6.0
```

Here it is on Windows:

```
setx GMOCK_HOME c:\Users\jlangr\gmock-1.6.0
```

Unix

For Unix, if you want to skip the README build instructions, you might also have success by following the steps I took. I chose to build Google Mock using CMake. From the root of your Google Mock installation ($GMOCK_HOME, hence-forth), do the following:

```
mkdir mybuild
cd mybuild
cmake ..
make
```

The build directory name mybuild is arbitrary. However, the build scripts used by the examples in the book assume this name. If you change it, you'll need to alter all of the CMakeLists.txt files.

You will also need to build Google Test, which is nested within Google Mock.

```
cd $GMOCK_HOME/gtest
mkdir mybuild
cd mybuild
cmake ..
make
```

Windows

Within the Google Mock distribution, you'll find the file .\msvc\2010\gmock.sln, which should work for Visual Studio 2010 and newer versions. (You'll also find .\msvc\2005.gmock.sln, which should presumably work for Visual Studio 2005 and 2008.)

To compile Google Mock from Visual Studio 2010 and Visual Studio 2012, you will need to configure the projects to use the November 2012 CTP. From the project properties, navigate to Configuration Properties→General→Platform Toolset and select the CTP.

The CTP does not have support for variadic templates (Visual Studio 2013 *might*). They are instead artificially simulated.[3] You will need to add a preprocessor definition to bump up _VARIADIC_MAX above its default of 5. A value of 10 should work fine.

When creating projects that use Google Mock, you'll need to point them to the proper location for include and library files. Under Configuration Properties→VC++ Directories, do the following:

- Add $(GMOCK_HOME)\msvc\2010\Debug to Library Directories.
- Add $(GMOCK_HOME)\include to Include Directories.
- Add $(GMOCK_HOME)\gtest\include to Include Directories.

Under Linker→Input, add gmock.lib to Additional Dependencies.

You'll want to ensure that both Google Mock and your project are built with the same memory model. By default, Google Mock builds using /MTd.

Creating a Main for Running Google Mock Tests

Code for each of the examples in this book includes a main.cpp file designed for use with Google Mock.

c2/1/main.cpp
```
#include "gmock/gmock.h"

int main(int argc, char** argv) {
    testing::InitGoogleMock(&argc, argv);
    return RUN_ALL_TESTS();
}
```

The main() function shown here first initializes Google Mock, passing along any command-line arguments. It then runs all of the tests.

Most of the time, this is all you need in main(). Google Mock also provides a default main() implementation that you can link to. Refer to http://code.google.com/p/googletest/wiki/Primer#Writing_the_main()_Function for further information.

1.6 CppUTest

CppUTest is another C++ unit testing framework that you might choose over Google Test/Google Mock. It offers many comparable features, plus provides a built-in memory leak detector. You can see more examples of CppUTest in *Test Driven Development for Embedded C [Gre10]* by James Grenning.

---

3. http://stackoverflow.com/questions/12558327/google-test-in-visual-studio-2012

Installing CppUTest

(Note: These instructions apply to CppUTest version 3.3. The newest version, 3.4, incorporates a number of changes, but was released just prior to my final deadline for major changes, preventing me from incorporating use of it into this book.)

You can find the project home for CppUTest at http://www.cpputest.org/, and you can find downloads at http://cpputest.github.io/cpputest/. Download the appropriate file and unpack, perhaps into a new directory named pputest within your home directory.

Create a CPPUTEST_HOME environment variable. Here's an example:

```
export CPPUTEST_HOME=/home/jeff/cpputest
```

You can build CppUTest using make. You will also need to build CppUTestExt, which provides mocking support.

```
cd $CPPUTEST_HOME
./configure
make
make -f Makefile_CppUTestExt
```

You can install CppUTest to /usr/local/lib using the command make install.

You can build CppUTest using CMake if you choose.

If you are running Windows, you will also find batch files for Visual Studio 2008 and 2010 that use MSBuild.

Creating a Main for Running CppUTest Tests

Code for the WAV Reader example in this book includes a testmain.cpp file designed for use with CppUTest.

wav/1/testmain.cpp
```cpp
#include "CppUTest/CommandLineTestRunner.h"

int main(int argc, char** argv) {
    return CommandLineTestRunner::RunAllTests(argc, argv);
}
```

1.7   libcurl

libcurl provides a client-side URL transfer library that supports HTTP and many other protocols. It supports the cURL command-line transfer tool. I refer to the library as cURL elsewhere in the book.

You can find the project home for cURL at http://curl.haxx.se/, and you can find downloads at http://curl.haxx.se/download.html. Download the appropriate file and unpack, perhaps into your home directory. Create a CURL_HOME environment variable; here's an example:

```
export CURL_HOME=/home/jeff/curl-7.29.0
```

You can build the library using CMake.

```
cd $CURL_HOME
mkdir build
cd build
cmake ..
make
```

1.8 JsonCpp

JsonCpp provides support for the data interchange format known as Java-Script Object Notation (JSON).

You can find the project home for JsonCpp at http://jsoncpp.sourceforge.net/, and you can find downloads at http://sourceforge.net/projects/jsoncpp/files/. Download the appropriate file and unpack, perhaps into your home directory. Create a JSONCPP_HOME environment variable; here's an example:

```
export JSONCPP_HOME=/home/jeff/jsoncpp-src-0.5.0
```

JsonCpp requires Scons, a Python build system. To install Scons under Ubuntu, use this:

```
sudo apt-get install scons
```

Navigate into $JSONCPP_HOME and use Scons to build the library.

```
scons platform=linux-gcc
```

For OS X, specifying a platform of linux-gcc worked for my install.

For my installation, building JsonCpp resulted in the creation of $JSON-CPP_HOME/libs/linux-gcc-4.7/libjson_linux-gcc-4.7_libmt.a. Create a symbolic link to this file with the following name:

```
cd $JSONCPP_HOME/libs/linux-gcc-4.7
ln -s libjson_linux-gcc-4.7_libmt.a libjson_linux-gcc-4.7.a
```

1.9 rlog

rlog provides a message logging facility for C++.

You can find the project home for rlog at https://code.google.com/p/rlog/. Download the appropriate file and unpack, perhaps into your home directory. Create an environment variable for RLOG_HOME. Here's an example:

```
export RLOG_HOME=/home/jeff/rlog-1.4
```

Under Ubuntu, you can build rlog using the following commands:

```
cd $RLOG_HOME
./configure
make
```

Under OS X, I was able to compile rlog only after applying a patch. See https://code.google.com/p/rlog/issues/detail?id=7 for information about the issue as well as the patch code. I used the code provided in the third comment ("This smaller diff..."). You can also find this patch code in the source distribution as code/wav/1/rlog.diff.

To apply the patch and build rlog, do the following:

```
cd $RLOG_HOME
patch -p1 [path to file]/rlog.diff
autoreconf
./configure
cp /opt/local/bin/glibtool libtool
make
sudo make install
```

The configure command copies a binary named libtool into the rlog directory, but it is *not* the binary that rlog expects. The command that copies glibtool atop libtool should correct this problem.

If the patch does not work for you, you can try making manual modifications. In the file $RLOG_HOME/rlog/common.h.in, you will find the following line:

```
# define RLOG_SECTION __attribute__ (( section("RLOG_DATA") ))
```

Replace that line with the following:

```
#ifdef _APPLE_
# define RLOG_SECTION __attribute__ (( section("__DATA, RLOG_DATA") ))
#else
# define RLOG_SECTION __attribute__ (( section("RLOG_DATA") ))
#endif
```

If you *still* have problems building rlog (it's quite the challenge under both MacOS and Windows), don't worry. When working through the legacy code example, skip ahead to Section 8.9, *Creating a Test Double for rlog,* on page 207, where you'll learn how to get rlog out of the mix entirely.

1.10 Boost

Boost provides a large set of essential C++ libraries.

You can find the project home for Boost at http://www.boost.org, and you can find downloads at http://sourceforge.net/projects/boost/files/boost. Boost is updated regularly to newer versions. Download the appropriate file and unpack, perhaps into your home directory. Create environment variables for both BOOST_ROOT and the Boost version you installed. Here's an example:

```
export BOOST_ROOT=/home/jeff/boost_1_53_0
export BOOST_VERSION=1.53.0
```

Many Boost libraries require only header files. Following the preceding instructions should allow you to build all of the examples that use Boost, with the exception of the code in *Legacy Challenges*.

To build the code in *Legacy Challenges*, you will need to build and link libraries from Boost. I used the following commands to build the appropriate libraries:

```
cd $BOOST_ROOT
./bootstrap.sh --with-libraries=filesystem,system
./b2
```

The commands I executed might work for you, but in the event they do not, refer to the instructions at http://ubuntuforums.org/showthread.php?t=1180792 (note, though, that the bootstrap.sh argument --with-library should be --with-libraries).

1.11 Building Examples and Running Tests

Once you've installed the appropriate software, you can build any of the example versions and subsequently execute tests. From within an example version directory, you'll first use CMake to create a makefile.

```
mkdir build
cd build
cmake ..
```

The legacy codebase (see *Legacy Challenges*) uses *libraries* from Boost, not just headers. CMakeLists.txt uses the BOOST_ROOT environment variable you defined twice: first, explicitly, by include_directories to indicate where Boost headers can be found, and second, implicitly, when CMake executes find_package to locate Boost libraries.

When building the legacy codebase, you might receive an error indicating that Boost cannot be found. If so, you can experiment with changing the location by passing a value for BOOST_ROOT when you execute CMake.

```
cmake -DBOOST_ROOT=/home/jeff/boost_1_53_0 ..
```

Otherwise, ensure that you have built the Boost libraries correctly.

Once you have created a make file using CMake, you can build an example by navigating into the example's build directory and then executing the following:

```
make
```

To execute tests, navigate into the example's build directory and then execute the following:

```
./test
```

For the library example in *Quality Tests*, you will find the test executable in build/libraryTests.

1.12 Teardown

In this chapter, you learned what you'll need in order to build and run the examples in this book. Remember that you'll learn best when you get your hands dirty and follow along with the examples.

If you get stuck with setting things up, first find a trusty pair partner to help. A second set of eyes can quickly spot something that you might struggle with for quite a while. You can also visit the book's home page at http://pragprog.com/titles/lotdd for helpful tips and a discussion forum. If you and your pair are both still stuck, please send me an email.

## CHAPTER 2

Test-Driven Development: A First Example

2.1 Setup

Write a test, get it to pass, clean up the design. That's all there is to TDD. Yet these three simple steps embody a significant amount of sophistication. Understand how to take advantage of TDD, and you will be rewarded with many benefits. Fail to heed what others have learned, and you will likely give up on TDD.

Rather than let you flounder, I'd like to guide you through test-driving some code in order to help you understand what happens at each step. You'll learn best by coding along with the example in this chapter. Make sure you've set up your environment properly (see Chapter 1, *Global Setup*, on page 1).

While not large, the example we'll work through isn't useless or trivial (but it's also not rocket science). It provides many teaching points and demonstrates how TDD can help you incrementally design a reasonably involved algorithm.

I hope you're ready to code!

2.2 The Soundex Class

Searching is a common need in many applications. An effective search should find matches even if the user misspells words. Folks misspell my name in endless ways: Langer, Lang, Langur, Lange, and Lutefisk, to name a few. I'd prefer they find me regardless.

In this chapter, we will test-drive a Soundex class that can improve the search capability in an application. The long-standing Soundex algorithm encodes words into a letter plus three digits, mapping similarly sounding words to the same encoding. Here are the rules for Soundex, per Wikipedia:[1]

---

1. http://en.wikipedia.org/wiki/Soundex

1. Retain the first letter. Drop all other occurrences of *a, e, i, o, u, y, h, w*.

2. Replace consonants with digits (after the first letter):

   - *b, f, p, v:* 1
   - *c, g, j, k, q, s, x, z:* 2
   - *d, t* : 3
   - *l:* 4
   - *m, n:* 5
   - *r:* 6

3. If two adjacent letters encode to the same number, encode them instead as a single number. Also, do so if two letters with the same number are separated by *h* or *w* (but code them twice if separated by a vowel). This rule also applies to the first letter.

4. Stop when you have a letter and three digits. Zero-pad if needed.

2.3 Getting Started

A common misconception of TDD is that you first define *all* the tests before building an implementation. Instead, you focus on one test at a time and incrementally consider the next behavior to drive into the system from there.

As a general approach to TDD, you seek to implement the next simplest rule in turn. (For a more specific, formalized approach to TDD, refer to the TPP [Section 10.4, *The Transformation Priority Premise*, on page 281].) What useful behavior will require the most straightforward, smallest increment of code to implement?

With that in mind, where do we start with test-driving the Soundex solution? Let's quickly speculate as to what implementing each rule might entail.

Soundex rule #3 appears most involved. Rule #4, indicating when to stop encoding, would probably make more sense once the implementation of other rules actually resulted in something getting encoded. The second rule hints that the first letter should already be in place, so we'll start with rule #1. It seems straightforward.

The first rule tells us to retain the first letter of the name and...*stop*! Let's keep things as small as possible. What if we have *only* a single letter in the word? Let's test-drive that scenario.

c2/1/SoundexTest.cpp
```
Line 1 #include "gmock/gmock.h"
     2 TEST(SoundexEncoding, RetainsSoleLetterOfOneLetterWord) {
     3     Soundex soundex;
     4 }
```

Test Lists

Each test you write in TDD and get to pass represents a new, working piece of behavior that you add to the system. Aside from getting an entire feature shipped, your passing tests represent your best measure of progress. You name each test to describe the small piece of behavior.

While you don't determine all the tests up front, you'll probably have an initial set of thoughts about what you need to tackle. Many test-drivers capture their thoughts about upcoming tests in a *test list* (described first in *Test Driven Development: By Example [Bec02]*). The list can contain names of tests or reminders of code cleanup that you need to do.

You can keep the test list on a scratch pad on the side of your workstation. (You could also type it at the bottom of your test file as comments—just make sure you delete them before checking in!) The list is yours alone, so you can make it as brief or cryptic as you like.

As you test-drive and think of new test cases, add them to the list. As you add code you know will need to be cleaned up, add a reminder to the list. As you complete a test or other task, cross it off the list. It's that simple. If you end up with outstanding list items at the end of your programming session, set the list aside for a future session.

You might think of the test list as a piece of initial design. It can help you clarify what you think you need to build. It can also help trigger you to think about other things you need to do.

Don't let the test list constrain what you do or the order in which you do it, however. TDD is a fluid process, and you should usually go where the tests suggest you go next.

Managing test lists can be particularly useful when you're learning TDD. Try it!

- On line 1, we include gmock, which gives us all the functionality we'll need to write tests.

- A simple test declaration requires use of the TEST macro (line 2). The TEST macro takes two parameters: the name of the test case and a descriptive name for the test. A *test case*, per Google's documentation, is a related collection of tests that can "share data and subroutines."[2] (The term is overloaded; to some, a test case represents a single scenario.)

Reading the test case name and test name together, left to right, reveals a sentence that describes what we want to verify: "Soundex encoding retains [the] sole letter of [a] one-letter word." As we write additional tests

---

2. http://code.google.com/p/googletest/wiki/V1_6_Primer#Introduction:_Why_Google_C++_Testing_Framework?

for Soundex encoding behavior, we'll use SoundexEncoding for the test case name to help group these related tests.

Don't discount the importance of crafting good test names—see the following sidebar.

The Importance of Test Names

Take great care with naming. The small investment of deriving highly descriptive test names pays well over time, as tests are read and reread by others who must maintain the code. Crafting a good test name will also help you, the test writer, better understand the intent of what you're about to build.

You'll be writing a number of tests for each new behavior in the system. Think about the set of test names as a concordance that quickly provides a developer with a concise summary of that behavior. The easier the test names are to digest, the more quickly you and other developers will find what you seek.

• On line 3, we create a Soundex object, then...stop! Before we proceed with more testing, we know we've just introduced code that won't compile—we haven't yet defined a Soundex class! We'll stop coding our test and fix the problem before moving on. This approach is in keeping with Uncle Bob's Three Rules of TDD:

  – Write production code only to make a failing test pass.

  – Write no more of a unit test than sufficient to fail. Compilation failures are failures.

  – Write only the production code needed to pass the one failing test.

(*Uncle Bob* is Robert C. Martin. See Section 3.4, *The Three Rules of TDD*, on page 59 for more discussion of the rules.)

Seeking incremental feedback can be a great approach in C++, where a few lines of test can generate a mountain of compiler errors. Seeing an error as soon as you write the code that generates it can make it easier to resolve.

The three rules of TDD aside, you'll find that sometimes it makes more sense to code the entire test before running it, perhaps to get a better feel for how you should design the interface you're testing. You might also find that waiting on additional slow compiles isn't worth the trade-off in more immediate feedback.

For now, particularly as you are learning TDD, seek feedback as soon as it can be useful. Ultimately, it's up to you to decide how incrementally you approach designing each test.

The compiler shows that we indeed need a Soundex class. We could add a compilation unit (.h/.cpp combination) for Soundex, but let's make life easier for ourselves. Instead of mucking with separate files, we'll simply declare everything in the same file as the test.

Once we're ready to push our code up or once we experience pain from having everything in one file, we'll do things the proper way and split the tests from the production code.

`c2/2/SoundexTest.cpp`

```
➤ class Soundex {
➤ };

#include "gmock/gmock.h"

TEST(SoundexEncoding, RetainsSoleLetterOfOneLetterWord) {
    Soundex soundex;
}
```

> *Q.: Isn't putting everything into a single file a dangerous shortcut?*
>
> *A.: It's a calculated effort to save time in a manner that incurs no short-term complexity costs. The hypothesis is that the cost of splitting files later is less than the overhead of flipping between files the whole time. As you shape the design of a new behavior using TDD, you'll likely be changing the interface often. Splitting out a header file too early would only slow you down.*
>
> *As far as "dangerous" is concerned: are you ever going to forget to split the files before checking in?*
>
> *Q.: But aren't you supposed to be cleaning up code as you go as part of following the TDD cycle? Don't you want to always make sure that your code retains the highest possible quality?*
>
> *A.: In general, yes to both questions. But our code is fine; we're simply choosing a more effective organization until we know we need something better. We're deferring complexity, which tends to slow us down, until we truly need it. (Some Agile proponents use the acronym YAGNI—"You ain't gonna need it.")*
>
> *If the notion bothers you deeply, go ahead and separate the files right off the bat. You'll still be able to follow through with the rest of the exercise. But I'd prefer you first try it this way. TDD provides you with safe opportunities to challenge yourself, so don't be afraid to experiment with what you might find to be more effective ways to work.*

We're following the third rule for TDD: write only enough production code to pass a test. Obviously, we don't have a complete test yet. The Retains-SoleLetterOfOneLetterWord test doesn't really execute any behavior, and it doesn't verify anything. Still, we can react to each incremental bit of negative feedback (in this case, failing compilation) and respond with just enough code to get past the negative feedback. To compile, we added an empty declaration for the Soundex class.

Building and running the tests at this point gives us positive feedback.

```
[==========] Running 1 test from 1 test case.
[----------] Global test environment set-up.
[----------] 1 test from SoundexEncoding
[ RUN      ] SoundexEncoding.RetainsSoleLetterOfOneLetterWord
[       OK ] SoundexEncoding.RetainsSoleLetterOfOneLetterWord (0 ms)
[----------] 1 test from SoundexEncoding (0 ms total)

[----------] Global test environment tear-down
[==========] 1 test from 1 test case ran. (0 ms total)
[  PASSED  ] 1 test.
```

Party time!

Well, not quite. After all, the test does nothing other than construct an instance of the empty Soundex class. Yet we have put some important elements in place. More importantly, we've proven that we've done so correctly.

Did you get this far? Did you mistype the include filename or forget to end the class declaration with a semicolon? If so, you've created your mistake within the fewest lines of code possible. In TDD, you practice safe coding by testing early and often, so you usually have but one reason to fail.

Since our test passes, it might be a good time to make a local commit. Do you have the right tool? A good version control system allows you to commit easily every time the code is *green* (in other words, when all tests are passing). If you get into trouble later, you can easily revert to a known good state and try again.

Part of the TDD mentality is that every passing test represents a proven piece of behavior that you've added to the system. It might not always be something you could ship, of course. But the more you think in such incremental terms and the more frequently you seek to integrate your locally proven behavior, the more successful you'll be.

Moving along, we add a line of code to the test that shows how we expect client code to interact with Soundex objects.

c2/3/SoundexTest.cpp

```
TEST(SoundexEncoding, RetainsSoleLetterOfOneLetterWord) {
    Soundex soundex;

➤    auto encoded = soundex.encode("A");
}
```

We are making decisions as we add tests. Here we decided that the Soundex class exposes a public member function called encode() that takes a string argument. Attempting to compile with this change fails, since encode() doesn't exist. The negative feedback triggers us to write just enough code to get everything to compile and run.

c2/4/SoundexTest.cpp

```
class Soundex
{
➤ public:
➤    std::string encode(const std::string& word) const {
➤        return "";
➤    }
};
```

The code compiles, and all the tests pass, which is still not a very interesting event. It's finally time to verify something useful: given the single letter A, can encode() return an appropriate Soundex code? We express this interest using an *assertion*.

c2/5/SoundexTest.cpp

```
TEST(SoundexEncoding, RetainsSoleLetterOfOneLetterWord) {
    Soundex soundex;

    auto encoded = soundex.encode("A");

➤    ASSERT_THAT(encoded, testing::Eq("A"));
}
```

An assertion verifies whether things are as we expect. The assertion here declares that the string returned by encode() is the same as the string we passed it. Compilation succeeds, but we now see that our first assertion has failed.

```
[==========] Running 1 test from 1 test case.
[----------] Global test environment set-up.
[----------] 1 test from SoundexEncoding
[ RUN      ] SoundexEncoding.RetainsSoleLetterOfOneLetterWord
SoundexTest.cpp:21: Failure
Value of: encoded
Expected: is equal to 0x806defb pointing to "A"
  Actual: "" (of type std::string)
[  FAILED  ] SoundexEncoding.RetainsSoleLetterOfOneLetterWord (0 ms)
[----------] 1 test from SoundexEncoding (0 ms total)
```

```
[----------] Global test environment tear-down
[==========] 1 test from 1 test case ran. (0 ms total)
[  PASSED  ] 0 tests.
[  FAILED  ] 1 test, listed below:
[  FAILED  ] SoundexEncoding.RetainsSoleLetterOfOneLetterWord

 1 FAILED TEST
```

At first glance, it's probably hard to spot the relevant output from Google Mock. We first read the very last line. If it says "PASSED," we stop looking at the test output—all our tests are working! If it says "FAILED" (it does in our example), we note how many test cases failed. If it says something other than "PASSED" or "FAILED," the test application itself crashed in the middle of a test.

With one or more failed tests, we scan upward to find the individual test that failed. Google Mock prints a [RUN] record with each test name when it starts and prints a [FAILED] or [OK] bookend when the test fails. On failure, the lines between [RUN] and [OK] might help us understand our failure. In the output for our first failed test shown earlier, we see the following:

```
[ RUN      ] SoundexEncoding.RetainsSoleLetterOfOneLetterWord
SoundexTest.cpp:21: Failure
Value of: encoded
Expected: is equal to 0x806defb pointing to "A"
  Actual: "" (of type std::string)
[  FAILED  ] SoundexEncoding.RetainsSoleLetterOfOneLetterWord (0 ms)
```

Paraphrasing this assertion failure, *Google Mock expected the local variable encoded to contain the string* "A", *but the actual string it contained was equal to the empty string.*

We expected a failing assertion, since we deliberately hard-coded the empty string to pass compilation. That negative feedback is a good thing and part of the TDD cycle. We want to first ensure that a newly coded assertion—representing functionality we haven't built yet—doesn't pass. (Sometimes it does, which is usually not a good thing; see Section 3.5, *Getting Green on Red*, on page 60.) We also want to make sure we've coded a legitimate test; seeing it first fail and then pass when we write the appropriate code helps ensure our test is honest.

The failing test prods us to write code, no more than necessary to pass the assertion.

```
c2/6/SoundexTest.cpp
std::string encode(const std::string& word) const {
    return "A";
}
```

We compile and rerun the tests. The final two lines of its output indicate that all is well.

```
[==========] 1 test from 1 test case ran. (0 ms total)
[  PASSED  ] 1 test.
```

Ship it!

I'm kidding, right? Well, no. We want to work incrementally. Let's put it this way: if someone told us to build a Soundex class that supported encoding only the letter *A*, we'd be done. We'd want to clean things up a little bit, but otherwise we'd need no additional logic.

Another way of looking at it is that the tests specify all of the behavior that we have in the system to date. Right now we have one test. Why would we have any more code than what that test states we need?

We're not done, of course. We have plenty of additional needs and requirements that we'll incrementally test-drive into the system. We're not even done with the current test. We *must, must, must* clean up the small messes we just made.

2.4 Fixing Unclean Code

What? We wrote one line of production code and three lines of test code and we have a problem? Indeed. It's extremely easy to introduce deficient code even in a small number of lines. TDD provides the wonderful opportunity to fix such small problems as they arise, before they add up to countless small problems (or even a few big problems).

We read both the test and production code we've written, looking for deficiencies. We decide that the assertion in our test isn't reader-friendly.

```
ASSERT_THAT(encoded, testing::Eq("A"));
```

Much as the test declaration (the combination of test case and test name) should read like a sentence, we want our asserts to do the same. We introduce a using directive to help.

```
c2/7/SoundexTest.cpp
#include "gmock/gmock.h"
using ::testing::Eq;

TEST(SoundexEncoding, RetainsSoleLetterOfOneLetterWord) {
    Soundex soundex;
    auto encoded = soundex.encode("A");
    ASSERT_THAT(encoded, Eq("A"));
}
```

Now we can paraphrase the assertion with no hiccups: *assert that the encoded value is equal to the string "A"*.

Our small change is a *refactoring*, a code transformation in which we retain existing behavior (as demonstrated by the test) but improve the design. In this case, we improved the test's design by enhancing its expressiveness. The namespace of Eq() is an implementation detail not relevant to the test's meaning. Hiding that detail improves the level of abstraction in the test.

Code duplication is another common challenge we face. The costs and risks of maintenance increase with the amount of code duplication.

Our Soundex class contains no obvious duplication. But looking at both the test and production code in conjunction reveals a common magic literal, the string "A". We want to eliminate this duplication. Another problem is that the test name (RetainsSoleLetterOfOneLetterWord) declares a general behavior, but the implementation supports only a specific, single letter. We want to eliminate the hard-coded "A" in a way that solves both problems.

How about simply returning the word passed in?

```
c2/8/SoundexTest.cpp
class Soundex
{
public:
    std::string encode(const std::string& word) const {
        return word;
    }
};
```

At any given point, your complete set of tests declares the behaviors you intend your system to have. That implies the converse: if no test describes a behavior, it either doesn't exist or isn't intended (or the tests do a poor job of describing behavior).

Where am I going with this? We have one test. It says we support one-letter words. Therefore, we can assume that the Soundex code needs to support only one-letter words—for now. And if all words are one letter, the simplest generalized solution for our test is to simply return the whole word passed to encode().

(There are other TDD schools of thought about what we might have coded at this point. One alternate technique is *triangulation*[3]—see *Triangulation*, on page 283—where you write a second, similar assertion but with a different data expectation in order to drive in the generalized solution. You'll discover more alternate approaches throughout the book, but we'll keep things simple for now.)

Our changes here are small, bordering on trivial, but now is the time to make them. TDD's refactoring step gives us an opportunity to focus on all issues, significant or minor, that arise from a small, isolated code change. As we drive through TDD cycles, we'll use the refactoring step as our opportunity to review the design impacts we just made to the system, fixing any problems we just created.

Our primary refactoring focus will be on increasing expressiveness and eliminating duplication, two concerns that will give us the most benefit when it comes to creating maintainable code. But we'll use other nuggets of design wisdom as we proceed, such as SOLID class design principles and code smells.

2.5 Incrementalism

It's question-and-answer (Q&A) time!

> *Q.:* *Do you really code like this, hard-coding things that you know you'll replace?*

> *A.:* *I always get this question. Yes.*

> *Q.:* *It seems stupid!*

> *A.:* *That's not a question, but yes, it's an OK first reaction to think this is stupid. It felt stupid to me at first, too. I got over it.*

> *Q.:* *Are we going to keep working like this? How will we get anything done if we hard-code everything?*

> *A.:* *That's two questions, but I'm happy to answer them both! Yes, we will keep working incrementally. This technique allows us to get a first passing test in place quickly. No worries, the hard-coded value will last only minutes at most. We know we're not done with what we need to build, so we'll have to write more tests to describe additional behavior. In this example, we know we must support the rest of the rules. As we write additional tests, we'll have to replace the hard-coding with interesting logic in order to get the additional tests to pass.*

---

3. *Test Driven Development: By Example [Bec02]*

Incrementalism is at the heart of what makes TDD successful. An incremental approach will seem quite unnatural and slow at first. However, taking small steps will increase your speed over time, partly because you will avoid errors that arise from taking large, complicated steps. Hang in there!

Astute readers will note that we've already coded something that does not completely meet the specification (*spec*) for Soundex. The last part of rule #4 says that we must "fill in zeros until there are three numbers." Oh, the joy of specs! We must read them comprehensively and carefully to fully understand how all their parts interact. (Better that we had a customer to interact with, someone who could clarify what was intended.) Right now it seems like rule #4 contradicts what we've already coded.

Imagine that the rules are being fed to us one by one. "Get the first part of rule #1 working, and then I'll give you a new rule." TDD aligns with this latter approach—each portion of a spec is an incremental addition to the system. An incremental approach allows us to build the system piecemeal, in any order, with continually verified, forward progress. There is a trade-off: we might spend additional time incorporating a new increment than if we had done a bit more planning. We'll return to this concern throughout the book. For now, let's see what happens when we avoid worrying about it.

We have two jobs: write a new test that describes the behavior, and change our existing test to ensure it meets the spec. Here's our new test:

`c2/9/SoundexTest.cpp`
```cpp
TEST(SoundexEncoding, PadsWithZerosToEnsureThreeDigits) {
    Soundex soundex;

    auto encoded = soundex.encode("I");

    ASSERT_THAT(encoded, Eq("I000"));
}
```

(One reviewer asks, "Why didn't we read the Soundex rules more carefully and write this first?" Good question. Indeed, we weren't careful. A strength of TDD is its ability to let you move forward in the face of incomplete information and in its ability to let you correct earlier choices as new information arises.)

Each test we add is independent. We don't use the outcome of one test as a precondition for running another. Each test must set up its own context. Our new test creates its own Soundex instance.

A failing test run shows that encode() returns the string "I" instead of "I000". Getting it to pass is straightforward.

```
c2/9/SoundexTest.cpp
std::string encode(const std::string& word) const {
    return word + "000";
}
```

Hard-coding an answer may again ruffle feathers, but it will help us keep on track. Per our tests so far, the Soundex class requires no additional behavior. Also, by building the smallest possible increment, we're forced to write additional tests in order to add more behavior to the system.

Our new test passes, but the first test we wrote now fails. The behavior it describes, by example, does not match the specification we derived from Wikipedia.

When done test-driving, you'll know that the tests correctly describe how your system works, as long as they pass. They provide examples that can read easier than specs, if crafted well. We'll continue to focus on making the tests readable in our exercises (and I might even casually refer to them as specs).

```
c2/9/SoundexTest.cpp
TEST(SoundexEncoding, RetainsSoleLetterOfOneLetterWord) {
    Soundex soundex;

    auto encoded = soundex.encode("A");

    ASSERT_THAT(encoded, Eq("A000"));
}
```

That wasn't too tough!

We now have two tests that perform the same steps, though the data differs slightly. That's OK; each test now discretely documents one piece of behavior. We not only want to make sure the system works as expected, we want everyone to understand its complete set of intended behaviors.

It's time for refactoring. The statement in encode() isn't as clear about what's going on as it could be. We decide to extract it to its own method with an intention-revealing name.

```
c2/10/SoundexTest.cpp
public:
    std::string encode(const std::string& word) const {
        return zeroPad(word);
    }

private:
    std::string zeroPad(const std::string& word) const {
        return word + "000";
    }
```

2.6 Fixtures and Setup

Not only do we want to look at production code for refactoring opportunities, we want to look at the tests, too. Both our tests require the same line of code to create a Soundex instance. We're not happy with even such seemingly trivial duplication. It adds up quickly and often turns into more complex duplication. It also clutters the tests, detracting from what's important for a reader to understand.

It's common for related tests to need common code. Google Mock lets us define a *fixture* class in which we can declare functions and member data for a related set of tests. (Technically, all Google Mock tests use a fixture that it generates behind the scenes.)

```
c2/10/SoundexTest.cpp
class SoundexEncoding: public testing::Test {
public:
    Soundex soundex;
};

TEST_F(SoundexEncoding, RetainsSoleLetterOfOneLetterWord) {
    auto encoded = soundex.encode("A");

    ASSERT_THAT(encoded, Eq("A000"));
}

TEST_F(SoundexEncoding, PadsWithZerosToEnsureThreeDigits) {
    auto encoded = soundex.encode("I");

    ASSERT_THAT(encoded, Eq("I000"));
}
```

We create the SoundexEncoding fixture (which must derive from ::testing::Test) so that creating a Soundex instance gets done in one place. Within the fixture, we declare a soundex member variable and make it public so that the tests have visibility to it. (If you're concerned about exposing soundex, remember that our fixture class lives in a .cpp file. We'd prefer to avoid every piece of unnecessary clutter in our tests.)

Google Mock instantiates the fixture class *once per test*. Before Google Mock executes RetainsSoleLetterOfOneLetterWord, it creates a SoundexEncoding instance, and before it executes PadsWithZerosToEnsureThreeDigits, it creates a separate SoundexEncoding instance. To code a custom fixture, we change the TEST macro invocation to TEST_F, with the F standing for "Fixture." If we forget to use TEST_F, any test code attempting to use fixture member errors will fail compilation.

We delete the local declarations of soundex, since the member is available to each test. We make this change incrementally. After coding the fixture and changing the macro, we delete the local declaration of soundex from the first test. We run all the tests to verify the change, remove the declaration from the second test, and run all the tests again.

Getting rid of the duplicate Soundex declaration does at least a couple things.

- It increases the *abstraction* level of our tests. We now see only two lines in each test, which allows us to focus on what's relevant. We *don't* see the irrelevant detail of how the Soundex object gets constructed (see Section 7.4, *Test Abstraction*, on page 181 for more information on why this is important).

- It can reduce future maintenance efforts. Imagine we have to change how we construct Soundex objects (perhaps we need to be able to specify a language as an argument). Moving Soundex construction into the fixture means we would need to make our change in only one place, as opposed to making the change across several tests.

With only two lines each, our tests are a little easier to read. What else might we do? We can reduce each test to a single line without losing any readability. I'm also not a fan of explicit using directives, so we clean that up too.

`c2/11/SoundexTest.cpp`
```cpp
#include "gmock/gmock.h"
#include "Soundex.h"

using namespace testing;

class SoundexEncoding: public Test {
public:
   Soundex soundex;
};

TEST_F(SoundexEncoding, RetainsSoleLetterOfOneLetterWord) {
   ASSERT_THAT(soundex.encode("A"), Eq("A000"));
}

TEST_F(SoundexEncoding, PadsWithZerosToEnsureThreeDigits) {
   ASSERT_THAT(soundex.encode("I"), Eq("I000"));
}
```

You'll note that the test now refers to Soundex.h. Having the tests and code in a single file was helpful for a short while. Now, the bouncing up and down in a single file is getting old. We split into the test and the header (we'll decide whether we should create an .impl file when we're done). Here's the header:

```
c2/11/Soundex.h
#ifndef Soundex_h
#define Soundex_h
#include <string>

class Soundex
{
public:
    std::string encode(const std::string& word) const {
        return zeroPad(word);
    }

private:
    std::string zeroPad(const std::string& word) const {
        return word + "000";
    }
};

#endif
```

2.7 Thinking and TDD

The cycle of TDD, once again in brief, is to write a small test, ensure it fails, get it to pass, review and clean up the design (including that of the tests), and ensure the tests all still pass. You repeat the cycle throughout the day, keeping it short to maximize the feedback it gives you. Though repetitive, it's not mindless—at each point you have many things to think about. *Thinking and TDD*, on page 58, contains a list of questions to answer at each small step.

To keep things moving, I'll assume you're following the steps of the cycle and remind you of them only occasionally. You may want to tack to your monitor a handy reminder card of the cycle.

For our next test, we tackle rule #2 ("replace consonants with digits after the first letter"). A look at the replacement table reveals that the letter *b* corresponds to the digit *1*.

```
c2/12/SoundexTest.cpp
TEST_F(SoundexEncoding, ReplacesConsonantsWithAppropriateDigits) {
    ASSERT_THAT(soundex.encode("Ab"), Eq("A100"));
}
```

The test fails as expected.

```
Value of: soundex.encode("Ab")
Expected: is equal to 0x80b8a5f pointing to "A100"
  Actual: "Ab000" (of type std::string)
```

As with most tests we will write, there might be infinite ways to code a solution, out of which maybe a handful are reasonable. Technically, our only job is to make the test pass, after which our job is to clean up the solution.

However, the implementation that we seek is one that generalizes our solution —but does not over-generalize it to support additional concerns—and doesn't introduce code that duplicates concepts already coded.

You could provide the following solution, which would pass all tests:

```
std::string encode(const std::string& word) const {
    if (word == "Ab") return "A100";
    return zeroPad(word);
}
```

That code, though, does not move toward a more generalized solution for the concern of replacing consonants with appropriate digits. It also introduces a duplicate construct: the special case for "Ab" resolves to zero-padding the text "A1", yet we already have generalized code that handles zero-padding any word.

You might view this argument as weak, and it probably is. You could easily argue any of the infinite alternate approaches for an equally infinite amount of time. But TDD is not a hard science; instead, think of it as a craftperson's tool for incrementally growing a codebase. It's a tool that accommodates continual experimentation, discovery, and refinement.

We'd rather move forward at a regular pace than argue. Here's our solution that sets the stage for a generalized approach:

c2/13/Soundex.h
```
std::string encode(const std::string& word) const {
➤    auto encoded = word.substr(0, 1);
➤
➤    if (word.length() > 1)
➤        encoded += "1";
➤    return zeroPad(encoded);
}
```

We run the tests, but our new test does not pass.

```
Expected: is equal to 0x80b8ac4 pointing to "A100"
  Actual: "A1000" (of type std::string)
```

The padding logic is insufficient. We must change it to account for the length of the encoded string.

c2/14/Soundex.h

```
std::string zeroPad(const std::string& word) const {
➤    auto zerosNeeded = 4 - word.length();
➤    return word + std::string(zerosNeeded, '0');
}
```

Our tests pass. That's great, but our code is starting to look tedious. Sure, we know how encode() works, because we built it. But someone else will have to spend just a little more time to carefully read the code in order to understand its intent. We can do better than that. We refactor to a more declarative solution.

c2/15/Soundex.h

```
class Soundex
{
public:
    std::string encode(const std::string& word) const {
➤        return zeroPad(head(word) + encodedDigits(word));
    }

private:
➤    std::string head(const std::string& word) const {
➤        return word.substr(0, 1);
➤    }

➤    std::string encodedDigits(const std::string& word) const {
➤        if (word.length() > 1) return "1";
➤        return "";
➤    }

    std::string zeroPad(const std::string& word) const {
    // ...
    }
};
```

We're fleshing out the algorithm for Soundex encoding, bit by bit. At the same time, our refactoring helps ensure that the core of the algorithm remains crystal clear, uncluttered by implementation details.

Structuring code in this declarative manner makes code considerably easier to understand. Separating interface (what) from implementation (how) is an important aspect of design and provides a springboard for larger design choices. You want to consider similar restructurings every time you hit the refactoring step in TDD.

Some of you may be concerned about a few things in our implementation details. First, shouldn't we use a stringstream instead of concatenating strings? Second, why not use an individual char where possible? For example, why not replace return word.substr(0, 1); with return word.front();? Third, wouldn't it perform better to use return std::string(); instead of return "";?

These code alternatives might all perform better. But they all represent premature optimization. More important now is a good design, with consistent interfaces and expressive code. Once we finish implementing correct behavior with a solid design, we might or might not consider optimizing performance (but not without first measuring; see Section 10.2, *TDD and Performance*, on page 269 for a discussion about handling performance concerns).

Premature performance optimizations aside, the code does need a bit of work. We eliminate the code smell of using a *magic literal* to represent the maximum length of a Soundex code by replacing it with an appropriately named constant.

c2/16/Soundex.h
```
static const size_t MaxCodeLength{4};
// ...
std::string zeroPad(const std::string& word) const {
    auto zerosNeeded = MaxCodeLength - word.length();
    return word + std::string(zerosNeeded, '0');
```

What about the hard-coded string "1" in encodedDigits()? Our code needs to translate the letter *b* to the digit *1*, so we can't eliminate it using a variable. We could introduce another constant, or we could return the literal from a function whose name explains its meaning.

We could even leave the hardcoded string "1" in place to be driven out by the next test. But can we guarantee we'll write that test before integrating code? What if we're distracted? Coming back to the code, we'll waste a bit more time deciphering what we wrote. Keeping with an incremental delivery mentality, we choose to fix the problem now.

c2/17/Soundex.h
```
std::string encodedDigits(const std::string& word) const {
    if (word.length() > 1) return encodedDigit();
    return "";
}
std::string encodedDigit() const {
    return "1";
}
```

2.8 Test-Driving vs. Testing

We need to test-drive more of the consonant conversion logic in order to generalize our solution. Should we add an assertion to ReplacesConsonantsWithAppropriateDigits, or should we create an additional test?

The rule of thumb for TDD is one assert per test (see Section 7.3, *One Assert per Test*, on page 178 for more information on this guideline). It's a good idea that promotes focusing on the behavior of the tests, instead of centering tests around functions. We will follow this rule most of the time.

An assertion that represents encoding a second consonant doesn't seem like distinct behavior. Were we to create a new test, how would we name it? ReplacesBWith1, ReplacesCWith2, and so on...yuk!

We make the rare choice of adding a second assertion, representing a discrete test case, to the test. We'd prefer that if one assertion fails, the others still execute. To accomplish that goal, we use the EXPECT_THAT macro provided by Google Mock, instead of ASSERT_THAT.

c2/18/SoundexTest.cpp
```
TEST_F(SoundexEncoding, ReplacesConsonantsWithAppropriateDigits) {
    EXPECT_THAT(soundex.encode("Ab"), Eq("A100"));
    EXPECT_THAT(soundex.encode("Ac"), Eq("A200"));
}
```

The second consonant drives in the need for an if statement to handle the special case.

c2/18/Soundex.h
```
std::string encodedDigits(const std::string& word) const {
    if (word.length() > 1) return encodedDigit(word[1]);
    return "";
}

std::string encodedDigit(char letter) const {
    if (letter == 'c') return "2";
    return "1";
}
```

We add a third data case.

c2/19/SoundexTest.cpp
```
TEST_F(SoundexEncoding, ReplacesConsonantsWithAppropriateDigits) {
    EXPECT_THAT(soundex.encode("Ab"), Eq("A100"));
    EXPECT_THAT(soundex.encode("Ac"), Eq("A200"));
    EXPECT_THAT(soundex.encode("Ad"), Eq("A300"));
}
```

The need for a third consonant makes it clear that we need to replace the if with a hash-based collection.

c2/19/Soundex.h
```
std::string encodedDigit(char letter) const {
    const std::unordered_map<char,std::string> encodings {
        {'b', "1"},
```

```
➤      {'c', "2"},
➤      {'d', "3"}
➤    };
➤    return encodings.find(letter)->second;
}
```

Now we need to code support for the rest of the consonant conversions. The question is, do we need to test-drive each one?

A mantra surfaced in the early TDD days that says, "Test everything that can possibly break." This is a glib response to the oft-asked question, "What do I have to test?" Realistically, coding encodings map is a low-risk activity. It's unlikely we'll break anything in doing so.

A counterargument is that you can break just about anything, no matter how simple (and I've done it). As the tedium of entering repetitive data increases, so does our likelihood to make a mistake and not even notice it. Having tests would decrease the chance that we create a defect.

Tests would provide a clear document of the conversions (though you could argue that the table itself is the clearest document). On the flip side, were we to create a table with hundreds of elements, having a test for each would be ridiculous.

What's the right answer? Maybe the most important consideration is that we are *test-driving*, not *testing*. "Is there a difference?" you ask. Yes. Using a testing technique, you would seek to exhaustively analyze the specification in question (and possibly the code) and devise tests that exhaustively cover the behavior. TDD is instead a technique for driving the design of the code. Your tests primarily serve the purpose of specifying the behavior of what you will build. The tests in TDD are almost a by-product of the process. They provide you with the necessary *confidence* to make subsequent changes to the code.

The distinction between test-driving and testing may seem subtle. The important aspect is that TDD represents more of a sufficiency mentality. You write as many tests as you need to drive in the code necessary and no more. You write tests to describe the next behavior needed. If you know that the logic won't need to change any further, you stop writing tests.

Of course, real experience provides the best determinant. Test-driving for confidence works great until you ship a defect. When you do, remind yourself to take smaller, safer steps.

We choose to test-drive. We complete the conversion table.

c2/20/Soundex.h

```
std::string encodedDigit(char letter) const {
    const std::unordered_map<char, std::string> encodings {
        {'b', "1"}, {'f', "1"}, {'p', "1"}, {'v', "1"},
        {'c', "2"}, {'g', "2"}, {'j', "2"}, {'k', "2"}, {'q', "2"},
                    {'s', "2"}, {'x', "2"}, {'z', "2"},
        {'d', "3"}, {'t', "3"},
        {'l', "4"},
        {'m', "5"}, {'n', "5"},
        {'r', "6"}
    };
    return encodings.find(letter)->second;
}
```

What about the tests? Do we need three assertions in ReplacesConsonantsWith-AppropriateDigits? To answer that question, we ask ourselves whether having the additional assertions provides increased understanding of how the feature works. We answer ourselves: probably not. We eliminate two assertions, change the remaining one to use ASSERT_THAT, and choose a different encoding just to bolster our confidence a little.

c2/20/SoundexTest.cpp

```
TEST_F(SoundexEncoding, ReplacesConsonantsWithAppropriateDigits) {
    ASSERT_THAT(soundex.encode("Ax"), Eq("A200"));
}
```

2.9 What If?

Our implementation assumes that the letter passed to encodedDigit() will be found in the encodings map. We make the assumption to allow moving forward incrementally, writing only the minimal code needed to pass each test. But we still have the responsibility of thinking about code that may need to be written.

Will it ever be possible for encodedDigit() to be passed a letter that doesn't appear in the lookup map? If so, what should the function do? Wikipedia doesn't answer the question. We could guess, but the better answer is to ask the customer. We don't have one, but we can find a customer proxy online. A web search quickly turns up a handful of Soundex calculator apps. We enter A# into one of them and receive A000 as a response. Question answered: we need to ignore unrecognized characters.

With TDD, you can choose to jot down the name of a would-be test, or you can write it now. At times I've found that driving in a few exceptional cases earlier would have saved me some debugging time later. Let's put the test in place now.

```
c2/21/SoundexTest.cpp
TEST_F(SoundexEncoding, IgnoresNonAlphabetics) {
    ASSERT_THAT(soundex.encode("A#"), Eq("A000"));
}
```

The test doesn't simply fail; it crashes. The find() call returns an iterator pointing to end() that we try to dereference. We change encodedDigit() to instead return an empty string in this case.

```
c2/21/Soundex.h
std::string encodedDigit(char letter) const {
    const std::unordered_map<char, std::string> encodings {
        {'b', "1"}, {'f', "1"}, {'p', "1"}, {'v', "1"},
        // ...
    };
➤   auto it = encodings.find(letter);
➤   return it == encodings.end() ? "" : it->second;
}
```

2.10 One Thing at a Time

We want to test-drive converting *multiple* characters in the tail of the word.

```
c2/22/SoundexTest.cpp
TEST_F(SoundexEncoding, ReplacesMultipleConsonantsWithDigits) {
    ASSERT_THAT(soundex.encode("Acdl"), Eq("A234"));
}
```

A simple solution would involve iterating through all but the first letter of the word, converting each. But our code isn't quite structured in a way that easily supports that. Let's restructure the code.

One thing at a time, however. When test-driving, you want to keep each step in the cycle distinct. When writing a test, don't go off and refactor. Don't refactor when trying to get a test to pass, either. Combining the two activities will waste your time when things go awry, which they will.

We comment out the test we just wrote, temporarily halting our "red" activity. (In Google Mock, prepending DISABLED_ to the test name tells Google Mock to skip executing it. See *Disabling Tests*, on page 76, to read about the implications of disabling tests.)

```
c2/23/SoundexTest.cpp
➤ TEST_F(SoundexEncoding, DISABLED_ReplacesMultipleConsonantsWithDigits) {
    ASSERT_THAT(soundex.encode("Acdl"), Eq("A234"));
}
```

We focus on refactoring activity and rework our solution a little. Rather than pass the entire word to encodedDigits(), we pass it the tail of the word—all characters except the first. Passing only the tail should simplify the code we'll need to iterate through the letters to be converted. It also allows us to use a couple string functions that help clarify what the code does: empty() and front().

c2/23/Soundex.h
```
    std::string encode(const std::string& word) const {
        return zeroPad(head(word) + encodedDigits(tail(word)));
    }

private:
    // ...
    std::string tail(const std::string& word) const {
        return word.substr(1);
    }

    std::string encodedDigits(const std::string& word) const {
        if (word.empty()) return "";
        return encodedDigit(word.front());
    }
```

We run our tests again to ensure our changes break no tests. That ends the refactoring activity.

We return to the start of the TDD cycle by reenabling ReplacesMultipleConsonantsWithDigits and watching it fail. We get our tests to pass by using a range-based for loop to iterate the tail of the word.

c2/24/Soundex.h
```
std::string encodedDigits(const std::string& word) const {
    if (word.empty()) return "";
    std::string encoding;
    for (auto letter: word) encoding += encodedDigit(letter);
    return encoding;
}
```

Now that we've added a loop to encodedDigits(), we think we don't need the *guard clause* to return early if the word passed in is empty. As a refactoring step, we remove it.

c2/25/Soundex.h
```
std::string encodedDigits(const std::string& word) const {
    std::string encoding;
    for (auto letter: word) encoding += encodedDigit(letter);
    return encoding;
}
```

We rerun our tests. Success! Deleting unnecessary code is extremely satisfying, but only when we can do so with confidence. Having tests to try these little bits of cleanup rocks.

2.11 Limiting Length

Rule #4 tells us the Soundex code must be four characters.

```
c2/26/SoundexTest.cpp
TEST_F(SoundexEncoding, LimitsLengthToFourCharacters) {
    ASSERT_THAT(soundex.encode("Dcdlb").length(), Eq(4u));
}
```

The code throws an exception when Google Mock runs this new test. No worries, because our test tool traps this exception, reports a test failure, and continues running any subsequent tests.

```
[ RUN      ] SoundexEncoding.LimitsLengthToFourCharacters
unknown file: Failure
C++ exception with description "basic_string::_S_create" thrown in the test body.
[  FAILED  ] SoundexEncoding.LimitsLengthToFourCharacters (1 ms)
```

By default, Google Mock swallows the problem and keeps running the rest of your tests. If you prefer to crash the tests on an uncaught exception, you can run Google Mock with the following command-line option:

```
--gtest_catch_exceptions=0
```

Looking at a backtrace in gdb (or a comparable debugging tool) tells us that our problem is in zeroPad(). A web search reveals that the _S_create error occurs when you attempt to create a string larger than the maximum allowed size. With those two facts, we focus on the string construction in zeroPad(). Aha! When the length of code exceeds MaxCodeLength, zerosNeeded overflows with a value that makes the string constructor unhappy.

TDD fosters an incremental approach that makes it easier to resolve problems, because it exposes them as soon as you create them. We didn't need to debug to pinpoint our problem; a glance at the backtrace was all we needed.

(Yet, any time things crash, we always wonder about our approach. How might we have better test-driven to make the source of problem more explicit? Once we wrote zeroPad(), we might have considered elevating it as a public utility method. At that point, our job would have been to more exhaustively test it in order to document to other developers how it could be used. We might have been more likely to stumble across the need to guard zeroPad() against creating a string with an invalid length.)

For our solution to the problem, we could fix zeroPad(). We could also change encodedDigits() to stop once it encodes enough letters. We choose the latter—once encoding gets filled with encoded digits, we break out of the loop.

c2/26/Soundex.h
```cpp
std::string encodedDigits(const std::string& word) const {
   std::string encoding;
   for (auto letter: word)
   {
      if (encoding.length() == MaxCodeLength - 1) break;
      encoding += encodedDigit(letter);
   }
   return encoding;
}
```

The new statement doesn't clearly and directly declare its intent. We immediately extract it to the intention-revealing function isComplete().

c2/27/Soundex.h
```cpp
std::string encodedDigits(const std::string& word) const {
   std::string encoding;
   for (auto letter: word) {
      if (isComplete(encoding)) break;
      encoding += encodedDigit(letter);
   }
   return encoding;
}
bool isComplete (const std::string& encoding) const {
   return encoding.length() == MaxCodeLength - 1;
}
```

2.12 Dropping Vowels

Rule #1 says to drop all occurrences of vowels and the letters *w*, *h*, and *y*. For lack of a better name, we'll refer to these as *vowel-like* letters.

c2/28/SoundexTest.cpp
```cpp
TEST_F(SoundexEncoding, IgnoresVowelLikeLetters) {
   ASSERT_THAT(soundex.encode("Baeiouhycdl"), Eq("B234"));
}
```

The test passes without us adding a lick of production code, because encodedDigit() answers an empty string if the letter to be encoded wasn't found. Any vowels thus encode to the empty string, which gets harmlessly appended.

A test that passes with no change to your classes is always cause for humility and pause (see Section 3.5, Getting Green on Red, on page 60). Ask yourself, "What might I have done differently?"

If a stream of subsequent tests continues to pass, consider reverting your effort. You're likely taking too-large steps, and you likely won't find as much benefit in TDD. In our case, we could have written a test that demonstrates what happens for any unrecognized characters and at that point chosen to have it return the same character instead of the empty string.

2.13 Doing What It Takes to Clarify Tests

For our next test, we tackle the case where two adjacent letters encode to the same digit. Per Soundex rule #3, such duplicate letters get encoded as a single digit. The rule also states that it applies to the first letter. Let's deal with the first case now and worry about the first letter next.

c2/29/SoundexTest.cpp

```cpp
TEST_F(SoundexEncoding, CombinesDuplicateEncodings) {
    ASSERT_THAT(soundex.encode("Abfcgdt"), Eq("A123"));
}
```

That's a confusing test! To understand why *Abfcgdt* encodes to *A123*, we have to know that *b* and *f* both encode to *1*, *c* and *g* both encode to *2*, and *d* and *t* both encode to *3*. We can learn these facts from reading other tests, such as ReplacesConsonantsWithAppropriateDigits, but maybe we should make the test more direct.

Let's add a series of *precondition* assertions to help readers make the connection.

c2/30/SoundexTest.cpp

```cpp
TEST_F(SoundexEncoding, CombinesDuplicateEncodings) {

➤    ASSERT_THAT(soundex.encodedDigit('b'), Eq(soundex.encodedDigit('f')));
➤    ASSERT_THAT(soundex.encodedDigit('c'), Eq(soundex.encodedDigit('g')));
➤    ASSERT_THAT(soundex.encodedDigit('d'), Eq(soundex.encodedDigit('t')));

    ASSERT_THAT(soundex.encode("Abfcgdt"), Eq("A123"));
}
```

The assertion doesn't compile, since encodedDigit() is private. We choose to simply make encodedDigit() public.

c2/30/Soundex.h

```cpp
➤ public:
    std::string encodedDigit(char letter) const {
        // ...
    }

➤ private:
    // ...
```

Uh-oh...I'm sensing consternation.

Q.:   *Wait, no! You can't just go making private functions public.*

A.:   *We do have other solutions. We could make the test code a friend of the Soundex class, but a friend is usually a poor choice, and that's no different when test-driving. We could move the function to another class, possibly named SoundexDigitEncoder, but that seems overkill. We could also forego the preconditions and find another way to make our test easier to read.*

Q.:   *We've always been taught to not expose private implementation details. Shouldn't you follow that time-honored rule?*

A.:   *First, we don't willy-nilly expose everything, just things we need. Second, we're not exposing implementation details so much as broadening the public interface of the Soundex class. Yes, we're adding to it a function that production clients of Soundex shouldn't need, but our test—a client—needs it. We take on a low risk of potential abuse and in return guarantee less wasted time for developers who must read our test in the future.*

We could make the case for precondition assertions in some of the other tests we've written for Soundex. Use them sparingly, though. Often, introducing a meaningfully named constant or local variable can be a simpler, as-effective solution. Also, the compulsion to add a precondition assertion might suggest you are missing another test. Are you? Go add it and then see whether having that test eliminates the need for the precondition assertion.

To make CombinesDuplicateEncodings pass, we could introduce a local variable that would track the last digit appended, updating it each iteration of the loop. But that seems muddy. Let's start with a declaration of intent.

`c2/31/Soundex.h`

```cpp
std::string encodedDigits(const std::string& word) const {
    std::string encoding;
    for (auto letter: word) {
        if (isComplete(encoding)) break;
        if (encodedDigit(letter) != lastDigit(encoding))
            encoding += encodedDigit(letter);
    }
    return encoding;
}
```

We know what lastDigit() needs to do. We think for a moment and come up with one way that provides the *how*.

`c2/31/Soundex.h`

```cpp
std::string lastDigit(const std::string& encoding) const {
    if (encoding.empty()) return "";
    return std::string(1, encoding.back());
}
```

2.14 Testing Outside the Box

Now we consider a test where the second letter duplicates the first. Hmm...our tests so far always use an uppercase letter followed by lowercase letters, but the algorithm shouldn't really care. Let's take a brief pause and implement a couple tests that deal with case considerations. (We could also choose to add to our test list and save the effort for later.)

We don't have explicit specs for dealing with case, but part of doing TDD well is thinking outside of what we're given. Creating a robust application requires finding answers to critical concerns that aren't explicitly specified. (Hint: ask your customer.)

Soundex encodes similar words to the same code to allow for quick and easy comparison. Case matters not in how words sound. To simplify comparing Soundex codes, we need to use the same casing consistently.

c2/32/SoundexTest.cpp
```cpp
TEST_F(SoundexEncoding, UppercasesFirstLetter) {
    ASSERT_THAT(soundex.encode("abcd"), StartsWith("A"));
}
```

We change the core algorithm outlined in encode() to include uppercasing the head of the word, which we expect to be only a single character. (The casting in upperFront() avoids potential problems with handling EOF.)

c2/32/Soundex.h
```cpp
  std::string encode(const std::string& word) const {
➤   return zeroPad(upperFront(head(word)) + encodedDigits(tail(word)));
  }

➤ std::string upperFront(const std::string& string) const {
➤   return std::string(1,
➤       std::toupper(static_cast<unsigned char>(string.front())));
➤ }
```

Thinking about case considerations prods us to revisit the test IgnoresVowelLikeLetters. Given what we learned earlier, we expect that our code will ignore uppercase vowels just like it ignores lowercase vowels. But we'd like to make sure. We update the test to verify our concern, putting us outside the realm of TDD and into the realm of testing after the fact.

c2/33/SoundexTest.cpp
```cpp
  TEST_F(SoundexEncoding, IgnoresVowelLikeLetters) {
➤   ASSERT_THAT(soundex.encode("BaAeEiIoOuUhHyYcdl"), Eq("B234"));
  }
```

It passes. We could choose to discard our updated test. In this case, we decide to retain the modified test in order to explicitly document the behavior for other developers.

Since we felt compelled to write yet another test that passed immediately, because we weren't quite sure what would happen, we decide to revisit our code. The code in encodedDigits() appears a bit too implicit and difficult to follow. We have to dig a bit to discover the following:

- Many letters don't have corresponding encodings.

- encodedDigit() returns the empty string for these letters.

- Concatenating an empty string to the encodings variable in encodedDigits() effectively does nothing.

We refactor to make the code more explicit. First, we change encodedDigit() to return a constant named NotADigit when the encodings map contains no entry for a digit. Then we add a conditional expression in encodedDigits() to explicitly indicate that NotADigit encodings get ignored. We also alter lastDigit() to use the same constant.

`c2/34/Soundex.h`

```
const std::string NotADigit{"*"};

std::string encodedDigits(const std::string& word) const {
    std::string encoding;
    for (auto letter: word) {
        if (isComplete(encoding)) break;

        auto digit = encodedDigit(letter);
        if (digit != NotADigit && digit != lastDigit(encoding))
            encoding += digit;
    }
    return encoding;
}

std::string lastDigit(const std::string& encoding) const {
    if (encoding.empty()) return NotADigit;
    return std::string(1, encoding.back());
}
// ...
std::string encodedDigit(char letter) const {
    const std::unordered_map<char, std::string> encodings {
        {'b', "1"}, {'f', "1"}, {'p', "1"}, {'v', "1"},
        // ...
    };
    auto it = encodings.find(letter);
    return it == encodings.end() ? NotADigit : it->second;
}
```

(That listing summarizes a few incremental refactoring changes, each verified with passing tests. In other words, we don't make these changes all at once.)

Let's move on to a test that deals with the casing of consonants.

```
c2/35/SoundexTest.cpp
TEST_F(SoundexEncoding, IgnoresCaseWhenEncodingConsonants) {
    ASSERT_THAT(soundex.encode("BCDL"), Eq(soundex.encode("Bcdl")));
}
```

Our assertion takes on a slightly different form. It declares that the encoding of "BCDL" should be equivalent to the encoding of "Bcdl". In other words, we don't care what the actual encoding is, as long as the uppercase input resolves to the same encoding as the corresponding lowercase input.

Our solution is to lowercase the letter when querying the encodings lookup table (in encodedDigit()).

```
c2/35/Soundex.h
        std::string encodedDigit(char letter) const {
            const std::unordered_map<char, std::string> encodings {
                {'b', "1"}, {'f', "1"}, {'p', "1"}, {'v', "1"},
                // ...
            };
➤           auto it = encodings.find(lower(letter));
            return it == encodings.end() ? NotADigit : it->second;
        }

private:
➤       char lower(char c) const {
➤           return std::tolower(static_cast<unsigned char>(c));
➤       }
```

2.15 Back on Track

When we started the work in this section, we were trying to write a test to handle the scenario where the second letter duplicates the first letter. That triggered us to make our algorithm case-insensitive. We can now return to our original goal and write this test:

```
c2/36/SoundexTest.cpp
TEST_F(SoundexEncoding, CombinesDuplicateCodesWhen2ndLetterDuplicates1st) {
    ASSERT_THAT(soundex.encode("Bbcd"), Eq("B230"));
}
```

Our solution involves a little bit of change to the overall policy embodied in encode(). We pass the entire word to encodedDigits() for encoding so that we can compare the encoding of the second letter to the first. We append only the tail of all encoded digits to the overall encoding.

In encodedDigits(), we encode the word's first character so that comparisons to the prior digit can compare against it. Since encodedDigits() now encodes the entire word, we alter isComplete() to accommodate one more character. We also change the core loop in encodedDigits() to iterate across the tail of the word.

c2/36/Soundex.h
```cpp
std::string encode(const std::string& word) const {
    return zeroPad(upperFront(head(word)) + tail(encodedDigits(word)));
}

std::string encodedDigits(const std::string& word) const {
    std::string encoding;

    encoding += encodedDigit(word.front());

    for (auto letter: tail(word)) {
        if (isComplete(encoding)) break;

        auto digit = encodedDigit(letter);
        if (digit != NotADigit && digit != lastDigit(encoding))
            encoding += digit;
    }
    return encoding;
}

bool isComplete (const std::string& encoding) const {
    return encoding.length() == MaxCodeLength;
}
```

2.16 Refactoring to Single-Responsibility Functions

The encodedDigits() function continues to increase in complexity. We inserted blank lines in order to visually group related statements, a dead giveaway that a function does too much.

The *single responsibility principle* (SRP) tells us that each function should have one reason to change.[4] encodedDigits() exhibits a classic violation of the SRP: it mixes high-level policy with implementation details.

Our encodedDigits() function accomplishes its goal using a two-step algorithm. First append the encoded first letter to the encoding, and then iterate through the rest of the letters and append them. The problem is that encodedDigits() also includes the low-level details to accomplish those two steps. encodedDigits() violates SRP, because it must change for two reasons: if we want to alter implementation details or if we need to change the overall policy for encoding.

---

4. *Agile Software Development, Principles, Patterns, and Practices [Mar02]*

We can extract the two steps from encodedDigits() into two separate functions, each containing implementation details for a simple abstract concept. What remains in encodedDigits() declares our solution's policy.

```
c2/37/Soundex.h
std::string encodedDigits(const std::string& word) const {
    std::string encoding;
    encodeHead(encoding, word);
    encodeTail(encoding, word);
    return encoding;
}

void encodeHead(std::string& encoding, const std::string& word) const {
    encoding += encodedDigit(word.front());
}

void encodeTail(std::string& encoding, const std::string& word) const {
    for (auto letter: tail(word)) {
        if (isComplete(encoding)) break;

        auto digit = encodedDigit(letter);
        if (digit != NotADigit && digit != lastDigit(encoding))
            encoding += digit;
    }
}
```

That's better. Let's go one step further and extract some of the body of the for loop in encodeTail().

```
c2/38/Soundex.h
void encodeTail(std::string& encoding, const std::string& word) const {
    for (auto letter: tail(word))
        if (!isComplete(encoding))
            encodeLetter(encoding, letter);
}

void encodeLetter(std::string& encoding, char letter) const {
    auto digit = encodedDigit(letter);
    if (digit != NotADigit && digit != lastDigit(encoding))
        encoding += digit;
}
```

The resulting refactored code creates some visual similarity that suggests the possibility for more tightening of the algorithm. Is encoding a single character in encodeHead() simply a special case of the encoding loop in encodeTail()? Feel free to experiment—you can do so safely, because you've got tests! We think the algorithm is clear enough for now and choose to move on.

2.17 Finishing Up

What about vowels? Rule #3 also states that otherwise-duplicate encodings separated by a vowel (not *h* or *w*) get coded twice.

```
c2/39/SoundexTest.cpp
TEST_F(SoundexEncoding, DoesNotCombineDuplicateEncodingsSeparatedByVowels) {
    ASSERT_THAT(soundex.encode("Jbob"), Eq("J110"));
}
```

Once again we solve our challenge by declaring *what* we want to accomplish. We change the conditional expression in encodeLetter() to append a digit only if it is not a duplicate *or* if the last letter is a vowel. This declaration drives a few corresponding changes.

```
c2/39/Soundex.h
void encodeTail(std::string& encoding, const std::string& word) const {
    for (auto i = 1u; i < word.length(); i++)
        if (!isComplete(encoding))
            encodeLetter(encoding, word[i], word[i - 1]);
}

void encodeLetter(std::string& encoding, char letter, char lastLetter) const {
    auto digit = encodedDigit(letter);
    if (digit != NotADigit &&
        (digit != lastDigit(encoding) || isVowel(lastLetter)))
        encoding += digit;
}

bool isVowel(char letter) const {
    return
        std::string("aeiouy").find(lower(letter)) != std::string::npos;
}
```

Is passing in the previous letter the best way to do this? It's direct and expressive. We'll stick with it for now.

2.18 What Tests Are We Missing?

We're rarely handed all the specs on a silver platter. Few are so lucky. Even our Soundex rules, seemingly complete, don't cover everything. While we were coding, some of the tests and some of our implementation triggered other thoughts. We'll either make mental notes or sometimes write down our thoughts on an index card or notepad. Here's a list for the Soundex exercise:

- What if we're passed a word with characters normally considered as word separators, such as periods (for example, "Mr.Smith")? Should we ignore the characters (like we currently do), throw an exception because the client should have split the word properly, or do something else?

Speaking of exceptions, how do we test-drive exception handling into our code? In *Exception-Based Tests*, on page 94, you'll learn how to design tests that expect exceptions to be thrown.

- What encoding should an empty string return? (Or can we assume we'll not be passed an empty string?)

- What should we do with non-English alphabet consonants (such as *ñ*)? Does the Soundex algorithm even apply? Our isVowel() function needs to support vowels with diacritical marks.

Many of these concerns are critical to designing a robust, fail-safe Soundex class. Without addressing them, our application may fail in production.

We don't have definitive answers for all of these "what ifs." As programmers, we've learned to make decisions at times on our own. But an oft-better route is to ask the *customer* or even collaborate with them to define acceptance tests (see Section 10.3, *Unit Tests, Integration Tests, and Acceptance Tests*, on page 278).

"Should the system do A, or should it do B?" In the old days, we would have simply coded our choice and moved on. What we lost in doing so was immediate documentation on which choice we made. Somewhere, the solution for B was encoded in the midst of a lot of other code. Sure, we could analyze the codebase to determine what decisions were made, but often at excessive cost. We've all spent too many hours trying to determine how code behaves.

In contrast, test-driving leaves behind a clear document. We waste no analysis time uncovering a choice made moons ago.

Test-driving solutions to any of our earlier "what if" questions is no different from what we've done so far. I'll leave coding the missing tests as an exercise for you.

2.19 Our Solution

We arrived at a test-driven solution for Soundex. Our solution is by no means the only one or even the best. But we have high confidence that we could ship it (barring the outstanding items discussed in Section 2.18, *What Tests Are We Missing?*, on page 48), and that's what's most important.

I've test-driven Soundex a handful of times, each time deriving a different solution. Most solutions differed only in a few small ways, but one was dramatically different (and poorly performing) when I actively sought to solve the problem in an extremely declarative manner. Each pass through the process of test-driving Soundex taught me a bit more about the algorithm, but I also learned more about what works well from a test-driving stance.

You might find similar value in test-driving the Soundex algorithm a few times. The notion of repeatedly practicing TDD against the same example is known as a *kata*. See Section 11.5, *Katas and Dojos*, on page 310 for further information on katas.

There is no one right way to code any solution. There *are* important solution characteristics.

- It implements what the customer asked for. If not, it's a bad solution, no matter what. The tests you build using TDD can help you understand whether your solution is in line with what the customer requested. Sufficient performance is one of those things your customer likely wants. Part of your job is to ensure you understand their specific performance needs, not introduce the costs of optimization when it's not needed.

- It works. If a solution exhibits significant defects, it's bad, no matter how elegant. TDD helps ensure that the software we deliver behaves the way we expect. *TDD is not a silver bullet.* You'll still ship defects, and you still need many other forms of testing. However, TDD gives you opportunities to ship code with considerably fewer defects.

- It's readily understood. Everyone wastes excessive time trying to understand poorly written code. Following TDD will provide you with safe opportunities to rename and restructure your code for better understanding.

- It's easily changed. Usually, ease of change aligns with design quality. TDD allows you to make the continual tweaks necessary to keep design quality high.

Our solution isn't very procedural. The complete algorithm isn't in one function that you can read from top to bottom. Instead, we implemented it in the form of numerous small member functions, most one or two lines long. Each of these functions contains code at a single level of abstraction. Initial encounters with code like this can cause fits of apoplexy: "Dagnabbit, where's all the work happening?" To learn more about why we code this way, refer to *Benefits of Small Methods*, on page 156.

2.20 The Soundex Class

Since we're ready to check in, let's take a look at our solution. We decide that we don't yet have a compelling reason to split out an implementation (.cpp) file, though that might be an essential part of making it production-ready in your system.

c2/40/SoundexTest.cpp

```cpp
#include "gmock/gmock.h"
#include "Soundex.h"
using namespace testing;

class SoundexEncoding: public Test {
public:
   Soundex soundex;
};

TEST_F(SoundexEncoding, RetainsSoleLetterOfOneLetterWord) {
   ASSERT_THAT(soundex.encode("A"), Eq("A000"));
}

TEST_F(SoundexEncoding, PadsWithZerosToEnsureThreeDigits) {
   ASSERT_THAT(soundex.encode("I"), Eq("I000"));
}

TEST_F(SoundexEncoding, ReplacesConsonantsWithAppropriateDigits) {
   ASSERT_THAT(soundex.encode("Ax"), Eq("A200"));
}

TEST_F(SoundexEncoding, IgnoresNonAlphabetics) {
   ASSERT_THAT(soundex.encode("A#"), Eq("A000"));
}

TEST_F(SoundexEncoding, ReplacesMultipleConsonantsWithDigits) {
   ASSERT_THAT(soundex.encode("Acdl"), Eq("A234"));
}

TEST_F(SoundexEncoding, LimitsLengthToFourCharacters) {
   ASSERT_THAT(soundex.encode("Dcdlb").length(), Eq(4u));
}

TEST_F(SoundexEncoding, IgnoresVowelLikeLetters) {
   ASSERT_THAT(soundex.encode("BaAeEiIoOuUhHyYcdl"), Eq("B234"));
}

TEST_F(SoundexEncoding, CombinesDuplicateEncodings) {
   ASSERT_THAT(soundex.encodedDigit('b'), Eq(soundex.encodedDigit('f')));
   ASSERT_THAT(soundex.encodedDigit('c'), Eq(soundex.encodedDigit('g')));
   ASSERT_THAT(soundex.encodedDigit('d'), Eq(soundex.encodedDigit('t')));

   ASSERT_THAT(soundex.encode("Abfcgdt"), Eq("A123"));
}

TEST_F(SoundexEncoding, UppercasesFirstLetter) {
   ASSERT_THAT(soundex.encode("abcd"), StartsWith("A"));
}
```

```cpp
TEST_F(SoundexEncoding, IgnoresCaseWhenEncodingConsonants) {
   ASSERT_THAT(soundex.encode("BCDL"), Eq(soundex.encode("Bcdl")));
}

TEST_F(SoundexEncoding, CombinesDuplicateCodesWhen2ndLetterDuplicates1st) {
   ASSERT_THAT(soundex.encode("Bbcd"), Eq("B230"));
}

TEST_F(SoundexEncoding, DoesNotCombineDuplicateEncodingsSeparatedByVowels) {
   ASSERT_THAT(soundex.encode("Jbob"), Eq("J110"));
}
```

c2/40/Soundex.h

```cpp
#ifndef Soundex_h
#define Soundex_h

#include <string>
#include <unordered_map>

#include "CharUtil.h"
#include "StringUtil.h"

class Soundex
{
public:
   static const size_t MaxCodeLength{4};

   std::string encode(const std::string& word) const {
      return stringutil::zeroPad(
         stringutil::upperFront(stringutil::head(word)) +
            stringutil::tail(encodedDigits(word)),
         MaxCodeLength);
   }

   std::string encodedDigit(char letter) const {
      const std::unordered_map<char, std::string> encodings {
         {'b', "1"}, {'f', "1"}, {'p', "1"}, {'v', "1"},
         {'c', "2"}, {'g', "2"}, {'j', "2"}, {'k', "2"}, {'q', "2"},
                     {'s', "2"}, {'x', "2"}, {'z', "2"},
         {'d', "3"}, {'t', "3"},
         {'l', "4"},
         {'m', "5"}, {'n', "5"},
         {'r', "6"}
      };
      auto it = encodings.find(charutil::lower(letter));
      return it == encodings.end() ? NotADigit : it->second;
   }

private:
   const std::string NotADigit{"*"};
```

```cpp
std::string encodedDigits(const std::string& word) const {
    std::string encoding;
    encodeHead(encoding, word);
    encodeTail(encoding, word);
    return encoding;
}

void encodeHead(std::string& encoding, const std::string& word) const {
    encoding += encodedDigit(word.front());
}

void encodeTail(std::string& encoding, const std::string& word) const {
    for (auto i = 1u; i < word.length(); i++)
        if (!isComplete(encoding))
            encodeLetter(encoding, word[i], word[i - 1]);
}
void encodeLetter(std::string& encoding, char letter, char lastLetter) const {
    auto digit = encodedDigit(letter);
    if (digit != NotADigit &&
            (digit != lastDigit(encoding) || charutil::isVowel(lastLetter)))
        encoding += digit;
}

std::string lastDigit(const std::string& encoding) const {
    if (encoding.empty()) return NotADigit;
    return std::string(1, encoding.back());
}

bool isComplete(const std::string& encoding) const {
    return encoding.length() == MaxCodeLength;
}
};
```

```
#endif
```

Wait...some things have changed! Where are the head(), tail(), and zeroPad() functions? Where are isVowel() and upper()? And lastDigit() looks different!

While you were busy reading, I did a bit of additional refactoring. Those missing functions, once defined in Soundex, now appear as free functions declared in StringUtil.h and CharUtil.h. With a small bit of refactoring, they now represent highly reusable functions.

Simply moving the functions out of Soundex isn't quite sufficient. The functions in their new home as public utilities need to be aptly described so other programmers can understand their intent and use. That means they need tests to show by example how a programmer might use them in their own client code. You can find both the utility functions and their tests in the downloadable source code for this book.

We test-drove one possible solution for Soundex. How a solution evolves is entirely up to you. The more you practice TDD, the more likely your style will evolve. Code I test-drove only two years ago differs dramatically from code I test-drive today.

2.21 Teardown

In this chapter, you experienced hands-on, nitty-gritty TDD. Did you work through the code on your own? If so, you implemented a Soundex class that you could almost introduce into a production application. If not, open your editor and build the Soundex class. Learning by writing code is more effective than reading code.

Ready to *really* learn TDD? Go again! Test-drive the Soundex class a second time, but this time do it on your own, without reading this chapter (unless you get stuck). What happens if you introduce the Soundex rules in a different order? What if you consider a different style of programming? What happens if, for example, you implement each rule as a separate function that transforms input text and build a Soundex implementation by chaining together a series of transforms?

When you're ready to move on, *Test-Driven Development Foundations* takes a step back and looks at TDD from a more holistic stance. It presents fundamental definitions for TDD and provides strategic as well as tactical advice for success.

## CHAPTER 3

Test-Driven Development Foundations

3.1 Setup

The detailed example from *Test-Driven Development: A First Example* shows what Test-Driven Development should look like in practice. As we worked through the example, we touched on a considerable number of concepts and good practices. (You might also have chosen to skip that chapter if you're already familiar with TDD.) This chapter explores these topics in more detail, providing a bit more background and rationale behind each.

- The definition of *unit*
- The TDD cycle of red-green-refactor
- The three rules of TDD
- Why you should never skip observing test failure
- Mind-sets for success
- Mechanics for success

When you've worked through each of these topics, you'll be well grounded in the process and concepts behind TDD.

3.2 Unit Test and TDD Fundamentals

TDD results in *unit tests*. A unit test verifies the behavior of a code unit, where a *unit* is the smallest testable piece of an application. You typically write a unit test in the programming language of the unit.

Unit Test Organization and Execution

A single unit test consists of a descriptive name and a series of code statements, conceptually divided into four (ordered) parts.

1. (Optional) statements that set up a context for execution
2. One or more statements to invoke the behavior you want to verify

3. One or more statements to verify the expected outcome

4. (Optional) cleanup statements (for example, to release allocated memory)

Some folks refer to the first three parts as *Given-When-Then*. In other words, *Given* a context, *When* the test executes some code, *Then* some behavior is verified. Other developers might call this breakdown *Arrange-Act-Assert* (see *Arrange-Act-Assert/Given-When-Then*, on page 84).

Typically you group related tests in a single source file. Google Mock, like most unit testing tools, allows you to logically group unit tests into *fixtures*. You might start with one fixture per C++ class being test-driven, but don't let that constrain you. It's not unusual to end up with more than one fixture for a single C++ class or one fixture that tests related behaviors from multiple classes. *File Organization*, on page 79, contains further detail on files and fixtures.

You use one of dozens of available C++ unit testing tools to execute your unit tests. While most of these tools share many similarities, no cross-tool standards exist. As a result, C++ unit tests are not directly portable between tools. Each tool defines its own rules for how tests are structured, what assertions look like, and how tests get executed.

Using the tool to execute all our tests is a *test run* or *suite run*. During a test run, the tool iterates all tests, executing each in isolation. For each test, the tool executes its statements from top to bottom. When the tool executes an assertion statement, the test fails if the condition expected by the assertion does not hold true. The test passes if no assertions fail.

Unit testing practice varies widely, as does the granularity of the tests involved. Most developers writing unit tests (but not doing TDD) seek only the verification it provides. These developers typically write tests once they complete functional portions of production code. Such tests written after development can be tougher to write and maintain, primarily because they weren't written with testing in mind. We'll do better and use TDD.

Test-Driving Units

In contrast to *plain ol' unit testing* (POUT), TDD is a more concisely defined process that *incorporates* the activity of unit testing. When doing TDD, you write the tests first, you strive to keep the granularity of tests small and consistent, and you seek myriad other benefits—most importantly the ability to safely change existing code.

You use TDD to *test-drive* new behavior into your system in quite small increments. In other words, to add a new piece of behavior to the system, you first write a test to define that behavior. The existence of a test that will not pass forces (drives) you to implement the corresponding behavior.

"Quite small?" No formal size constraint exists, so you want to move in the direction of an ideal instead. Each test should represent the smallest meaningful increment you can think of. Your favorite tests contain one, two, or three lines (see *Arrange-Act-Assert/Given-When-Then*, on page 84) with one assertion (Section 7.3, *One Assert per Test*, on page 178). You'll of course have plenty of tests that are longer, and that may be OK, but having an ideal will remind you to question the size of each longer test—is it doing too much?

Tests with no more than three lines and a single assertion take only minutes to write and usually only minutes to implement—how much code can you meaningfully verify in a single assert? These small bits of related new code you add to the system in response to a failing test are logical groupings, or *units* of code.

You don't seek to write tests that cover a wide swath of functionality. The responsibility for such end-to-end tests lies elsewhere, perhaps in the realm of acceptance tests/customer tests or system tests. The term this book uses for tests against such aggregate code behavior is *integration tests* (see Section 10.3, *Unit Tests, Integration Tests, and Acceptance Tests*, on page 278). Integration tests verify code that must *integrate* with other code or with external entities (the file system, databases, web protocols, and other APIs). In contrast, unit tests allow you to verify units in isolation from other code.

The first rule of TDD (Section 3.4, *The Three Rules of TDD*, on page 59) states that you cannot write production code unless to make a failing test pass. Following the first rule of TDD, you'll inevitably need to test-drive code that interacts with external entities. Doing so puts you in the realm of integration tests, but that may be OK; nothing about TDD *prevents* you from creating them. Don't sweat the terminology distinction much. What's more important is that you are systematically driving every piece of code into the system by first specifying its behavior.

In *Test Doubles*, you'll learn how to use test doubles to break dependencies on external entities. Your integration tests, slow by their nature, will morph into fast unit tests.

3.3 The TDD Cycle: Red-Green-Refactor

When doing TDD, you repeat a short cycle of the following:

1. Write a test ("red").
2. Get the test to pass ("green").
3. Optimize the design ("refactor").

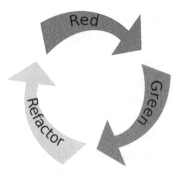

This cycle is often summarized as *red-green-refactor*, a phrase that stems from unit testing tools used for TDD. Red (fail) and pass (green) derive from SUnit (the first unit testing tool designed to support TDD[1]) and similar GUI tools that use the colors to provide immediate feedback on test results. The text-based output of Google Mock uses red and green when executed in a terminal with color support.

During the refactoring step, you seek to ensure your codebase has the best possible design, which allows you to extend and maintain your system at reasonable cost. You *refactor* (a term popularized by Martin Fowler's *Refactoring: Improving the Design of Existing Code [FBBO99]*) when you improve your code's design without changing its behavior, something that having tests allows you to safely do. The *Incremental Design* chapter covers refactoring.

Thinking and TDD

The goal of "burning the TDD cycle in your brain" is to make you comfortable with writing tests first to specify behavior and with cleaning up code each time through the cycle. Ingraining this habit will free your mind to instead think about the more challenging problem of growing a solution incrementally.

At each point in the TDD cycle, you must be able to answer many questions.

- *Write a small test.* What's the smallest possible piece of behavior you can increment the system by (*What's the Next Test?*, on page 73, offers a few ideas)? Does the system already have that behavior? How can you concisely describe the behavior in the test's name? Does the interface expressed in the test represent the best possible way for client code to use the behavior?

- *Ensure the new test fails.* If it doesn't, why not? Does the behavior already exist? Did you forget to compile? Did you take too large a step in the prior test? Is its assertion valid?

---

1. http://sunit.sourceforge.net

- *Write the code you think makes the test pass.* Are you writing no more code than needed to meet the current set of behaviors specified by the tests? Are you recognizing where the code you just wrote will need to be cleaned up? Are you following your team's standards?

- *Ensure all the tests pass.* If not, did you code things incorrectly, or is your specification incorrect?

- *Clean up the code changes you just made.* What do you need to do in order to get your code to follow team standards? Does your new code duplicate other code in the system that you should clean up, too? Does the code exhibit questionable smells? Are you following good design principles? What else do you know about design and clean code that you should apply here? Otherwise, is the design evolving in a good direction? Does your code change impact the design of other code areas that you should also change?

- *Ensure the tests all still pass.* Do you trust that you have adequate unit test coverage? Should you run a slower set of tests to have the confidence to move on? What's the next test?

You'll find ample resources in this book to help you answer these questions.

There's plenty to think about every few moments throughout your development day. The cycle of TDD is simple, but the reality of building production-quality code rarely is. Doing TDD is not a mindless exercise.

3.4 The Three Rules of TDD

Robert C. Martin ("Uncle Bob") provides a concise set of rules for practicing TDD.[2]

1. Write production code only to pass a failing unit test.

2. Write no more of a unit test than sufficient to fail (compilation failures are failures).

3. Write no more production code than necessary to pass the one failing unit test.

Rule #1 says to write tests *first*—understand and specify, in the form of a unit test example, behavior you must build into the system.

Rule #2 says to proceed as incrementally as possible—after each line you write, get feedback (via compilation or test run) if you can before moving on.

---

2.   http://butunclebob.com/ArticleS.UncleBob.TheThreeRulesOfTdd

When test-driving a RetweetCollection class, we stop as soon as we write this much of a first test:

```cpp
c3/1/RetweetCollectionTest.cpp
#include "gmock/gmock.h"

TEST(ARetweetCollection, IsEmptyWhenCreated) {
   RetweetCollection retweets;

}
```

We haven't yet defined RetweetCollection, so we know that this one line of test code shouldn't compile. We write the code that defines the RetweetCollection class and recompile until we get it right. Only then do we move on to writing the assertion that demonstrates the collection is empty.

Rule #2 is controversial and by no means universally accepted as a TDD standard. In C++, it might not be effective if compilation requires you to wait long. You might also find it's more effective to flesh out the design of a complete test first. But before you abandon the rule, give it an honest effort. (As a long-time TDD practitioner, I employ rule #2 on a case-by-case basis.)

Rule #3 says to write no more code than your tests specify. That's why rule #1 says "to pass a *failing* unit test." If you write more code than needed—if you implement behavior for which no test exists—you'll be unable to follow rule #1, because you'll soon be writing tests that immediately pass.

As you grow in your mastery of TDD, you'll find cases where it's near impossible to lead with a failing test. (The following section, *Getting Green on Red*, talks about this further.)

Learning by following the rules will help you later understand the adverse implications of breaking them.

3.5 Getting Green on Red

The first rule of TDD requires you to first demonstrate test failure before you can write any code. In spirit, this is a simple rule to follow. If you write only just enough code to make a test to pass, another test for additional functionality should fail automatically. In practice, however, you'll find yourself sometimes writing tests that pass right off the bat. I refer to these undesired events as *premature passes*.

You might experience a premature pass for one of many reasons:

- Running the wrong tests
- Testing the wrong code

- Unfortunate test specification
- Invalid assumptions about the system
- Suboptimal test order
- Linked production code
- Overcoding
- Testing for confidence

Running the Wrong Tests

The first thing to do when sitting down is run your test suite. How many tests do you have? Each time you add a new test, anxiously await the new count when your run your test suite. "Hmm...why am I getting a green? Well, I should have forty-three tests now...but wait! There are only forty-two. The test run doesn't include my new test."

Tracking your test count helps you quickly determine when you've made one of the following silly mistakes:

- You ran the wrong suite.

- Your Google Mock filter (see *Running a Subset of the Tests*, on page 87) omits the new test.

- You didn't compile or link in the new test.

- You disabled (*Disabling Tests*, on page 76) the new test.

If you don't first observe test failure, things get worse. You write the test, skip running the test suite, write the code, and run the tests. You think they're all passing because you wrote the right code, but in reality they pass because the test run doesn't include the new test. You might blissfully chug along for a good while before you discover that you've coded a broken heap of sludge.

Keeping to the TDD cycle can prevent you from wasting a lot of time.

Testing the Wrong Code

Similar to running the wrong tests, you can test the wrong code. Usually it's related to a build error but not always. Here are a few reasons why you might end up running the wrong code:

- You forgot to save or build, in which case the "wrong" code is the last compiled version that doesn't incorporate your new changes. Ways to eliminate this mistake include making the unit test run dependent upon compilation or running tests as part of a postbuild step.

- The build failed and you didn't notice, thinking it had passed.

- The build script is flawed. Did you link the wrong object module? Is another object module with a same-named module clashing?

- You are testing the wrong class. If you're doing interesting things with *test doubles*, which allow you to use polymorphic substitution in order to make testing easier, your test might be exercising a different implementation than you think.

Unfortunate Test Specification

You accidentally coded a test to assert one thing when you meant another.

Suppose we code a test as follows:

```
TEST_F(APortfolio, IsEmptyWhenCreated) {
   ASSERT_THAT(portfolio.isEmpty(), Eq(false));
}
```

Well, no. Portfolios should be empty when created, per the test name; therefore, we should expect the call to isEmpty() to return true, not false. Oops.

On a premature pass, always reread your test to ensure it specifies the proper behavior.

Invalid Assumptions About the System

Suppose you write a test and it passes immediately. You affirm you're running the right tests and testing the right code. You reread the test to ensure it does what you want. That means the system already has the behavior you just specified in the new test. Hmmm.

You wrote the test because you assumed the behavior didn't already exist (unless you were testing out of insecurity—see Testing for Confidence on page 69). A passing test tells you that your assumption was wrong. The behavior is already in the system! You must stop and analyze the system in the light of the behavior you thought we were adding, until you understand the circumstances enough to move on.

Getting a passing test in this case represents a good thing. You've been alerted to something important. Perhaps it is your misunderstanding of how a third-party component behaves. Taking the time to investigate may well save you from shipping a defect.

Suboptimal Test Order

The interface for RetweetCollection requires size() and a convenience member function called isEmpty(). After getting our first two tests for these concepts to pass, we refactor the implementation of isEmpty() to delegate to size() so that we don't have variant algorithms for two related concepts.

c3/2/RetweetCollectionTest.cpp

```
#include "gmock/gmock.h"
#include "RetweetCollection.h"

using namespace ::testing;

class ARetweetCollection: public Test {
public:
   RetweetCollection collection;
};

TEST_F(ARetweetCollection, IsEmptyWhenCreated) {
   ASSERT_TRUE(collection.isEmpty());
}

TEST_F(ARetweetCollection, HasSizeZeroWhenCreated) {
   ASSERT_THAT(collection.size(), Eq(0u));
}
```

c3/2/RetweetCollection.h

```
#ifndef RetweetCollection_h
#define RetweetCollection_h
class RetweetCollection {
public:
   bool isEmpty() const {
      return 0 == size();
   }

   unsigned int size() const {
      return 0;
   }
};
#endif
```

To expand on the concept of emptiness, we write a subsequent test to ensure a retweet collection isn't empty once tweets are added to it.

c3/3/RetweetCollectionTest.cpp

```
#include "Tweet.h"

TEST_F(ARetweetCollection, IsNoLongerEmptyAfterTweetAdded) {
   collection.add(Tweet());

   ASSERT_FALSE(collection.isEmpty());
}
```

(For now, we don't care about the content of a tweet, so all we need to supply for the Tweet class definition in Tweet.h is simply class Tweet {};.)

Getting IsNoLongerEmptyAfterTweetAdded to pass is a simple matter of introducing a member variable to track the collection's size.

c3/3/RetweetCollection.h
```cpp
#include "Tweet.h"

class RetweetCollection {
public:
    RetweetCollection()
        : size_(0) {
    }

    bool isEmpty() const {
        return 0 == size();
    }

    unsigned int size() const {
        return size_;
    }

    void add(const Tweet& tweet) {
        size_ = 1;
    }

private:
    unsigned int size_;
};
```

But we now have a problem. If we want to explore the behavior of size() after adding a tweet, it will pass immediately.

c3/4/RetweetCollectionTest.cpp
```cpp
TEST_F(ARetweetCollection, HasSizeOfOneAfterTweetAdded) {
    collection.add(Tweet());

    ASSERT_THAT(collection.size(), Eq(1u));
}
```

What might we have done to avoid writing a test that passed?

Before answering that question, maybe we need a different perspective. Did we need to even write this test? TDD is about confidence, not exhaustive testing. Once we have an implementation we are confident is sufficient, we can stop writing tests. Perhaps we should delete HasSizeOfOneAfterTweet-Added and move on. Or, perhaps we should retain it for its documentation value.

Otherwise, any time we get a premature pass, we look at the code we wrote to pass the prior test. Did we write too much code? In this case, no, the code was as simple as it could have been. But what if we had explored the emptiness behavior further before introducing the size() behavior? With tests in the order IsEmptyWhenCreated, IsNoLongerEmptyAfterTweetAdded, and HasSizeZeroWhenCreated, we would have ended up with a slightly different scenario.

```
c3/5/RetweetCollection.h
class RetweetCollection {
public:
    RetweetCollection()
        : empty_(true) {
    }

    bool isEmpty() const {
        return empty_;
    }

    void add(const Tweet& tweet) {
        empty_ = false;
    }

    unsigned int size() const {
        return 0;
    }

private:
    bool empty_;
};
```

We can't link size() to isEmpty() at this point, since we have no tests that define how size() behaves after a purchase. Thus, we can't refactor size(); it remains as is with a hard-coded return. Now when we code HasSizeOfOneAfterTweetAdded, it will fail. The simplest implementation to get it to pass is a little odd, but that's OK!

```
c3/6/RetweetCollection.h
unsigned int size() const {
    return isEmpty() ? 0 : 1;
}
```

It's easy to be lazy as a programmer. You'll likely resist reverting your changes and starting over in order to find a path that avoids a premature pass. Yet you'll learn some of the most valuable lessons in the rework. If you choose not to, at least rack your brain and think how you might have avoided the premature pass, which might help you avoid the problem next time.

Linked Production Code

In *Suboptimal Test Order*, on page 62, isEmpty() is a convenience method designed to make client code clearer. We know it's linked to the concept of size (we coded it!). The collection is empty when the size is zero and not empty when the size is greater than zero.

Adding a convenience method such as isEmpty() creates duplication on the side of the code's interface. It represents a different way for clients to interface with behavior that we've already test-driven. That means a test against isEmpty() will pass automatically. We still want to clearly document its behavior, though.

As we add new functionality to RetweetCollection, such as combining similar tweets, we'll want to verify that the new behavior properly impacts the collection's size and emptiness. We have several ways to address verifying both attributes.

The first option is for every size-related assertion, add a second assertion around emptiness. This choice produces unnecessarily repetition and cluttered tests.

c3/7/RetweetCollectionTest.cpp
```cpp
TEST_F(ARetweetCollection, DecreasesSizeAfterRemovingTweet) {
   collection.add(Tweet());

   collection.remove(Tweet());

   ASSERT_THAT(collection.size(), Eq(0u));
   ASSERT_TRUE(collection.isEmpty()); // DON'T DO THIS
}
```

The second option is for every test around size, write a second test for emptiness. While keeping in line with the notion of one assert per test, this choice would also produce too much duplication.

c3/8/RetweetCollectionTest.cpp
```cpp
TEST_F(ARetweetCollection, DecreasesSizeAfterRemovingTweet) {
   collection.add(Tweet());
   collection.remove(Tweet());
   ASSERT_THAT(collection.size(), Eq(0u));
}
// AVOID doing this
TEST_F(ARetweetCollection, IsEmptyAfterRemovingTweet) {
   collection.add(Tweet());
   collection.remove(Tweet());
   ASSERT_TRUE(collection.isEmpty());
}
```

The third option is to create a helper method or custom assertion. Since the code contains a conceptual link between size and emptiness, perhaps we should link the concepts in the assertions.

c3/9/RetweetCollectionTest.cpp
```
MATCHER_P(HasSize, expected, "") {
    return
        arg.size() == expected &&
        arg.isEmpty() == (0 == expected);
}

TEST_F(ARetweetCollection, DecreasesSizeAfterRemovingTweet) {
    collection.add(Tweet());

    collection.remove(Tweet());

    ASSERT_THAT(collection, HasSize(0u));
}
```

The MATCHER_P macro in Google Mock defines a custom matcher that accepts a single argument. See https://code.google.com/p/googlemock/wiki/CheatSheet for further information. You can use a simple helper method if your unit testing tool doesn't support custom matchers.

The fourth option is to create tests that explicitly document the link between the two concepts. In a sense, these tests are a form of documenting invariants. From there on out, we can stop worrying about testing for emptiness in any additional tests.

c3/10/RetweetCollectionTest.cpp
```
TEST_F(ARetweetCollection, IsEmptyWhenItsSizeIsZero) {
    ASSERT_THAT(collection.size(), Eq(0u));

    ASSERT_TRUE(collection.isEmpty());
}

TEST_F(ARetweetCollection, IsNotEmptyWhenItsSizeIsNonZero) {
    collection.add(Tweet());
    ASSERT_THAT(collection.size(), Gt(0u));

    ASSERT_FALSE(collection.isEmpty());
}
```

(In the expression Gt(0), Gt stands for *greater than*.)

The asserts that relate to checking size in these two tests act as *precondition* assertions. They are technically unnecessary but in this case serve to bolster the relationship between the two concepts.

I will usually prefer the fourth option, though sometimes find the third useful. TDD is not an exact science. It provides room for many different approaches, meaning that you must stop and assess the situation from time to time and choose a solution that works best in context.

Overcoding

If you've programmed for any length of time, you have a normal tendency to jump right with what you *know* is needed for an end solution. "I *know* we're gonna need a dictionary data structure, so let's just code in the map now." Or, "Yeah, that could throw an exception that we need to handle. Let's code for that case and log the error in the catch block and then rethrow."

These inclinations and intuitions about what the code needs to do are what makes a good programmer. You don't have to discard these thoughts that come to mind. Knowing about hash-based structures can help guide you to better solutions, and knowing what errors can arise is important.

But to succeed with TDD, you must ensure that you introduce these concepts incrementally and with tests. Keeping to the red-green-refactor rhythm provides many safeguards and also helps grow the number and coverage of unit tests.

Introducing a map prematurely can present you with premature passes for some time, since it will immediately cover many of the cases your code needs to handle. You might omit a number of useful tests as a result. You can instead incrementally grow the underlying data structure, using failing tests as proof for a need to generalize the solution.

Sometimes you'll realize that you don't even need a map. Resisting a more-than-necessary implementation allows you to keep the code simpler in the meantime. You'll also avoid permanent over-complexity when there's a simpler end solution.

Writing tests for things like exception handling means that client programmers will have an easier time understanding how to interact with your class. You force yourself to clearly understand and document the scenarios in which problems can occur.

Learning to produce just enough code is one of the more challenging facets of TDD, but it can pay off dramatically. Sticking to red-green-refactor can help reinforce the incremental approach of TDD.

Testing for Confidence

Sometimes you just don't know what the code does in certain cases. Test-driving generated what you believe to be a complete solution, but you're not sure. "Does our algorithm handle this case?" You write the corresponding test as a probe of the solution. If it fails, you're still in the red-green-refactor cycle, with a failing test prodding you to write the code that handles the new case.

If your probe passes, great! The system works as you hoped. You can move on. But should you keep or discard the new test? Your answer should reflect its documentation value. Does it help a future consumer or developer to understand something important? Does it help better document why another test fails? If so, retain the test. Otherwise, remove it.

Writing a test to probe behavior represents an assumption you're making about the system that you want to verify. You might liken testing for confidence to *Invalid Assumptions About the System*, on page 62. The distinction is that every time you write a test, you should know whether you expect it to fail or pass. If you expect a test to fail and you're surprised when it doesn't, you've made an invalid assumption. If you write a test that you expect to pass, you're testing for confidence.

Stop and Think

Premature passes should be fairly rare. But they're significant, particularly when you're learning to practice TDD. Each time one occurs, ask yourself these questions: What did I miss? Did I take too large a step? Did I make a dumb mistake? What might I have done differently? Like compiler warnings, you always want to listen to what premature passes are telling you.

3.6 Mind-Sets for Successful Adoption of TDD

TDD is a discipline to help you grow a quality design, not just a haphazard approach to verifying pieces of a system. Success with TDD derives from adopting a proper mentality about how to approach it. Here are a half-dozen useful mind-sets to adopt when doing TDD.

Incrementalism

TDD is a way to grow a codebase from nothing into a fully functional system, bit by bit (or unit by unit). Every time you add a new unit of behavior into the system, you know it all still works—you wrote a test for the new behavior, and you have tests for every other unit already built. You don't move on unless everything still works with the new feature in place. Also, you know exactly what the system was designed to do, because your unit tests describe the behaviors you drove into the system.

The incremental approach of TDD meshes well with an Agile process (though you can certainly use TDD in any process, Agile or not). Agile defines short iterations (typically a week or two) in which you define, build, and deliver a small amount of functionality. Each iteration represents the highest-priority features the business wants. The business may completely change priorities with each subsequent iteration. They may even choose to cancel the project prematurely. That's OK, because by definition you will have delivered the features that the business wanted most. Contrast the result with a classic approach, where you first spend months on analysis and then on design, before proceeding to code. No real value is delivered until well after you complete analysis and design and usually not until all coding is considered complete.

TDD offers support *in the small* for a similar incremental mind-set. You tackle units one by one, defining and verifying them with tests. At any given point, you can stop development and know that you have built everything the tests say the system does. Anything not tested is not implemented, and anything tested is implemented correctly and completely.

Test Behavior, Not Methods

A common mistake for TDD newbies is to focus on testing member functions. "We have an add() member function. Let's write TEST(ARetweetCollection, Add)." But fully covering add behavior requires coding to a few different scenarios. The result is that you must lump a bunch of different behaviors into a single test. The documentation value of the tests diminishes, and the time to understand a single test increases.

Instead, focus on behaviors or *cases* that describe behaviors. What happens when you add a tweet that you've already added before? What if a client passes in an empty tweet? What if the user is no longer a valid Twitter user?

We translate the set of concerns around adding tweets into separate tests.

```
TEST(ARetweetCollection, IgnoresDuplicateTweetAdded)
TEST(ARetweetCollection, UsesOriginalTweetTextWhenEmptyTweetAdded)
TEST(ARetweetCollection, ThrowsExceptionWhenUserNotValidForAddedTweet)
```

As a result, you can holistically look at the test names and know exactly the behaviors that the system supports.

Using Tests to Describe Behavior

Think of your tests as examples that describe, or document, the behavior of your system. The full understanding of a well-written test is best gleaned by combining two things: the test name, which summarizes the behavior exhibited given a specific context, and the test statements themselves, which demonstrate the summarized behavior for a single example.

```
c3/11/RetweetCollectionTest.cpp
TEST_F(ARetweetCollection, IgnoresDuplicateTweetAdded) {
    Tweet tweet("msg", "@user");
    Tweet duplicate(tweet);
    collection.add(tweet);

    collection.add(duplicate);

    ASSERT_THAT(collection.size(), Eq(1u));
}
```

The test name provides a high-level summary: a duplicate tweet added should be ignored. But what makes a tweet a duplicate, and what does it mean to ignore a tweet? The test provides a simple example that makes the answers to those two questions clear in a matter of seconds. A duplicate tweet is an exact copy of another, and the size remains unchanged after the duplicate is added.

The more you think about TDD as documentation, the more you understand the importance of a high-quality test. The documentation aspect of the tests is a by-product of doing TDD. To ensure your investment in unit tests returns well on value, you must ensure that others can readily understand your tests. Otherwise, your tests will waste their time.

Good tests will save time by acting as a trustworthy body of comprehensive documentation on the behaviors your system exhibits. As long as all your tests pass, they accurately impart what the system does. Your documentation won't get stale.

Keeping It Simple

The cost of unnecessary complexity never ends. You've no doubt wasted countless hours struggling to decipher a complex member function or convoluted design. Most of the time, you could have programmed the solution more simply and saved everyone a lot of time.

Developers create unnecessary complexity for numerous reasons.

- *Time pressure.* "We just need to ship this code and move on. We have no time to make it pretty." Sooner or later, you'll have no time, period, because it's taking ten times longer to do *anything*. Haste allows complexity to grow, which slows you down in so many ways (comprehension, cost of change, build time).

- *Lack of education.* You need to want better code, and you need to admit when your code sucks, but that means you must know the difference. Seek honest feedback from teammates through pairing and other review forms. Learn how to recognize design deficiencies and code smells. Learn how to correct them with better approaches—take advantage of the many great books on creating clean designs and code.

- *Existing complexity.* A convoluted legacy codebase will make you code through hoops to add new behavior. Long methods promote longer methods, and tightly coupled designs promote even more coupling.

- *Fear of changing code.* Without fast tests, you don't always do the right things in code. "If it ain't broke, don't fix it." Fear inhibits proper refactoring toward a good, sustainable design. With TDD, every green bar you get represents an opportunity to improve the codebase (or at least prevent it from degrading). *Incremental Design* is dedicated to doing the right things in code.

- *Speculation.* "We're probably going to have a many-to-many relationship between customers and accounts down the road, so let's just build that in now." Maybe you'll be right most of the time, but you'll live with premature complexity in the meantime. Sometimes you'll travel a different road entirely and end up paying for the (unused) additional complexity forever, or at least paying dearly to undo the *wrong* complexity. Instead, wait until you really need it. It usually won't cost anything more.

Simplicity is how you survive in a continually changing environment. In an Agile shop, you deliver new features each iteration, some of which you might never have considered before. That's a challenge; you'll find yourself force-fitting new features if the existing system can't accommodate change. Your best defense is a simple design: code that is readable, code that doesn't exhibit duplication, and code that eschews other unnecessary complexities. These characteristics maximally reduce your maintenance costs.

Sticking to the Cycle

Not following red-green-refactor will cost you. See Section 3.5, *Getting Green on Red*, on page 60 for many reasons why it's important to first observe a red bar. Obviously, not getting a green when you want one means you're not adding code that works. More importantly, not taking advantage of the refactoring step of the cycle means that your design will degrade. Without following a disciplined approach to TDD, you will slow down.

3.7 Mechanics for Success

The prior section, Section 3.6, *Mind-Sets for Successful Adoption of TDD*, on page 69, emphasizes a philosophy for success with TDD. This section discusses various specific techniques that will help keep you on track.

What's the Next Test?

As you embark on learning TDD, one of the biggest questions always on your mind will be, "What's the next test I should write?" The examples in this book should suggest a few answers to this question.

One answer is to write the test that results in the simplest possible increment of production code. But just what does that mean?

Uncle Bob has devised a scheme to categorize each increment as a transformation form (see Section 10.4, *The Transformation Priority Premise*, on page 281). All transformations are prioritized from simplest (highest priority) to most complex (lowest priority). Your job is to choose the transformation with the highest-priority order and write the test that generates that transformation. Incrementing in transformation priority order will produce an ideal ordering of tests. That's the premise—the *Transformation Priority Premise* (TPP).

If the TPP sounds complex, that's because it is. It's a theory. So far, it's been demonstrated to provide value for many algorithmic-oriented solutions.

Otherwise, you can use the following list of questions to help decide:

- What's the next most logically meaningful behavior?
- What's the smallest piece of that meaningful behavior you can verify?
- Can you write a test that demonstrates that the current behavior is insufficient?

Let's work through an example and test-drive a class named SQL whose job is to generate SQL statements (select, insert, delete, and so on) given database metadata about a table.

We seek meaningful behavior with each new test. That means we don't directly test-drive getters, setters, or constructors. (They'll get coded as needed when driving in useful behaviors.) Generating a SQL statement that operates on a table seems useful and small enough. We can choose from drop table or truncate table.

Test name	GeneratesDropUsingTableName
Implementation	return "drop" + tableName_

That's trivial and represents a couple minutes coding. We can quickly add support for truncate.

SQL generation so far seems to involve appending the table name to a command string, which suggests a refactored implementation that simplifies creating drop and truncate statements. (The variables Drop and Truncate represent constant strings, each with a trailing space, in the example.)

```
std::string dropStatement() const {
    return createCommand(Drop);
}

std::string truncateStatement() const {
    return createCommand(Truncate);
}

std::string createCommand(const std::string& name) const {
    return name + tableName_;
}
```

We recognize that our behavior is insufficient. We'll have a problem if client code passes in an empty table name.

Sometimes it's worth considering exceptional cases early on, before you get too deep in all the happy path cases. Other times, you can save them until later. You can often code an exceptional test in a short time, needing only a small bit of minimally invasive code to make it pass.

Test name	ConstructionThrowsWhenTableNameEmpty
Implementation	if (tableName_.empty()) throw ...

Next we tackle the select statement as a meaningful increment. The simplest case is to support select *.

Test name	GeneratesSelectStar
Implementation	return createCommand(SelectStarFrom)

It's important to support iterating columns, since most developers consider it better practice than select *.

Test name	GeneratesSelectWithColumnList
Implementation	return Select + columnList() + From + tableName_

Now we're hitting a tiny bit more complexity. It might take a few minutes to implement columnList(), but getting the test to pass is still not an extensive effort.

Our select statement is insufficient. We explore the ability to specify a where clause.

Test name	GeneratesSelectWhereColumnEqual
Implementation	return selectStatement() + whereEq(columnName, value)

The implementation for GeneratesSelectWithColumnList would probably reside in a member function with signature std::string selectStatement() const. The subsequent test, GeneratesSelectWhereColumnEqual, can simply reuse selectStatement(). This is what we want: each small test increment builds upon a prior small increment with minimal impact.

Over time, you'll get a good mental picture of the implementation required to get a given test to pass. Your job is to make life easy on yourself, so you'll get better at choosing the test that corresponds to the implementation with the simplest increment.

You will make less than ideal choices from time to time when choosing the next test. See *Suboptimal Test Order*, on page 62, for an example. A willingness to backtrack and discard a small bit of code can help you better learn how to take more incremental routes through an implementation.

Ten-Minute Limit

TDD depends on short feedback cycles. As long as you're sticking to the red-green-refactor cycle, you should do well with TDD. But it's still possible to bog down. From time to time, you'll struggle getting a test to pass. Or you'll attempt to clean up some code but break a few tests in the process. Or you'll feel compelled to bring up the debugger to understand what's going on.

Struggle is expected, but set a limit on the length of your suffering. Allow no more than ten minutes to elapse from the time your tests last passed. Some developers go as far as to use a timer. You need not be quite so strict about the time, but it is important to realize when your attempt at a solution derails.

If the time limit hits, discard your current effort and start over. A good version control tool like git makes reverting easy, rapid, effective, and very safe. (If you don't use git, consider running it locally with a bridging tool like git-svn.)

Don't get overly attached to code, particularly not code you struggled with. Throw it out with extreme prejudice. It's at most ten minutes of code, and your solution was likely poor. Take a short break, clear your mind, and approach the problem with a new, improved outlook.

If you were stymied by something that didn't work before, take smaller steps this second time and see where that gets you. Introduce additional asserts to verify all questionable assumptions. You'll at least pinpoint the very line of code that caused the problem, and you'll probably build a better solution.

Defects

You will have defects. It's inevitable. However, TDD gives you the potential to have close to zero defects in your new code. I saw one test-driving team's defect report for software that showed only fifteen defects during its first eleven months in production. Other great TDD success stories exist.

Your dumb logic defects will almost disappear with TDD. What will remain? It will be all the other things that can and do go wrong: conditions no one ever expected, external things out of sync (for example, config files), and curious combinations of behavior involving several methods and/or classes. You'll also have defects because of specification problems, including inadvertent omissions and misunderstandings between you and the customer.

TDD isn't a silver bullet. But it *is* a great way to help eliminate dumb logic mistakes we all make. (More importantly, it's a beautiful way to shape your system's design well.)

When QA or support finally does shove a defect in your face, what do you do? Well, you're test-driving. You might first write a few simple tests to probe the existing system. Tests with a tighter focus on related code might help you better understand how the code behaves, which in turn might help you decipher the failure. You can sometimes retain these probes as useful characterization tests (Chapter 8, *Legacy Challenges*, on page 195). Other times, you discard them as one-time tools.

Once you think you've pinpointed the problem source, don't simply fix it and move on. This is TDD! Instead, write a test that you think emulates the behavior that exposed the defect. Ensure that the test fails (red!). Fix it (green!). Refactor (refactor!).

Disabling Tests

Normally, work on one thing at a time when test-driving code. Occasionally you'll find yourself with a second test that fails while you're working on getting a first test to pass. Having another test always fail means that you won't be able to follow the red-green-refactor cycle for the first test (unless they are both failing for the same reason).

Instead of allowing the second, failing test to distract you or divert your attention, you can disable it temporarily. Commenting out the test code would work, but a better mechanism is to mark the test as disabled. Many tools support the ability to explicitly disable a test and can remind you when you run your tests that one or more tests are disabled. The reminder should help prevent you from the crime of accidentally checking in disabled tests.

Using Google Mock, you disable a test by prepending DISABLED_ to its name.

```
TEST(ATweet, DISABLED_RequiresUserNameToStartWithAnAtSign)
```

When you run your test suite, Google Mock will print a reminder at the end to let you know you have one or more disabled tests.

```
[----------] Global test environment tear-down
[==========] 17 tests from 3 test cases ran. (2 ms total)
[  PASSED  ] 17 tests.

  YOU HAVE 1 DISABLED TEST
```

Don't check in code with disabled (or commented-out) tests unless you have a really good reason. The code you integrate should reflect current capabilities of the system. Commented-out tests (and production code too) waste time for other developers. "Is this test commented out because the behavior no longer exists? Is it broken? In-flux? Does it run slowly and people enable it when they want to run it? Should I talk to someone else about it?"

3.8 Teardown

In this chapter, you learned key fundamentals about TDD, including how it differs from unit testing, how to follow the TDD cycle (and what to do when it doesn't go as expected), and some important mind-sets and mechanisms for success with TDD. The underlying concepts and philosophies covered here provide the foundation for moving forward with TDD. In the next chapter, you'll learn some nuts and bolts about how to translate these concepts into actual tests.

## CHAPTER 4

Test Construction

4.1 Setup

By now you should have a solid understanding of the process and concepts behind TDD. This chapter delves into the specifics of implementing your tests: file organization, fixtures, setup, teardown, filters, assertions, and exception-based assertions, plus a few other odds and ends.

4.2 Organization

How do you organize your tests, from both a file standpoint and a logical one? In this section, you'll learn about how to group your tests using fixtures, as well as how to take advantage of their setup and teardown hooks. You'll learn how to approach organization within your tests as well, using the concept of Given-When-Then (also known as Arrange-Act-Assert).

File Organization

You test-drive related behavior by defining tests in a single test file. For example, to test-drive a RetweetCollection class (implemented in RetweetCollection.cpp/h), start with RetweetCollectionTest.cpp. Don't create a header file for your test functions—it demands extra effort for no value.

You may end up with multiple test files that verify related behavior. You may also have one test file cover behavior located in a few areas. Don't limit yourself to one test file per class. *Setup and Teardown*, on page 81, provides one reason why you'd want multiple test files per class.

Name the file based on the tests it contains. Summarize the related behavior and encode it in the test name. Decide on a naming scheme, something like *BehaviorDescription*Test.cpp, *BehaviorDescription*Tests.cpp, or Test*BehaviorDescription*.cpp. It doesn't matter which as long as your codebase consistently adheres to the standard. A consistent naming convention will help programmers readily locate the tests they seek.

Fixtures

Most unit testing tools let you logically group related tests. In Google Mock, you group related tests using what Google calls the *test case name*. The following test declaration has a test case name of ARetweetCollection. IncrementsSizeWhenTweetAdded is the name of a test within the test case.

```
TEST(ARetweetCollection, IncrementsSizeWhenTweetAdded)
```

Related tests need to run in the same environment. You'll have many tests that require common initialization or helper functions. Many test tools let you define a *fixture*—a class that provides support for cross-test reuse.

In Google Mock, you define a fixture as a class derived from ::testing::Test. You typically define the fixture at the beginning of your test file.

```
using namespace ::testing;

class ARetweetCollection: public Test {
};
```

The following two tests exhibit duplication; they both create an instance of RetweetCollection:

```
TEST(ARetweetCollection, IsEmptyWhenCreated) {
    RetweetCollection collection;

    ASSERT_THAT(collection.isEmpty(), Eq(true));
}

TEST(ARetweetCollection, IsNoLongerEmptyAfterTweetAdded) {
    RetweetCollection collection;
    collection.add(Tweet());

    ASSERT_THAT(collection.isEmpty(), Eq(false));
}
```

You can eliminate the local definitions of RetweetCollection by defining RetweetCollection once in the fixture.

```
class ARetweetCollection: public Test {
public:
    RetweetCollection collection;
};
```

To give a test access to members defined in the fixture class, you must change the TEST macro definition to TEST_F (the trailing *F* stands for *fixture*). Here are the cleaned-up tests:

```
TEST_F(ARetweetCollection, IsEmptyWhenCreated) {
   ASSERT_THAT(collection.isEmpty(), Eq(true));
}

TEST_F(ARetweetCollection, IsNoLongerEmptyAfterTweetAdded) {
   collection.add(Tweet());

   ASSERT_THAT(collection.isEmpty(), Eq(false));
}
```

The test case name *must* match the fixture name! If not or if you forget to append _F to the macro name, you'll get a compile error where the tests reference elements from the fixture (collection in this example).

Creation of a collection variable is a detail that test readers don't usually need to see in order to understand what's going on. Moving the instantiation to a fixture removes that distraction from each of the two tests in this example. If you remove an element from a test in this manner, reread the test. If its intent remains clear, great. If not, undo the change, or consider renaming the variable to make the intent obvious.

You can and should also move all common *functions* into the fixture, particularly if you are not enclosing your tests within a namespace.

Setup and Teardown

If all of the tests in a test case require one or more statements of common initialization, you can move that code into a *setup* function that you define in the fixture. In Google Mock, you must name this member function SetUp (it overrides a virtual function in the base class ::testing::Test).

For each test belonging to the fixture, Google Mock creates a new, separate instance of the fixture. This isolation helps minimize problems created when the statements executed in one test impact another test. The implication is that each test must create its own context from scratch and not depend upon the context created by any other tests. After creating the fixture instance, Google Mock executes the code in SetUp() and then executes the test itself.

Both of the following tests add a Tweet object to the collection in order to create an initial context:

```
c3/14/RetweetCollectionTest.cpp
```
```cpp
TEST_F(ARetweetCollection, IsNoLongerEmptyAfterTweetAdded) {
   collection.add(Tweet());
   ASSERT_FALSE(collection.isEmpty());
}

TEST_F(ARetweetCollection, HasSizeOfOneAfterTweetAdded) {
   collection.add(Tweet());
   ASSERT_THAT(collection.size(), Eq(1u));
}
```

We define a new fixture for RetweetCollection tests that represents a collection populated with a single tweet. We choose a fixture name that describes that context: ARetweetCollectionWithOneTweet.

```
c3/15/RetweetCollectionTest.cpp
```
```cpp
class ARetweetCollectionWithOneTweet: public Test {
public:
   RetweetCollection collection;
   void SetUp() override {
      collection.add(Tweet());
   }
};
```

We take advantage of the common initialization, creating tests that are ever-so-simpler to read.

```
c3/15/RetweetCollectionTest.cpp
```
```cpp
TEST_F(ARetweetCollectionWithOneTweet, IsNoLongerEmpty) {
   ASSERT_FALSE(collection.isEmpty());
}

TEST_F(ARetweetCollectionWithOneTweet, HasSizeOfOne) {
   ASSERT_THAT(collection.size(), Eq(1u));
}
```

When removing duplication, be careful not to remove information critical to understanding the test. Does the fixture name clearly describe the context? ARetweetCollectionWithOneTweet seems self-explanatory, but then again it's easy to convince yourself. Ask another programmer. If they're compelled to read the fixture's setup code, find a way to make the test more explicit.

The first test previously had the *test case.test name* combination ARetweet-Collection.IsNoLongerEmptyAfterTweetAdded (Google Mock refers to this combination as its *full name*). Now the full name is ARetweetCollectionWith-OneTweet.IsNoLongerEmpty. We can avoid having to encode redundant descriptions of our context into each test name by using fixtures with names that describe the context.

We have one more test we can clean up.

c3/15/RetweetCollectionTest.cpp
```cpp
TEST_F(ARetweetCollection, IgnoresDuplicateTweetAdded) {
   Tweet tweet("msg", "@user");
   Tweet duplicate(tweet);
   collection.add(tweet);
   collection.add(duplicate);

   ASSERT_THAT(collection.size(), Eq(1u));
}
```

The first Tweet object added in the test differs from the Tweet objects created in the other tests; it passes values for both of the Tweet's constructor arguments, whereas the other Tweet objects are initialized using default arguments. But we don't really care what Tweet object ends up in the collection in those tests, just that the collection contains a tweet, any tweet. We choose to use the more interesting tweet for all tests.

c3/16/RetweetCollectionTest.cpp
```cpp
class ARetweetCollectionWithOneTweet: public Test {
public:
   RetweetCollection collection;
   void SetUp() override {
      collection.add(Tweet("msg", "@user"));
   }
};
```

But we need to reference that tweet from IgnoresDuplicateTweetAdded in order to create a second, duplicate Tweet object. We'll want to introduce a member variable to the ARetweetCollectionWithOneTweet fixture. That means we'll have to declare it as a pointer type that we initialize in setup. We can use regular ol' C++ pointers that we delete in a *teardown* function.

c3/17/RetweetCollectionTest.cpp
```cpp
class ARetweetCollectionWithOneTweet: public Test {
public:
   RetweetCollection collection;
   Tweet* tweet;
   void SetUp() override {
      tweet = new Tweet("msg", "@user");
      collection.add(*tweet);
   }

   void TearDown() override {
      delete tweet;
      tweet = nullptr;
   }
};
```

The teardown function is essentially the opposite of the setup function. It executes after each test, even if the test threw an exception. You use the teardown function for cleanup purposes—to release memory (as in this example), to relinquish expensive resources (for example, database connections), or to clean up other bits of state, such as data stored in static variables.

Using pointers requires a small change to our test, since the tweet variable now requires pointer semantics. The exciting payoff is that we are able to reduce the number of lines in the test from five to three that represent the core of what we're demonstrating in the test.

c3/17/RetweetCollectionTest.cpp

```
TEST_F(ARetweetCollectionWithOneTweet, IgnoresDuplicateTweetAdded) {
    Tweet duplicate(*tweet);
    collection.add(duplicate);

    ASSERT_THAT(collection.size(), Eq(1u));
}
```

Here's a version of the fixture that uses smart pointers:

c3/18/RetweetCollectionTest.cpp

```
class ARetweetCollectionWithOneTweet: public Test {
public:
    RetweetCollection collection;
    shared_ptr<Tweet> tweet;

    void SetUp() override {
        tweet = shared_ptr<Tweet>(new Tweet("msg", "@user"));
        collection.add(*tweet);
    }
};
```

Setup initialization code should apply to *all* associated tests. Setup context that only a fraction of tests use creates unnecessary confusion. If some tests require a tweet and some tests don't, create a second fixture and apportion the tests appropriately.

Don't hesitate to create additional fixtures. But each time you create a new fixture, determine whether that need represents a design deficiency in the production code. The need for two distinct fixtures might indicate that the class you're testing violates the SRP, and you might want to split it into two.

Arrange-Act-Assert/Given-When-Then

Tests have a common flow. A test first sets up proper conditions, then executes code representing the behavior that you want to verify, and finally verifies that the expected behavior occurred as expected. (Some tests may also need to clean up after themselves. For example, a test may need to close a database connection opened by earlier-executing test code.)

Your tests should declare intent with as much immediacy as possible. That means your tests shouldn't require readers to slowly slog through each line of the test, trying to discern what's going on. A reader should readily understand the essential elements of a test's setup (*arrange*), what behavior it executes (*act*), and how that behavior gets verified (*assert*).

The mnemonic Arrange, Act, Assert (AAA, usually spoken as *triple-A*), devised by Bill Wake,[1] reminds you to visually organize your tests for rapid recognition. Looking at this next test, can you quickly discern which lines of the test relate to setting up a context, which line represents execution of the behavior we want to verify, and which lines relate to the actual assertion?

c3/14/RetweetCollectionTest.cpp
```
TEST_F(ARetweetCollection, IgnoresDuplicateTweetAdded) {
   Tweet tweet("msg", "@user");
   Tweet duplicate(tweet);
   collection.add(tweet);
   collection.add(duplicate);
   ASSERT_THAT(collection.size(), Eq(1u));
}
```

With the lines clumped together, it takes a few extra moments to see exactly what's being tested. Contrast that version of the test with code that makes the Arrange, Act, and Assert portions of the test obvious.

c3/13/RetweetCollectionTest.cpp
```
TEST_F(ARetweetCollection, IgnoresDuplicateTweetAdded) {
   Tweet tweet("msg", "@user");
   Tweet duplicate(tweet);
   collection.add(tweet);

   collection.add(duplicate);

   ASSERT_THAT(collection.size(), Eq(1u));
}
```

Some test-drivers prefer the mnemonic *Given-When-Then*. *Given* a context, *When* the test invokes some behavior, *Then* some result is verified. (The cleanup task isn't part of the mnemonic; it's considered housekeeping with minimal significance to an understanding of the behavior your test verifies.) You might also hear the phrase *Setup—Execute—Verify (—Teardown)*. Given-When-Then provides a slight additional connotation that your focus when

---

1. http://xp123.com/articles/3a-arrange-act-assert

doing TDD is on verifying behavior, not executing tests. It also aligns with an analogous concept used for Acceptance Test–Driven Development (see Section 10.3, *Unit Tests, Integration Tests, and Acceptance Tests*, on page 278).

The concept of AAA won't shatter any earths, but applying it consistently will eliminate unnecessary friction that haphazardly organized tests create for the reader.

4.3 Fast Tests, Slow Tests, Filters, and Suites

If you test-drive small, isolated units of code, each of your tests has the ability to run blazingly fast. A typical test might run in less than a millisecond on a decent machine. With that speed, you can run at least thousands of unit tests in a couple seconds.

Dependencies on collaborators that interact with slow resources such as databases and external services will slow things down. Simply establishing a database connection might take 50ms. If a large percentage of your tests must interact with a database, your thousands of tests will require minutes to run. Some shops wait more than a half hour for all their tests to run.

You'll learn how to begin breaking those dependencies on slow collaborators in the chapter *Test Doubles*. Building fast tests might represent the difference between succeeding with TDD and abandoning it prematurely. Why?

A core goal of doing TDD is to obtain as much feedback as possible as often as possible. When you change a small bit of code, you want to know immediately whether your change was correct. Did you break something in a far-flung corner of the codebase?

You want to run *all* of your unit tests with each small change. A significant payoff of TDD is the ability to obtain this ridiculously rapid and powerful feedback. If you built fast unit tests, it's absolutely possible, as suggested, to run all your tests in a few seconds. Running all your tests all the time is not unreasonable with such short wait times.

If instead your tests complete executing in more than a few seconds, you won't run them as often. How often would you wait two minutes for your tests to run—perhaps five times an hour? What if the tests take twenty minutes to run? You might run those tests a handful of times per day.

TDD begins to diminish in power as the feedback cycle lengthens. The longer the time between feedback, the more questionable code you will create. It's easy and typical to introduce small, or even large, problems as you code. In contrast, running tests after every small change allows you to incrementally address these problems. If your test reveals a defect after you've added a couple minutes of new code, you can easily pinpoint code that caused the problem. If you created a few lines of difficult code, you can clean it up readily and safely.

Slow tests create such a problem for TDD that some folks no longer call them unit tests but instead refer to them as integration tests. (See Section 10.3, *Unit Tests, Integration Tests, and Acceptance Tests*, on page 278.)

Running a Subset of the Tests

You might already have a set of tests (a *suite*) that verifies a portion of your system. Chances are good that your test suite isn't so fast, since most existing systems exhibit countless dependencies on slow collaborators.

The first natural reaction to a slow test suite is to run tests less frequently. That strategy doesn't work if you want to do TDD. The second reaction is to run a subset of the tests all the time. While less than ideal, this strategy might just work, as long as you understand the implications.

Google Mock makes it easy to run a subset of the tests by specifying what is known as a *test filter*. You specify a test filter as a command-line argument to your test executable. The filter allows you to specify tests to execute in the form *test case name.test name*. For example, to run a single, specific test, do this:

```
./test --gtest_filter=ATweet.CanBeCopyConstructed # weak
```

Don't get in a regular habit of running only one test at a time, however. You can use a wildcard character (*) to run numerous tests. Let's at least run all of the tests associated with the ATweet test case.

```
./test --gtest_filter=ATweet.*  # slightly less weak
```

If you're test-driving a class related to tweets, perhaps the best thing you can do is find a way to run all other tests related to tweets, too. You have wildcards, dude (or dude-ess)! Take advantage of them.

```
./test --gtest_filter=*weet*.*
```

Now we're talking! That filter also includes all of the tests against RetweetCollection. (I cleverly omitted the capital T since it doesn't match the lowercase t of RetweetCollection.)

What if you want to run all tests related to tweets but avoid any construction tests for the Tweet class? Google Mock lets you create complex filters.

```
./test --gtest_filter=*Retweet*.*:ATweet.*:-ATweet*.*Construct*
```

You use a colon (:) to separate individual filters. Once Google Mock encounters a negative sign (hyphen), all filters thereafter are subtractive. In the previous example, -ATweet*.*Construct* tells Google Mock to ignore all ATweet tests with the word Construct somewhere in their name.

So, what's the problem with running a subset of the tests? The more tests you can run in a short time, the more likely you will know the moment you introduce a defect. The fewer tests you run, the longer it will be on average before you discover a defect. In general, the longer the time between introducing a defect and discovering it, the longer it will take to correct. There are a few simple reasons. First, if you've worked on other things in the interim, you will often expend additional time to understand the original solution. Second, newer code in the area may increase the comprehension effort required as well as the difficulty of making a fix.

Many unit test tools (but not Google Mock) directly support the ability to permanently specify arbitrary suites. For example, CppUnit provides a Test-Suite class that allows you to programmatically add tests to a collection of tests to run.

Test Triaging

I worked recently with a customer that had a sizable C++ codebase. They had embarked on TDD not long before my arrival and had built a few hundred tests. The majority of their tests ran slowly, and the entire test run took about three minutes, far too long for the number of tests in place. Most tests took about 300 or more milliseconds to execute.

Using Google Mock, we quickly wrote a test listener whose job was to produce a file, slowTests.txt, containing a list of tests that took longer than 10ms to execute. We then altered Google Mock code to support reading a list of filters from a file. That change essentially provided suite support for Google Mock. We then changed Google Mock to support running the *converse* of a specified filter. Using the slowTests.txt file, the team could run either the *slow* subset of all tests or the *fast* subset of all tests. The slow suite took most of the three minutes to run (see Section 10.3, *Unit Tests, Integration Tests, and Acceptance Tests*, on page 278); the fast suite took a couple seconds.

We altered Google Mock to fail if an individual test exceeded a specified number of milliseconds (passed in as a command-line argument named slow_test_threshold). The customer then configured the continuous integration (CI) build to first run the *fast* test suite, triggering it to fail if any test was too slow, and then to run the slow suite.

We told the developers to run the fast suite continually at their desk as they test-drove code. The developers were to specify the slow_test_threshold value as they ran fast tests, so they knew as soon as they introduced an unacceptably slow test. Upon check-in, they were to run both slow and fast suites. We asked the developers to try to shrink the size of slowTests.txt over time, by finding ways to eliminate bad dependencies that made those tests run slowly (see the chapter *Test Doubles*).

The team got the message and ended up with the bulk of their unit tests as fast tests. Last I heard, they were rapidly growing their test-driven codebase successfully.

I've helped a few teams through a similar process of test triaging. Often it's the 80-20 rule: 20 percent of the tests take 80 percent of the execution time. Bucketing the tests into fast and slow suites allows a team to quickly improve their ability to do TDD.

The ability to define suites provides the basis for splitting tests so that you can run fast tests only. The identification of the slow tests allows you to incrementally transform crummy slow tests into spiffy fast tests.

You will usually need integration tests (tests that must *integrate* with external services; see Section 10.3, *Unit Tests, Integration Tests, and Acceptance Tests*, on page 278). They will be slow. Having the ability to arbitrarily define suites allows you to maintain many collections of tests that you run in the CI build as appropriate.

4.4 Assertions

Assertions turn a test into an automated test. In the absence of an assertion, Google Mock simply executes a block of code. If you want to verify that the block of code worked, you'd need to manually inspect the results (perhaps by step-debugging or printing the contents of some variables).

You don't have time for manual verification. TDD generates automated unit tests, which self-verify (see Section 7.2, *Tests Come FIRST*, on page 173), saving you from the risky and tedious work of visually inspecting results. There's hardly anything more wasteful than manually bringing up the GUI for an application, time and time again, in order to verify something that a unit test could have verified automatically.

When your test framework runs an individual test, it executes statements from the top to the bottom of the test's code block. Each assertion encountered represents an attempt to verify that something occurred as expected. If the assertion's condition is not met, the test framework aborts execution of the remainder of the test. (This is often accomplished by having the assertion throw an exception that the framework traps.) The framework stores information about the test failure, runs any teardown logic, and moves on to another test.

Some tools, Google Mock included, provide an alternate assertion mechanism that allows a test to continue executing even if the assertion fails. These assertions are known as *nonfatal assertions* (in contrast to *fatal assertions* that abort the test).

Your production tests should use fatal assertions. A test should abort once an assertion failure occurs. It makes little sense to continue executing a test once an assumption verified by an assertion no longer holds true. If you strive for one assert per test (Section 7.3, *One Assert per Test*, on page 178), you'll rarely have code that executes after that sole assertion.

When designing tests or deciphering test failures, you might use additional assertions as probes. Is a member variable initialized to a specific value? Does setup put things into the state I expect? If a nonfatal assertion fails, the rest of the test still runs, perhaps providing you with additional useful knowledge. You would normally remove such probes when you're ready to check in code.

Classic Form Assertions

Most, if not all, frameworks support what I'll refer to as *classic*-form asserts. They follow a pattern first set out with SUnit, a Smalltalk unit testing framework built in the 1990s. Nothing is wrong with using this form, but you might also consider the more literary form of assertions known as Hamcrest (see *Hamcrest Assertions*, on page 91). You'll want to learn both, since you'll encounter plenty of code using classic assertions.

The table here shows the two core workhorse assertions for Google Mock. Your framework will use similar verbiage.

Form	Description	(Passing) Example
ASSERT_TRUE(expression)	Fail the test if *expression* returns a false (or 0) value.	ASSERT_TRUE(4 < 7)
ASSERT_EQ(expected, actual)	Fail the test if expected == actual returns false.	ASSERT_EQ(4, 20 / 5)

Google Mock, like most C++ unit-testing frameworks, uses macros to implement the behavior for assertions. The assertion implementations for equality comparisons are generally overloaded to support comparison of all primitive types.

Most frameworks provide several additional assertion forms designed to improve expressiveness. For example, Google Mock supports ASSERT_FALSE (assert that an expression returns false) plus a series of relational assertions such as ASSERT_GT (assert that a first argument is greater than a second). You would express the first assertion in the preceding table as ASSERT_LT(4, 7).

Hamcrest Assertions

Your unit testing tool provides a small fixed set of classic-form assertions. The most prevalent assertion, comparing two values for equality (ASSERT_EQ in Google Mock), is idiomatic. You have to remember that the expected value comes first. Were you to read an assertion out loud, it would sound like "Assert equals the expected value of 5 to the actual value of x." It's not a big deal, because you'll be reading thousands of asserts over time, but the awkward phrasing slightly detracts from the readability of a test. Also, it's easier for newbies to mistakenly invert the order of actual and expected values.

Hamcrest assertions were introduced into unit testing tools several years ago in an attempt to improve the expressiveness of tests, the flexibility of creating complex assertions, and the information supplied by failure messages. Hamcrest uses *matchers* ("Hamcrest" is an anagram of "matchers") to declare comparisons against actual results. Matchers can be combined to build complex yet easily understood comparison expressions. You can also create custom matchers.

A few simple examples are worth a thousand words, or at least the number of words in the preceding paragraph.

```
string actual = string("al") + "pha";
ASSERT_THAT(actual, Eq("alpha"));
```

The assertion reads left to right: assert that the actual value is Equal to the string "alpha". For simple equality comparisons, the improved readability comes at the low cost of a few extra characters.

Hamcrest can seem like overkill initially. But the wealth of matchers should make it clear that Hamcrest provides ample opportunities for high levels of expressiveness in your tests. Many of the matchers can actually reduce the amount of code you write at the same time they increase the abstraction level in your tests.

```
ASSERT_THAT(actual, StartsWith("alx"));
```

A list of the provided matchers appears in the Google Mock documentation.[2]

You'll want to add a using declaration to your test file.

```
using namespace ::testing;
```

Otherwise, the assertions that you so dearly want to be expressive will be filled with clutter.

```
ASSERT_THAT(actual, ::testing::StartsWith("al"));
```

---

2. http://code.google.com/p/googlemock/wiki/V1_6_CheatSheet#Matchers

The value of using Hamcrest increases even more with the improved readability of the failure messages.

```
Expected: starts with "alx"
  Actual: "alpha" (of type std::string)
```

The ability to combine matchers can reduce multiple lines needed to assert something into a single-line assertion.

```
ASSERT_THAT(actual,
     AllOf(StartsWith("al"), EndsWith("ha"), Ne("aloha")));
```

In this example, AllOf indicates that all of the matcher arguments must succeed in order for the entire assert to pass. Thus, the actual string must start with "al", end with "ha", and not be equal to "aloha".

Most developers eschew the use of Hamcrest for assertions against boolean values and prefer to use the classic-form assertion instead.

```
ASSERT_TRUE(someBooleanExpression);
ASSERT_FALSE(someBooleanExpression);
```

Finally, if the set of matchers Google Mock provides is insufficient for your needs, you can create custom matchers.[3]

Choosing the Right Assertion

The goal of an assertion in your test is to succinctly describe the expected outcome of preceding statements executed in the test. Usually you want the assertion to be specific. If you know that the value of a variable should be 3, use an equality assertion form and assert exactly that.

```
ASSERT_THAT(tweetsAdded, Eq(3));
```

Weaker comparisons can at times be more expressive, but most of the time you want to avoid them.

```
ASSERT_THAT(tweetsAdded, Gt(0)); // avoid broad assertions
```

Most of your assertions should use the equality form. You could technically use the ASSERT_TRUE form for everything, but the equality form assertions (Hamcrest or not) provide a better message when an assertion does fail. When the following assertion fails...

```
unsigned int tweetsAdded(5);
ASSERT_TRUE(tweetsAdded == 3);
```

the failure message provides minimal information.

---

3.   http://code.google.com/p/googlemock/wiki/V1_6_CheatSheet#Defining_Matchers

```
Value of: tweetsAdded == 3
  Actual: false
Expected: true
```

However, when you use an equality form...

```
ASSERT_THAT(tweetsAdded, Eq(3));
```

the failure message tells you what the assertion expected plus what was actually received.

```
Value of: tweetsAdded
Expected: is equal to 3
  Actual: 5 (of type unsigned int)
```

The wording of the failure message is why you always want to specify the *expected* and *actual* values in the correct order. Unintentionally reversing the order creates a confusing failure message that will take additional time to decipher. If you use ASSERT_THAT(), the actual value comes first; if you use ASSERT_EQ(), the expected value comes first.

Comparing Floats

Floating-point numbers are imprecise binary representations of real numbers. As such, the result of a float-based calculation might not exactly match another float value, even though it appears as if they should. Here's an example:

```
double x{4.0};
double y{0.56};
ASSERT_THAT(x + y, Eq(4.56));
```

On my machine, I receive the following failure when I execute the previous assertion:

```
Value of: x + y
Expected: is equal to 4.56
  Actual: 4.56 (of type double)
```

Google Mock and other tools provide special assertion forms that allow you to compare two floating-point quantities using a tolerance. If the two quantities differ by an amount greater than the tolerance, the assertion fails. Google Mock provides a simpler comparison by using units in the last place (ULPs) as the default tolerance.

```
ASSERT_THAT(x + y, DoubleEq(4.56));
```

(In a forthcoming version of Google Test, you can also specify the tolerance value itself if you are daring enough—ULPs and comparing floating-point numbers are complex topics (http://www.cygnus-software.com/papers/comparingfloats/comparingfloats.htm).

Exception-Based Tests

As a good programmer, you know the possibilities for failure that could arise from executing code. You know when to throw exceptions and also when you might need to protect your application by introducing try-catch blocks. Your intimate knowledge of the code paths is what allows you to know when you need to worry about handling exceptions.

When doing TDD, you drive code to handle these concerns into your system by first writing a failing test. The result is a test that documents to other developers—who don't have your intimate knowledge of the code paths—what could go wrong and what should happen when it does. A client developer armed with this knowledge can consume your classes with much higher confidence.

Suppose you are testing a bit of code that throws an exception under certain circumstances. Your job as a professional is to document that case in a test.

Some unit testing frameworks allow you to declare that an exception should be thrown and fail the test if an exception is not thrown. Using Google Mock, we code the following:

c3/12/TweetTest.cpp
```
TEST(ATweet, RequiresUserToStartWithAtSign) {
    string invalidUser("notStartingWith@");
    ASSERT_ANY_THROW(Tweet tweet("msg", invalidUser));
}
```

The ASSERT_ANY_THROW macro fails the test if the expression it encloses does *not* throw an exception. We run all the tests and await the failure of this test.

```
Expected: Tweet tweet("msg", invalidUser) throws an exception.
  Actual: it doesn't.
```

Here is corresponding code that gets the test to pass:

c3/12/Tweet.h
```
Tweet(const std::string& message="",
      const std::string& user=Tweet::NULL_USER)
    : message_(message)

    , user_(user) {
    if (!isValid(user_)) throw InvalidUserException();
}

bool isValid(const std::string& user) const {
    return '@' == user[0];
}
```

(The implementation of isValid() is sufficient for the one new test we added to TweetTest. Its implementation assumes that Tweet's constructor is passed a nonempty string for the user argument. So, what other test do we need to write?)

If you know the type of the exception that will be thrown, you can specify it.

```
c3/12/TweetTest.cpp
TEST(ATweet, RequiresUserToStartWithAnAtSign) {
    string invalidUser("notStartingWith@");
    ASSERT_THROW(Tweet tweet("msg", invalidUser), InvalidUserException);
}
```

The failure message tells you when the expected exception type does not match what was actually thrown.

```
Expected: Tweet tweet("msg", invalidUser) throws an exception
          of type InvalidUserException.
  Actual: it throws a different type.
```

If your framework does not support a single-line declarative assert that ensures an exception is thrown, you can use the following structure in your test:

```
c3/12/TweetTest.cpp
TEST(ATweet, RequiresUserNameToStartWithAnAtSign) {
    string invalidUser("notStartingWith@");
    try {
        Tweet tweet("msg", invalidUser);
        FAIL();
    }
    catch (const InvalidUserException& expected) {}
}
```

We could code this in a number of ways, but I prefer the technique shown here. It's the generally preferred idiom in the TDD community. You might also need to use the try-catch structure if you must verify any postconditions after the exception is thrown. For example, you may want to verify the text associated with the thrown exception object.

```
c3/13/TweetTest.cpp
TEST(ATweet, RequiresUserNameToStartWithAtSign) {
    string invalidUser("notStartingWith@");
    try {
        Tweet tweet("msg", invalidUser);
        FAIL();
    }
    catch (const InvalidUserException& expected) {
        ASSERT_STREQ("notStartingWith@", expected.what());
    }
}
```

Note the use of ASSERT_STREQ. Google Mock supplies four assertion macros (ASSERT_STREQ, ASSERT_STRNE, ASSERT_STRCASEEQ, and ASSERT_STRCASENE) designed to support C-style (null-terminated) strings, in other words, char* variables.

4.5 Inspecting Privates

New test-drivers inevitably ask two questions: Is it OK to write tests against private member data? What about private member functions? These are two related but distinct topics that both relate to design choices you must make.

Private Data

The *Tell-Don't-Ask* design concept says that you should tell an object to do something and let that object go off and complete its work. If you ask lots of questions of the object, you're violating Tell-Don't-Ask. A system consisting of excessive queries to other objects will be entangled and complex. Client C asks an object S for information, does some work that's possibly a responsibility S could take on, asks another question of S, and so on, creating a tight interaction between C and S. Since S is not taking on the responsibility it should, clients other than C are likely asking similar questions and thus coding duplicate bits of logic to handle the responses.

An object told to do something will sometimes delegate the work to a collaborator object. Accordingly, a test would verify the interaction—"Did the collaborator receive the message?"—using a test double (see *Test Doubles*). This is known as *interaction-based testing*.

Still, not all interactions require spying on collaborators. When test-driving a simple container, for example, you'll want to verify that the container holds on to any objects added. Simply ask the container what it contains using its public interface and assert against the answer. Tests that verify by inspecting attributes of an object are known as *state-based tests*.

It's only fair game to allow clients to know what they themselves stuffed into an object. Add an accessor. (If you're worried about evil clients using this access for cracking purposes, have the accessor return a copy instead.)

You might have the rare need to hold onto the result of some intermediate calculation—essentially a side effect of making a function call that will be used later. It's acceptable to create an accessor to expose this value that might not otherwise need to be part of the interface for the class. You might declare the test as a friend of the target class, but don't do that. Add a brief comment to declare your intent.

```cpp
public:
   // exposed for testing purposes; avoid direct production use:
   unsigned int currentWeighting;
```

Exposing data solely for the purpose of testing will bother some folks, but it's more important to know that your code works as intended.

Excessive state-based testing is a design smell, however. Any time you expose data *solely* to support an assertion, think about how you might verify behavior instead. Refer to *Schools of Mock*, on page 134, for further discussion of state vs. interaction testing.

Private Behavior

When test-driving, everything flows from the public interface design of your class. To add detailed behavior, you test-drive it as if your test were a production client of the class. As the details get more detailed and the code more complex, you'll find yourself naturally refactoring to additional extracted methods. You might find yourself wondering if you should directly write tests against those extracted methods.

The library system defines a HoldingService class that provides the public API for checking out and checking in holdings. Its CheckIn() method provides a reasonable (though slightly messy) high-level policy implementation for checking in holdings.

c7/2/library/HoldingService.cpp
```cpp
void HoldingService::CheckIn(
      const string& barCode, date date, const string& branchId)
{
   Branch branch(branchId);
   mBranchService.Find(branch);

   Holding holding(barCode);
   FindByBarCode(holding);

   holding.CheckIn(date, branch);
   mCatalog.Update(holding);

   Patron patronWithBook = FindPatron(holding);

   patronWithBook.ReturnHolding(holding);

   if (IsLate(holding, date))
      ApplyFine(patronWithBook, holding);

   mPatronService.Update(patronWithBook);
}
```

The challenge is the ApplyFine() function. The programmer who originally test-drove the implementation of CheckIn() started with a simple implementation for a single case but extracted the function as it became complex.

c7/2/library/HoldingService.cpp

```cpp
void HoldingService::ApplyFine(Patron& patronWithHolding, Holding& holding)
{
    int daysLate = CalculateDaysPastDue(holding);

    ClassificationService service;
    Book book = service.RetrieveDetails(holding.Classification());

    switch (book.Type()) {
      case Book::TYPE_BOOK:
          patronWithHolding.AddFine(Book::BOOK_DAILY_FINE * daysLate);
          break;
      case Book::TYPE_MOVIE:
          {
              int fine = 100 + Book::MOVIE_DAILY_FINE * daysLate;
              if (fine > 1000)
                  fine = 1000;
              patronWithHolding.AddFine(fine);
          }
          break;
      case Book::TYPE_NEW_RELEASE:
          patronWithHolding.AddFine(Book::NEW_RELEASE_DAILY_FINE * daysLate);
          break;
    }
}
```

Each test built around ApplyFine() must run in a context that requires a patron first check a book out and then check it in. Wouldn't it make more sense to exhaust all of the ApplyFine() code paths by testing it directly?

Writing tests against ApplyFine() directly should make us feel a twinge bad because of the information-hiding violation. More importantly, our design senses should be tingling. ApplyFine() violates the SRP for HoldingService: a HoldingService should provide a high-level workflow only for clients. Implementation details for each step should appear elsewhere. Viewed another way, ApplyFine() exhibits feature envy—it wants to live in another class, perhaps Patron.

Most of the time, when you feel compelled to test private behavior, instead move the code to another class or to a new class.

ApplyFine() isn't yet a candidate for moving wholesale to Patron, because it does a few things: it asks another function on the service to calculate the number of days past due, determines the book type for the given book, and applies a calculated fine to the patron. The first two responsibilities require access to other HoldingService features, so they need to stay in HoldingService for now. But we can split apart and move the fine calculation.

c7/3/library/HoldingService.cpp

```
void HoldingService::ApplyFine(Patron& patronWithHolding, Holding& holding)
{
    unsigned int daysLate = CalculateDaysPastDue(holding);

    ClassificationService service;
    Book book = service.RetrieveDetails(holding.Classification());
    patronWithHolding.ApplyFine(book, daysLate);
}
```

c7/3/library/Patron.cpp

```
void Patron::ApplyFine(Book& book, unsigned int daysLate)
{
    switch (book.Type()) {
      case Book::TYPE_BOOK:
          AddFine(Book::BOOK_DAILY_FINE * daysLate);
          break;

      case Book::TYPE_MOVIE:
          {
              int fine = 100 + Book::MOVIE_DAILY_FINE * daysLate;
              if (fine > 1000)
                  fine = 1000;
              AddFine(fine);
          }
          break;

      case Book::TYPE_NEW_RELEASE:
          AddFine(Book::NEW_RELEASE_DAILY_FINE * daysLate);
          break;
    }
}
```

Now that we look at the moved function in its new home, we see that we still have problems. Asking about the type of book still exhibits possible feature envy. The switch statement represents another code smell. Replacing it with a polymorphic hierarchy would allow us to create more direct, more focused tests. For now, though, we've put ApplyFine() in a place where we should feel comfortable about making it public so that we can directly test it.

Q.: Won't I end up with thousands of extra special-purpose classes by coding this way?

A.: You will end up with more classes, certainly, but not thousands more. Each class will be significantly smaller, easier to understand/test/maintain, and faster to build! (See Section 4.3, Fast Tests, Slow Tests, Filters, and Suites, on page 86.)

Q.: I'm not a fan of creating more classes.

A.: It's where you start truly taking advantage of OO. As you start creating more single-purpose classes, each containing a small number of single-purpose methods, you'll start to recognize more opportunities for reuse. It's impossible to reuse large, highly detailed classes. In contrast, SRP-compliant classes begin to give you the hope of reducing your overall amount of code.

What if you're dealing with legacy code? Suppose you want to begin refactoring a large class with dozens of member functions, many private. Like private behavior, simply relax access and add a few tests around some of the private functions. (Again, don't worry about abuse; it doesn't happen.) Seek to move the function to a better home later. See *Legacy Challenges* for more on getting legacy code under control.

4.6 Testing vs. Test-Driving: Parameterized Tests and Other Toys

Despite the word *test* appearing in its name, TDD is less about testing than it is about design. Yes, you produce unit tests as a result of practicing TDD, but they are almost a by-product. It might seem like a subtle difference, but the true goal is to allow you to keep the design clean over time so that you may introduce new behavior or change existing behavior with high confidence and reasonable cost.

With a testing mentality, you seek to create tests that cover a breadth of concerns. You create tests for five types of cases: zero, one, many, boundary, and exceptional cases. With a test-*driving* mentality, you write tests in order to drive in code that you believe meets desired specifications. While both testing and test-driving are about providing enough confidence to ship code, you stop test-driving as soon you have the confidence that you've built all you need (and your tests all pass, of course). In contrast, a good tester seeks to cover the five types of cases as exhaustively as reasonable.

Nothing prohibits you from writing additional after-the-fact tests when doing TDD. Usually, though, you stop as soon as you believe you have a correct and clean implementation that covers the cases you know you must support. Stated another way, stop once you can't think of how to write a test that would fail.

As an example, consider the Roman number converter (see *Code Kata: Roman Numeral Converter*), which converts an Arabic numeral to a corresponding Roman numeral. A good tester would probably test at least a couple dozen conversions to ensure that all the various digits and combinations thereof were covered. In contrast, when test-driving the solution, I could stop at about a dozen tests. At that point, I have the confidence that I've built the right algorithm, and the remainder of the work is simply filling in a digit-to-digit conversion table. (In the appendix, I drive through a few more assertions for confidence and demonstration purposes.)

The genesis of many code-level testing tools was to support the writing of tests, not to support doing TDD. As such, many tools provide sophisticated features to make testing easier. For example, some tools allow you to define dependencies between tests. It's a nice optimization feature if you have a suite of integration tests (see Section 10.3, *Unit Tests, Integration Tests, and Acceptance Tests*, on page 278) that run slowly; you can speed up your test run by stringing tests together in a certain order. (The maintenance costs of and pains from using such tightly coupled tests increase.) But when doing TDD, you seek fast, independent tests and therefore don't need the complexity of test dependencies.

Nothing is wrong with wanting or using any of these testing features from time to time. However, question the desire: Does this feature suggest that I'm outside the bounds of TDD? Is there an approach that better aligns with the goals of TDD?

This section will cover, briefly, some tempting test tool features. Refer to your test tool for further details about these features if you still feel compelled to use them (even after I attempt to dissuade you).

Parameterized Tests

The Roman numeral converter (*Code Kata: Roman Numeral Converter*) must convert the numbers from 1 through 3999. Perhaps it would be nice if you could simply iterate a list of expected inputs and outputs and pump this into a single test that took an input and an output as arguments. The *parameterized tests* feature exists in some test tools (Google Mock included) to support this need.

Let's demonstrate with this very trivial class called Adder:

```
c3/18/ParameterizedTest.cpp
class Adder {
public:
    static int sum(int a, int b) {
        return a + b;
    }
};
```

Here is a normal TDD-generated test that drove in the implementation for sum():

c3/18/ParameterizedTest.cpp
```cpp
TEST(AnAdder, GeneratesASumFromTwoNumbers) {
    ASSERT_THAT(Adder::sum(1, 1), Eq(2));
}
```

But that test covers only a single case! Yes, and we're confident that the code works, and we shouldn't feel the need to create a bunch of additional cases.

For more complex code, it might make us a tad more confident to blast through a bunch of cases. For the Adder example, we first define a fixture that derives from TestWithParam<T>, where T is the parameter type.

c3/18/ParameterizedTest.cpp
```cpp
class AnAdder: public TestWithParam<SumCase> {
};
```

Our parameter type is SumCase, designed to capture two input numbers and an expected sum.

c3/18/ParameterizedTest.cpp
```cpp
struct SumCase {
    int a, b, expected;
    SumCase(int anA, int aB, int anExpected)
      : a(anA), b(aB), expected(anExpected) {}
};
```

With these elements in place, we can write a parameterized test. We use TEST_P, P for parameterized, to declare the test.

c3/18/ParameterizedTest.cpp
```cpp
TEST_P(AnAdder, GeneratesLotsOfSumsFromTwoNumbers) {
    SumCase input = GetParam();
    ASSERT_THAT(Adder::sum(input.a, input.b), Eq(input.expected));
}
SumCase sums[] = {
    SumCase(1, 1, 2),
    SumCase(1, 2, 3),
    SumCase(2, 2, 4)
};
INSTANTIATE_TEST_CASE_P(BulkTest, AnAdder, ValuesIn(sums));
```

The last line kicks off calling the test with injected parameters. INSTANTI-ATE_TEST_CASE_P takes the name of the fixture as its second argument and takes the values to be injected as the third argument. (The first argument, BulkTest, represents a prefix that Google Mock appends to the test name.) The ValuesIn() function indicates that the injection process should use an element from the array sums to inject into the test (GeneratesLotsOfSumsFromTwoNumbers) each time it's called. The first line in the test calls GetParam(), which returns the injected value (a SumCase object).

Cool! But in the dozen-plus years I've been doing TDD, I've used parameterized tests less than a handful of times. It works well if you have a lot of simple data you want to crunch through. Perhaps someone gave you a spreadsheet with a bunch of data cases. You might dump those values as parameters (and maybe even write a bit of code to pull the parameters directly from the spreadsheet). These are perfectly fine ideas, but you're no longer in the realm of TDD.

Also, remember that a goal of TDD is to have tests that document behaviors by example, each named to aptly describe the unique behavior being driven in. Parameterized tests can meet this need, but more often than not, they simply act as tests.

Comments in Tests

The code examples distributed as part of the documentation for a prominent test tool include a number of well-annotated tests. Comments appear, I presume, for pedantic reasons.

```
// Tests the c'tor that accepts a C string.
TEST(MyString, ConstructorFromCString)
```

It takes a lot to offend me, but this comment comes pretty close. What a waste of typing effort, space, and time for those who must read the code.

Of course, comments aren't a test tool feature but a language feature. In both production code and test code, your best choice is to transform as many comments as you can into more-expressive code. The remaining comments will likely answer questions like "Why in the world did I code it that way?"

Outside of perhaps explaining a "why," if you need a comment to explain your test, it stinks. Tests should clearly document class capabilities. You can always rename and structure your tests in a way (see Section 7.3, *One Assert per Test*, on page 178 and *Arrange-Act-Assert/Given-When-Then*, on page 84) that obviates explanatory comments.

In case I haven't quite belabored the point, don't summarize a test with a descriptive comment. Fix its name. Don't guide readers through the test with comments. Clean up the steps in the test.

4.7 Teardown

Armed with the mechanics of constructing tests provided in this chapter and the concepts of TDD from the prior chapter, you're ready to tackle some bigger issues. How do you write tests against objects that must interact with other objects, particularly when those objects exhibit troublesome dependencies?

## CHAPTER 5

Test Doubles

5.1 Setup

In the prior three chapters, you test-drove a stand-alone class and learned all about the fundamentals of TDD. If only life were so simple! The reality is that objects must work with other objects (collaborators) in a production OO system. Sometimes the dependencies on collaborators can cause pesky challenges for test-driving—they can be slow, unstable, or not even around to help you yet.

In this chapter, you'll learn how to brush away those challenges using test doubles. You'll first learn how to break dependencies using handcrafted test doubles. You'll then see how you might simplify the creation of test doubles by using a tool. You'll learn about different ways of setting up your code so that it can use test doubles (also known as *injection* techniques). Finally, you'll read about the design impacts of using test doubles, as well as strategies for their best use.

5.2 Dependency Challenges

Objects often must collaborate with other objects in order to get their work done. An object tells another to do something or asks it for information. If an object *A* depends upon a collaborator object *B* in order to accomplish its work, *A* is *dependent upon B*.

Story: Place Description Service

As a programmer on map-based applications, I want a service that returns a one-line description of the named place nearest a given location (latitude and longitude).

An important part of building the Place Description Service involves calling an external API that takes a location and returns place data. I found an open, free Representational State Transfer (REST) service that returns the place data in JSON format, given a GET URL. This Nominatim Search Service is part of the Open MapQuest API.[1,2]

Test-driving the Place Description Service presents a challenge—the dependency on the REST call is problematic for at least a few reasons.

- Making an actual HTTP call to invoke a REST service is very slow and will bog down your test run. (See Section 4.3, *Fast Tests, Slow Tests, Filters, and Suites*, on page 86.)

- The service might not always be available.

- You can't guarantee what results the call will return.

Why do these dependency concerns create testing challenges? First, a dependency on slow collaborators results in undesirably slow tests. Second, a dependency on a volatile service (either unavailable or returning different answers each time) results in intermittently failing tests.

The dependency concern of sheer *existence* can exist. What if you have no utility code that supports making an HTTP call? In a team environment, the job of designing and implementing an appropriate HTTP utility class might be on someone else's plate. You don't have the time to sit and wait for someone else to complete their work, and you don't have the time to create an HTTP class yourself.

What if *you* are the person on the hook for building HTTP support? Maybe you'd like to first explore the design of the Place Description Service implementation overall and worry about the implementation details of an HTTP utility class later.

5.3 Test Doubles

You can avoid being blocked, in any of these cases, by employing a *test double*. A test double is a stand-in—a doppelgänger (literally: "double walker")—for a production class. HTTP giving you trouble? Create a test double HTTP implementation! The job of the test double will be to support the needs of the test. When a client sends a GET request to the HTTP object, the test double can return a canned response. The test itself determines the response that the test double should return.

---

1. You can find details on the API at http://open.mapquestapi.com/nominatim.
2. Wikipedia provides an overview of REST at https://en.wikipedia.org/wiki/Representational_state_transfer.

Imagine you are on the hook to build the service but you aren't concerned with unit testing it (perhaps you plan on writing an integration test). You have access to some classes that you can readily reuse.

- CurlHttp, which uses cURL[3] to make HTTP requests. It derives from the pure virtual base class Http, which defines two functions, get() and initialize(). Clients must call initialize() before they can make calls to get().
- Address, a struct containing a few fields.
- AddressExtractor, which populates an Address struct from a JSON[4] string using JsonCpp.[5]

You might code the following:

```
CurlHttp http;
http.initialize();
auto jsonResponse = http.get(createGetRequestUrl(latitude, longitude));

AddressExtractor extractor;
auto address = extractor.addressFrom(jsonResponse);

return summaryDescription(address);
```

Now imagine you want to add tests for that small bit of code. It won't be so easy, because the CurlHttp class contains unfortunate dependencies you don't want. Faced with this challenge, many developers would choose to run a few manual tests and move on.

You're better than that. You're test-driving! That means you want to add code to your system *only* in order to make a failing test pass. But how will you write a test that sidesteps the dependency challenges of the CurlHttp class? In the next section, we'll work through a solution.

5.4   A Hand-Crafted Test Double

To use a test double, you must be able to supplant the behavior of the Curl-Http class. C++ provides many different ways, but the predominant manner is to take advantage of polymorphism. Let's take a look at the Http interface that the CurlHttp class implements (realizes):

```
c5/1/Http.h
virtual ~Http() {}
virtual void initialize() = 0;
virtual std::string get(const std::string& url) const = 0;
```

---

3.   http://curl.haxx.se/libcurl/cplusplus/

4.   http://www.json.org

5.   http://jsoncpp.sourceforge.net

Your solution is to override the virtual methods on a derived class, provide special behavior to support testing in the override, and pass the Place Description Service code a base class pointer.

Let's see some code.

```
c5/1/PlaceDescriptionServiceTest.cpp
TEST_F(APlaceDescriptionService, ReturnsDescriptionForValidLocation) {
   HttpStub httpStub;
   PlaceDescriptionService service{&httpStub};

   auto description = service.summaryDescription(ValidLatitude, ValidLongitude);

   ASSERT_THAT(description, Eq("Drury Ln, Fountain, CO, US"));
}
```

We create an instance of HttpStub in the test. HttpStub is the type of our test double, a class that derives from Http. We define HttpStub directly in the test file so that we can readily see the test double's behavior along with the tests that use it.

```
c5/1/PlaceDescriptionServiceTest.cpp
class HttpStub: public Http {
   void initialize() override {}
   std::string get(const std::string& url) const override {
      return "???";
   }
};
```

Returning a string with question marks is of little use. What do we need to return from get()? Since the external Nominatim Search Service returns a JSON response, we should return an appropriate JSON response that will generate the description expected in our test's assertion.

```
c5/2/PlaceDescriptionServiceTest.cpp
class HttpStub: public Http {
   void initialize() override {}
   std::string get(const std::string& url) const override {
      return R"({ "address": {
         "road":"Drury Ln",
         "city":"Fountain",
         "state":"CO",
         "country":"US" }})";
   }
};
```

How did I come up with that JSON? I ran a live GET request using my browser (the Nominatim Search Service API page shows you how) and captured the resulting output.

From the test, we *inject* our HttpStub instance into a PlaceDescriptionService object via its constructor. We're changing our design from what we speculated. Instead of the service constructing its own Http instance, the client of the service will now need to construct the instance and inject it into (pass it to) the service. The service constructor holds on to the instance via a base class pointer.

c5/2/PlaceDescriptionService.cpp
```
PlaceDescriptionService::PlaceDescriptionService(Http* http) : http_(http) {}
```

Simple polymorphism gives us the test double magic we need. A PlaceDescriptionService object knows not whether it holds a production Http instance or an instance designed solely for testing.

Once we get our test to compile and fail, we code summaryDescription().

c5/2/PlaceDescriptionService.cpp
```
string PlaceDescriptionService::summaryDescription(
        const string& latitude, const string& longitude) const {
    auto getRequestUrl = "";
    auto jsonResponse = http_->get(getRequestUrl);

    AddressExtractor extractor;
    auto address = extractor.addressFrom(jsonResponse);
    return address.road + ", " + address.city + ", " +
            address.state + ", " + address.country;
}
```

(We're fortunate: someone else has already built AddressExtractor for us. It parses a JSON response and populates an Address struct.)

When the test invokes summaryDescription(), the call to the Http method get() is received by the HttpStub instance. The result is that get() returns our hard-coded JSON string. A test double that returns a hard-coded value is a *stub*. You can similarly refer to the get() method as a *stub method*.

We test-drove the relevant code into summaryDescription(). But what about the request URL? When the code you're testing interacts with a collaborator, you want to make sure that you pass the correct elements to it. How do we know that we pass a legitimate URL to the Http instance?

In fact, we passed an empty string to the get() function in order to make incremental progress. We need to drive in the code necessary to populate getRequestUrl correctly. We could triangulate and assert against a second location (see *Triangulation*, on page 283).

Better, we can add an assertion to the get() stub method we defined on HttpStub.

```
c5/3/PlaceDescriptionServiceTest.cpp
class HttpStub: public Http {
  void initialize() override {}
  std::string get(const std::string& url) const override {
➤     verify(url);
    return R"({ "address": {
      "road":"Drury Ln",
      "city":"Fountain",
      "state":"CO",
      "country":"US" }})";
  }
  void verify(const string& url) const {
    auto expectedArgs(
      "lat=" + APlaceDescriptionService::ValidLatitude + "&" +
      "lon=" + APlaceDescriptionService::ValidLongitude);
      ASSERT_THAT(url, EndsWith(expectedArgs));
  }
};
```

(Why did we create a separate method, verify(), for our assertion logic? It's because of a Google Mock limitation: you can use assertions that cause fatal failures only in functions with void return.[6])

Now, when get() gets called, the stub implementation ensures the parameters are as expected. The stub's assertion tests the most important aspect of the URL: does it contain correct latitude/longitude arguments? Currently it fails, since we pass get() an empty string. Let's make it pass.

```
c5/3/PlaceDescriptionService.cpp
string PlaceDescriptionService::summaryDescription(
    const string& latitude, const string& longitude) const {
➤   auto getRequestUrl = "lat=" + latitude + "&lon=" + longitude;
    auto jsonResponse = http_->get(getRequestUrl);
    // ...
}
```

Our URL won't quite work, since it specifies no server or document. We bolster our verify() function to supply the full URL before passing it to get().

```
c5/4/PlaceDescriptionServiceTest.cpp
void verify(const string& url) const {
➤   string urlStart(
➤     "http://open.mapquestapi.com/nominatim/v1/reverse?format=json&");
➤   string expected(urlStart +
      "lat=" + APlaceDescriptionService::ValidLatitude + "&" +
      "lon=" + APlaceDescriptionService::ValidLongitude);
➤   ASSERT_THAT(url, Eq(expected));
}
```

---

6. http://code.google.com/p/googletest/wiki/AdvancedGuide#Assertion_Placement

Once we get the test to pass, we undertake a bit of refactoring. Our summary-Description() method violates cohesion, and the way we construct key-value pairs in both the test and production code exhibits duplication.

c5/4/PlaceDescriptionService.cpp
```cpp
string PlaceDescriptionService::summaryDescription(
      const string& latitude, const string& longitude) const {
   auto request = createGetRequestUrl(latitude, longitude);
   auto response = get(request);
   return summaryDescription(response);
}
string PlaceDescriptionService::summaryDescription(
      const string& response) const {
   AddressExtractor extractor;
   auto address = extractor.addressFrom(response);
   return address.summaryDescription();
}

string PlaceDescriptionService::get(const string& requestUrl) const {
   return http_->get(requestUrl);
}

string PlaceDescriptionService::createGetRequestUrl(
      const string& latitude, const string& longitude) const {
   string server{"http://open.mapquestapi.com/"};
   string document{"nominatim/v1/reverse"};
   return server + document + "?" +
      keyValue("format", "json") + "&" +
      keyValue("lat", latitude) + "&" +
      keyValue("lon", longitude);
}
string PlaceDescriptionService::keyValue(
      const string& key, const string& value) const {
   return key + "=" + value;
}
```

What about all that other duplication? ("*What* duplication?" you ask.) The text expressed in the test matches the text expressed in the production code. Should we strive to eliminate this duplication? There are several approaches we might take; for further discussion, refer to *Implicit Meaning*, on page 191.

Otherwise, our production code design appears sufficient for the time being. Functions are composed and expressive. As a side effect, we're poised for change. The function keyValue() appears ripe for reuse. We can also sense that generalizing our design to support a second service would be a quick increment, since we'd be able to reuse some of the structure in PlaceDescriptionService.

Our test's design is insufficient, however. For programmers not involved in its creation, it is too difficult to follow. Read on.

5.5 Improving Test Abstraction When Using Test Doubles

It's easy to craft tests that are difficult for others to read. When using test doubles, it's even easier to craft tests that obscure information critical to their understanding.

ReturnsDescriptionForValidLocation is difficult to understand because it hides relevant information, violating the concept of test abstraction (see Section 7.4, *Test Abstraction*, on page 181).

c5/4/PlaceDescriptionServiceTest.cpp
```cpp
TEST_F(APlaceDescriptionService, ReturnsDescriptionForValidLocation) {
   HttpStub httpStub;
   PlaceDescriptionService service{&httpStub};

   auto description = service.summaryDescription(ValidLatitude, ValidLongitude);

   ASSERT_THAT(description, Eq("Drury Ln, Fountain, CO, US"));
}
```

Why do we expect the description to be an address in Fountain, Colorado? Readers must poke around to discover that the expected address *correlates* to the JSON address in the HttpStub implementation.

We must refactor the test so that stands on its own. We can change the implementation of HttpStub so that the test is responsible for setting up the return value of its get() method.

c5/5/PlaceDescriptionServiceTest.cpp
```cpp
class HttpStub: public Http {
public:
   string returnResponse;
   void initialize() override {}
   std::string get(const std::string& url) const override {
      verify(url);
      return returnResponse;
   }

   void verify(const string& url) const {
      // ...
   }
};

TEST_F(APlaceDescriptionService, ReturnsDescriptionForValidLocation) {
   HttpStub httpStub;
   httpStub.returnResponse = R"({"address": {
                                 "road":"Drury Ln",
                                 "city":"Fountain",
                                 "state":"CO",
                                 "country":"US" }})";
```

```
    PlaceDescriptionService service{&httpStub};
    auto description = service.summaryDescription(ValidLatitude, ValidLongitude);
    ASSERT_THAT(description, Eq("Drury Ln, Fountain, CO, US"));
}
```

Now the test reader can correlate the summary description to the JSON object returned by HttpStub.

We can similarly move the URL verification to the test.

c5/6/PlaceDescriptionServiceTest.cpp
```
class HttpStub: public Http {
public:
    string returnResponse;
➤   string expectedURL;
    void initialize() override {}
    std::string get(const std::string& url) const override {
        verify(url);
        return returnResponse;
    }
    void verify(const string& url) const {
➤       ASSERT_THAT(url, Eq(expectedURL));
    }
};

TEST_F(APlaceDescriptionService, ReturnsDescriptionForValidLocation) {
    HttpStub httpStub;
    httpStub.returnResponse = // ...
➤   string urlStart{
➤       "http://open.mapquestapi.com/nominatim/v1/reverse?format=json&"};
➤   httpStub.expectedURL = urlStart +
➤       "lat=" + APlaceDescriptionService::ValidLatitude + "&" +
➤       "lon=" + APlaceDescriptionService::ValidLongitude;
    PlaceDescriptionService service{&httpStub};

    auto description = service.summaryDescription(ValidLatitude, ValidLongitude);

    ASSERT_THAT(description, Eq("Drury Ln, Fountain, CO, US"));
}
```

Our test is now a little longer but expresses its intent clearly. In contrast, we pared down HttpStub to a simple little class that captures expectations and values to return. Since it also verifies those expectations, however, HttpStub has evolved from being a stub to becoming a *mock*. A mock is a test double that captures expectations and self-verifies that those expectations were met.[7] In our example, an HttpStub object verifies that it will be passed an expected URL.

---

7. *xUnit Test Patterns [Mes07]*

To test-drive a system with dependencies on things such as databases and external service calls, you'll need several mocks. If they're only "simple little classes that manage expectations and values to return," they'll all start looking the same. Mock tools can reduce some of the duplicate effort required to define test doubles.

5.6   Using Mock Tools

Mock tools such as Google Mock, CppUMock, or Hippo Mocks simplify your effort to define mocks and set up expectations. You'll learn how to use Google Mock in this section.

Defining a Derivative

Let's test-drive summaryDescription() again. We'll need to mock the HTTP methods get() and initialize().

c5/7/Http.h
```
virtual ~Http() {}
virtual void initialize() = 0;
virtual std::string get(const std::string& url) const = 0;
```

The first step in using the mock support built into Google Mock is to create a derived class that declares mock methods. Google Mock allows us to define the HttpStub derivative succinctly.

c5/7/PlaceDescriptionServiceTest.cpp
```
class HttpStub: public Http {
public:
    MOCK_METHOD0(initialize, void());
    MOCK_CONST_METHOD1(get, string(const string&));
};
```

To declare a mock method, you use one of a few macro forms. MOCK_CONST_METHOD1 tells Google Mock to define a const member function taking one argument (that's the 1 at the end of MOCK_CONST_METHOD1). The first macro argument, get(), represents the name of the member function. You supply the rest of the member function's signature—its return value and argument declarations—as the second macro argument (string(const string&)).

To mock initialize(), you use MOCK_METHOD0, which creates a nonconst, zero-argument override. The second macro argument, void(), says to declare a function that takes no arguments and returns void.

Google Mock also provides support for mocking template functions and for specifying the calling convention.[8]

---

8.   http://code.google.com/p/googlemock/wiki/V1_6_CheatSheet#Defining_a_Mock_Class

Google Mock translates a mock declaration into a member function defined on the derived class. Behind the scenes, Google Mock synthesizes an implementation for that function to manage interactions with it. If the member function doesn't override the appropriate base class function, you won't get the behavior you want.

(Under C++11, the override keyword lets the compiler verify that you've properly overridden a function. However, the MOCK_METHOD macros don't yet accommodate the override keyword. See https://code.google.com/p/googlemock/issues/detail?id=157 for a patch that you can apply to Google Mock to fix this shortfall.)

Setting Expectations

We decide to delete our implementation of summaryDescription() and test-drive it again. We choose to shrink the scope of the first test. Instead of driving an implementation for all of summaryDescription(), we'll drive in only the code that sends off an HTTP request. A new test name captures our intent.

```
c5/7/PlaceDescriptionServiceTest.cpp
TEST_F(APlaceDescriptionService, MakesHttpRequestToObtainAddress) {
   HttpStub httpStub;
   string urlStart{
      "http://open.mapquestapi.com/nominatim/v1/reverse?format=json&"};
   auto expectedURL = urlStart +
      "lat=" + APlaceDescriptionService::ValidLatitude + "&" +
      "lon=" + APlaceDescriptionService::ValidLongitude;
   EXPECT_CALL(httpStub, get(expectedURL));
   PlaceDescriptionService service{&httpStub};

   service.summaryDescription(ValidLatitude, ValidLongitude);
}
```

We use the EXPECT_CALL() macro to set up expectations as part of the test's Arrange step (see *Arrange-Act-Assert/Given-When-Then,* on page 84). The macro configures Google Mock to verify that a message get() gets sent to the httpStub object with an argument that matches expectedURL.

Where's the assertion? Google Mock does its verification when the mock object goes out of scope. Visually, our test doesn't follow AAA, but the assertion step still executes—it just does so implicitly. Some mock tools require you to add an explicit verification call, which would once again make your assert step visible.

If needed, you can force Google Mock to run its verification before the mock goes out of scope.

```
Mock::VerifyAndClearExpectations(&httpStub);
```

Seeing an explicit assert step might make some folks happy, but it's not necessary. You'll quickly learn how to read a test when you see mock expectations being set.

We implement just enough of summaryDescription() to compile.

c5/7/PlaceDescriptionService.cpp
```
string PlaceDescriptionService::summaryDescription(
    const string& latitude, const string& longitude) const {
  return "";
}
```

Running our tests produces the following failure:

```
Actual function call count doesn't match EXPECT_CALL(httpStub, get(expectedURL))...
        Expected: to be called once
          Actual: never called - unsatisfied and active
```

The expectation was not met. No code called get() on httpStub by the time our test completed. That's a good failure! We implement enough code to pass the test.

c5/8/PlaceDescriptionService.cpp
```
string PlaceDescriptionService::summaryDescription(
    const string& latitude, const string& longitude) const {
  string server{"http://open.mapquestapi.com/"};
  string document{"nominatim/v1/reverse"};
  string url = server + document + "?" +
               keyValue("format", "json") + "&" +
               keyValue("lat", latitude) + "&" +
               keyValue("lon", longitude);
  http_->get(url);
  return "";
}
```

We write a second test to flesh out summaryDescription().

c5/9/PlaceDescriptionServiceTest.cpp
```
TEST_F(APlaceDescriptionService, FormatsRetrievedAddressIntoSummaryDescription) {
   HttpStub httpStub;
➤  EXPECT_CALL(httpStub, get(_))
➤    .WillOnce(Return(
➤      R"({ "address": {
➤        "road":"Drury Ln",
➤        "city":"Fountain",
➤        "state":"CO",
➤        "country":"US" }})"));
   PlaceDescriptionService service(&httpStub);
   auto description = service.summaryDescription(ValidLatitude, ValidLongitude);
   ASSERT_THAT(description, Eq("Drury Ln, Fountain, CO, US"));
}
```

The EXPECT_CALL() invocation in the test tells Google Mock what to return from a call to get(). To paraphrase the code, a call on the HttpStub object to get() *will once* (and only once) *return* a specific JSON string value.

We don't care what gets passed in the get() call, since we verified that behavior in MakesHttpRequestToObtainAddress. Our EXPECT_CALL() uses the wildcard matcher _ (an underscore; its qualified name is testing::_) as an argument to get(). The wildcard allows Google Mock to match on any call to the function, regardless of the argument.

The wildcard increases the test's level of abstraction by removing an irrelevant detail. However, the lack of concern over the URL argument means that we'd better have that other test (MakesHttpRequestToObtainAddress) that *is* concerned with proper argument passing. In other words, don't use wildcard matchers unless you truly don't care about the arguments or if you already have other tests that do care.

(The wildcard is one of many matchers provided by Google Mock. The matchers are the same ones you've been using for your assertions. See the Google Mock documentation[9] for the full list of matchers.)

We get the test to pass.

```
c5/9/PlaceDescriptionService.cpp
string PlaceDescriptionService::summaryDescription(
        const string& latitude, const string& longitude) const {
    string server{"http://open.mapquestapi.com/"};
    string document{"nominatim/v1/reverse"};
    string url = server + document + "?" +
                 keyValue("format", "json") + "&" +
                 keyValue("lat", latitude) + "&" +
                 keyValue("lon", longitude);
➤   auto response = http_->get(url);

➤   AddressExtractor extractor;
➤   auto address = extractor.addressFrom(response);
➤   return address.summaryDescription();
}
```

We can refactor to the same implementation as when we test-drove using a hand-crafted mock (see code/c5/10 in the source distribution).

Nice Mocks and Strict Mocks

Astute readers may have noted that we don't follow the proper CurlHttp protocol in our implementations of summaryDescription(). We don't call initialize() before

---

9.   http://code.google.com/p/googlemock/wiki/V1_6_CheatSheet#Matchers

calling get(). (Don't forget to run your integration tests!) To drive in a call to initialize(), we can add an expectation to the MakesHttpRequestToObtainAddress test.

c5/11/PlaceDescriptionServiceTest.cpp

```
TEST_F(APlaceDescriptionService, MakesHttpRequestToObtainAddress) {
   HttpStub httpStub;
   string urlStart{
      "http://open.mapquestapi.com/nominatim/v1/reverse?format=json&"};
   auto expectedURL = urlStart +
      "lat=" + APlaceDescriptionService::ValidLatitude + "&" +
      "lon=" + APlaceDescriptionService::ValidLongitude;
   EXPECT_CALL(httpStub, initialize());
   EXPECT_CALL(httpStub, get(expectedURL));
   PlaceDescriptionService service{&httpStub};

   service.summaryDescription(ValidLatitude, ValidLongitude);
}
```

The high-level policy in summaryDescription() remains untouched. We make an isolated change to get() to update its implementation detail.

c5/11/PlaceDescriptionService.cpp

```
string PlaceDescriptionService::get(const string& url) const {
   http_->initialize();
   return http_->get(url);
}
```

When we run the tests, we receive a warning—not for MakesHttpRequestToObtainAddress but for FormatsRetrievedAddressIntoSummaryDescription, which is the other test.

```
GMOCK WARNING:
Uninteresting mock function call - returning directly.
   function call: initialize()
```

Google Mock captures all interactions with a mock object, not just the ones for which you set expectations. The warning is intended to help by telling you about an interaction you might not have expected.

Your goal should always be zero warnings. Either turn them all off or fix them as soon as they arise. Any other strategy that allows warnings to stick around will breed hundreds or thousands of warnings over time. At that point, they're all pretty much useless. Ignoring the Google Mock warning is unacceptable; we must eliminate it.

We have other choices. We could add the expectation to FormatsRetrievedAddressIntoSummaryDescription, but that adds a bit of clutter to the test that has nothing to do with its goal. We'll avoid this solution that goes against the concept of test abstraction.

Always question design when you're presented with a challenge like this. The initialization call is required, but does it belong elsewhere (perhaps in an initialization() function called after construction of PlaceDescriptionService)? Moving the call to a different place wouldn't eliminate the warning, though.

What about the test design? We split one test into two when we changed from a hand-rolled mock solution to one using Google Mock. If we expressed everything in a single test, that one test could set up the expectations to cover all three significant events (initialization, message passing to get(), and return from get()). That's an easy fix, but we'd end up with a cluttered test. See Section 7.3, *One Assert per Test*, on page 178 for further discussion about this choice. For now, let's stick with separate tests.

We could also create a fixture helper function that added the expectation on initialize() and then returned the HttpStub instance. We might name such a function createHttpStubExpectingInitialization().

Google Mock provides a simpler solution (and many other mock tools provide similar solutions). The NiceMock template effectively tells Google Mock to track interactions only for methods on which expectations exist.

c5/12/PlaceDescriptionServiceTest.cpp

```
TEST_F(APlaceDescriptionService, FormatsRetrievedAddressIntoSummaryDescription) {
    NiceMock<HttpStub> httpStub;
    EXPECT_CALL(httpStub, get(_))
      .WillOnce(Return(
      // ...
}
```

In contrast, wrapping a mock in StrictMock turns the uninteresting mock call warning into an error.

```
StrictMock<HttpStub> httpStub;
```

By using NiceMock, we take on a small risk. If the code later somehow changes to invoke another method on the Http interface, our tests aren't going to know about it. You should use NiceMock when you need it, not habitually. Seek to fix your design if you seem to require it often.

You can read more about NiceMock and StrictMock in the Google Mock documentation.[10]

---

10. http://code.google.com/p/googlemock/wiki/CookBook#Nice_Mocks_and_Strict_Mocks

Order in the Mock

It's unlikely, but what if we inadvertently swapped the order of the calls to Http's initialize() and get() functions?

c5/13/PlaceDescriptionService.cpp
```
string PlaceDescriptionService::get(const string& url) const {
➤    auto response = http_->get(url);
➤    http_->initialize();
➤    return response;
}
```

Surprise, the tests still pass! By default, Google Mock doesn't concern itself with verifying the order in which expectations are met. If you're concerned about order, you can tell Google Mock (and many other C++ mocking tools) to verify it. The simplest way is to declare an instance of InSequence at the top of the test and ensure that subsequent EXPECT_CALLs appear in the order you expect.

c5/13/PlaceDescriptionServiceTest.cpp
```
TEST_F(APlaceDescriptionService, MakesHttpRequestToObtainAddress) {
➤    InSequence forceExpectationOrder;
    HttpStub httpStub;

    string urlStart{
        "http://open.mapquestapi.com/nominatim/v1/reverse?format=json&"};

    auto expectedURL = urlStart +
        "lat=" + APlaceDescriptionService::ValidLatitude + "&" +
        "lon=" + APlaceDescriptionService::ValidLongitude;
    EXPECT_CALL(httpStub, initialize());
    EXPECT_CALL(httpStub, get(expectedURL));
    PlaceDescriptionService service{&httpStub};

    service.summaryDescription(ValidLatitude, ValidLongitude);
}
```

Google Mock provides finer control over order if you require it. The After() clause says that an expectation is met only if it executes after another expectation. Google Mock also lets you define an ordered list of expected calls. Refer to the Google Mock documentation[11] for further information.

Making a Mockery of Things: Clever Mock Tool Features

The EXPECT_CALL macro supports a number of additional modifiers. Here's its syntax:

---

11. http://code.google.com/p/googlemock/wiki/CheatSheet#Expectation_Order

```
EXPECT_CALL(mock_object, method(matchers))
    .With(multi_argument_matcher)    ?
    .Times(cardinality)              ?
    .InSequence(sequences)           *
    .After(expectations)             *
    .WillOnce(action)                *
    .WillRepeatedly(action)          ?
    .RetiresOnSaturation();          ?
```

(The ? and * represent the cardinality of each modifier: ? indicates that you can optionally call the modifier once, and * indicates that you can call the modifier any number of times.)

The most likely useful modifier is Times(), which lets you specify the exact number of times you expect a method to be called. You can specify WillRepeatedly() if you know a method will be called many times but aren't concerned with exactly how many. Refer to the Google Mock documentation[12] for further nuances and details.

Google Mock is a general-purpose unit testing tool that supports mocking for just about any convolution that you can code. For example, suppose you need to mock a function to populate an out parameter. Yup, Google Mock can do that. The following interface, defined on a class named DifficultCollaborator, represents a function that both returns a value and populates an argument:

c5/13/OutParameterTest.cpp
```
virtual bool calculate(int* result)
```

You can specify one action for a Google Mock expectation, using either WillOnce() or WillRepeatedly(). Most of the time, that action will be to return a value. In the case of a function that needs to do more, you can use DoAll(), which creates a composite action from two or more actions.

c5/13/OutParameterTest.cpp
```
DifficultCollaboratorMock difficult;
Target calc;
EXPECT_CALL(difficult, calculate(_))
➤     .WillOnce(DoAll(
➤         SetArgPointee<0>(3),
➤         Return(true)));

auto result = calc.execute(&difficult);

ASSERT_THAT(result, Eq(3));
```

---

12. http://code.google.com/p/googlemock/wiki/CheatSheet#Setting_Expectations, http://code.google.com/p/googlemock/wiki/ForDummies#Setting_Expectations

Our additional action for this example is SetArgPointee<0>(3), which tells Google Mock to set the pointee (the thing that's getting pointed at) for the 0th argument to the value 3.

Google Mock has solid support for other side-effect actions, including the ability to throw exceptions, set variable values, delete arguments, and invoke functions or functors. Refer to the Google Mock documentation[13] for the complete list.

Just because you can doesn't necessarily mean you should, though. Most of the time, the basic Google Mock mechanisms you learned earlier will suffice. When test-driving, if you find yourself seeking esoteric mock tool features frequently, stop and take a look at your design. Are you testing a method that's doing too much? Can you restructure your design in a manner so that you don't need such complex mocking? More often than not, you can.

Where you may need the more powerful features of your mock tool is when you tackle the challenge of writing tests around non-test-driven, poorly structured code. You'll learn about these challenges in *Legacy Challenges*.

Troubleshooting Mock Failures

You will invariably struggle with defining mocks properly. I'll come clean: in coding our current example for this book, I scratched my head for several minutes when I received the following failure message:

```
Actual function call count doesn't match EXPECT_CALL(httpStub, get(expectedURL))...
        Expected: to be called once
          Actual: never called - unsatisfied and active
```

The first thing to determine is whether the production code actually makes the proper call. (Have you even coded anything yet?) Second, have you defined the mock method properly? If you're not sure, you either can add a cout statement as the first line of the production implementation or can crank up the debugger.

Did you make the member function getting mocked virtual?

Did you botch the MOCK_METHOD() declaration? All type information must match precisely; otherwise, the mock method is not an override. Ensure all const declarations match.

---

13. http://code.google.com/p/googlemock/wiki/CheatSheet#Actions

If you're still stuck, eliminate any concerns about argument matching. Use the wildcard matcher (testing::_) for all arguments and rerun the tests. If they pass, then one of the arguments is not recognized as a match by Google Mock.

My stupidity was that I had inadvertently stripped the const declaration from the URL argument.

One Test or Two?

When using a handcrafted mock, we ended up with a single test to verify the true end goal, the ability to generate a summary description for a location. In the second example, however, we ended up with two tests. Which is right?

From the stance of documenting public behaviors—those a client would care about—PlaceDescriptionService's sole goal is to return a summary string given a location. Describing this behavior in a single test might be simpler for a reader. The interaction of summaryDescription() with its Http collaborator isn't of interest to the client. It's an implementation detail (you might imagine a solution where we have all the geolocation data locally). Does it make sense to create a second test to document that interaction?

Absolutely. TDD's most important value is in helping you drive and shape the design of your system. Interactions with collaborators are a key aspect of that design. Having tests that describe those interactions will be of high value to other developers.

Having two tests provides additional benefits. First, a mock verification *is* an assertion. We already require an assertion to verify the summary string. Splitting into two tests falls in line with one assert per test (Section 7.3, *One Assert per Test*, on page 178). Second, the separated tests are eminently more readable. Setting expectations in Google Mock makes it harder to spot the assertion points (and also to keep in line with *Arrange-Act-Assert/Given-When-Then*, on page 84), so anything we can do to simplify mock-based tests pays off.

5.7 Getting Test Doubles in Place

You have two jobs when introducing a test double. First, code the test double. Second, get the target to use an instance of it. Certain techniques for doing so are known as *dependency injection* (DI).

In the PlaceDescriptionService example, we injected the test double via a constructor. In some circumstances, you might find it more appropriate to pass the test double using a setter member function. These ways to inject a test double are known as (surprise!) *constructor injection* or *setter injection*.

Other techniques for getting test doubles in place exist. Use the one that's most appropriate for your circumstance.

Override Factory Method and Override Getter

To apply Override Factory Method, you must change the production code to use a factory method any time a collaborator instance is needed. Here's one way to implement the change in the PlaceDescriptionService:

```
c5/15/PlaceDescriptionService.h
#include <memory>
// ...
   virtual ~PlaceDescriptionService() {}
// ...
protected:
   virtual std::shared_ptr<Http> httpService() const;
```

```
c5/15/PlaceDescriptionService.cpp
#include "CurlHttp.h"
string PlaceDescriptionService::get(const string& url) const {
➤    auto http = httpService();
➤    http->initialize();
➤    return http->get(url);
   }

➤ shared_ptr<Http> PlaceDescriptionService::httpService() const {
➤    return make_shared<CurlHttp>();
➤ }
```

Instead of referring to the member variable http_ for interactions with the HTTP service, the code now calls the protected member function httpService() to obtain an Http pointer.

In the test, we define a derivative of PlaceDescriptionService. The primary job of this subclass is to override the factory method (httpService()) that returns an Http instance.

```
c5/15/PlaceDescriptionServiceTest.cpp
class PlaceDescriptionService_StubHttpService: public PlaceDescriptionService {
public:
   PlaceDescriptionService_StubHttpService(shared_ptr<HttpStub> httpStub)
     : httpStub_{httpStub} {}
   shared_ptr<Http> httpService() const override { return httpStub_; }
   shared_ptr<Http> httpStub_;
};
```

We change our tests to create an HttpStub shared pointer and store it in the PlaceDescriptionService_StubHttpService instance. Here's what MakesHttpRequest-ToObtainAddress now looks like:

```
c5/15/PlaceDescriptionServiceTest.cpp
TEST_F(APlaceDescriptionService, MakesHttpRequestToObtainAddress) {
   InSequence forceExpectationOrder;
   shared_ptr<HttpStub> httpStub{new HttpStub};

   string urlStart{
      "http://open.mapquestapi.com/nominatim/v1/reverse?format=json&"};

   auto expectedURL = urlStart +
      "lat=" + APlaceDescriptionService::ValidLatitude + "&" +
      "lon=" + APlaceDescriptionService::ValidLongitude;
   EXPECT_CALL(*httpStub, initialize());
   EXPECT_CALL(*httpStub, get(expectedURL));
   PlaceDescriptionService_StubHttpService service{httpStub};

   service.summaryDescription(ValidLatitude, ValidLongitude);
}
```

Override Factory Method demonstrates the hole in coverage created by using test doubles. Since our test overrides the production implementation of httpService(), code in that method never gets exercised by the tests. As stated before, make sure you have an integration test that requires use of the real service! Also, don't let any real logic sneak into the factory method; otherwise, you'll grow the amount of untested code. The factory method should return only an instance of the collaborator type.

As an alternative to Override Factory Method, you can use Override Getter. With respect to our example, the difference is that the httpServer() function is a simple getter that returns a member variable referencing an existing instance, whereas in Override Factory, httpServer() is responsible for constructing the instance. The test remains the same.

```
c5/16/PlaceDescriptionService.h
class PlaceDescriptionService {
public:
   PlaceDescriptionService();
   virtual ~PlaceDescriptionService() {}
   std::string summaryDescription(
      const std::string& latitude, const std::string& longitude) const;

private:
   // ...
   std::shared_ptr<Http> http_;

protected:
   virtual std::shared_ptr<Http> httpService() const;
};
```

```
c5/16/PlaceDescriptionService.cpp
PlaceDescriptionService::PlaceDescriptionService()
    : http_{make_shared<CurlHttp>()} {}
// ...
shared_ptr<Http> PlaceDescriptionService::httpService() const {
    return http_;
}
```

Used sparingly, Override Factory Method and Override Getter are simple and
effective, particularly in legacy code situations (see *Legacy Challenges*). Prefer
constructor or setter injection, however.

Introduce via Factory

A factory class is responsible for creating and returning instances. If you have
an HttpFactory, you can have your tests tell it to return an HttpStub instance
instead of an Http (production) instance. If you don't already have a legitimate
use for a factory, don't use this technique. Introducing a factory only to support testing is a poor choice.

Here's our factory implementation:

```
c5/18/HttpFactory.cpp
#include "HttpFactory.h"
#include "CurlHttp.h"
#include <memory>

using namespace std;

HttpFactory::HttpFactory() {
    reset();
}

shared_ptr<Http> HttpFactory::get() {
    return instance;
}

void HttpFactory::reset() {
    instance = make_shared<CurlHttp>();
}

void HttpFactory::setInstance(shared_ptr<Http> newInstance) {
    instance = newInstance;
}
```

During setup, the test creates a factory and injects an HttpStub instance into
it. Subsequent requests to get() on the factory return this test double.

c5/18/PlaceDescriptionServiceTest.cpp

```cpp
class APlaceDescriptionService: public Test {
public:
   static const string ValidLatitude;
   static const string ValidLongitude;

   shared_ptr<HttpStub> httpStub;
   shared_ptr<HttpFactory> factory;
   shared_ptr<PlaceDescriptionService> service;

   virtual void SetUp() override {
      factory = make_shared<HttpFactory>();
      service = make_shared<PlaceDescriptionService>(factory);
   }

   void TearDown() override {
      factory.reset();
      httpStub.reset();
   }
};

class APlaceDescriptionService_WithHttpMock: public APlaceDescriptionService {
public:
   void SetUp() override {
      APlaceDescriptionService::SetUp();
      httpStub = make_shared<HttpStub>();
      factory->setInstance(httpStub);
   }
};

TEST_F(APlaceDescriptionService_WithHttpMock, MakesHttpRequestToObtainAddress) {
   string urlStart{
      "http://open.mapquestapi.com/nominatim/v1/reverse?format=json&"};
   auto expectedURL = urlStart +
      "lat=" + APlaceDescriptionService::ValidLatitude + "&" +
      "lon=" + APlaceDescriptionService::ValidLongitude;
   EXPECT_CALL(*httpStub, initialize());
   EXPECT_CALL(*httpStub, get(expectedURL));
   service->summaryDescription(ValidLatitude, ValidLongitude);
}
```

We change the production code in summaryDescription() to obtain its Http instance from the factory.

c5/18/PlaceDescriptionService.cpp

```cpp
string PlaceDescriptionService::get(const string& url) const {
➤    auto http = httpFactory_->get();
   http->initialize();
   return http->get(url);
}
```

Since we're passing the factory through the constructor, this pattern is little different from constructor injection, except that we now have an extra layer of indirection.

Introduce via Template Parameter

Some of the injection techniques can be somewhat clever. Injecting via a template parameter is another option that doesn't require clients to pass a collaborator instance. Its use is best constrained to legacy situations where a template already exists.

We declare the PlaceDescriptionService class as a template that can be bound to a single typename, HTTP. We add a member variable, http_, of the parameter type HTTP. Since we want clients to use the class name PlaceDescriptionService, we rename the template class to PlaceDescriptionServiceTemplate. After the template definition, we supply a typedef that defines the type PlaceDescriptionService as PlaceDescriptionServiceTemplate bound to the *production* class Http. Here's the code:

c5/19/PlaceDescriptionService.h
```
template<typename HTTP>
class PlaceDescriptionServiceTemplate {
public:
    // ...
    // mocks in tests need the reference
    HTTP& http() {
        return http_;
    }
private:
    // ...
    std::string get(const std::string& url) {
        http_.initialize();
        return http_.get(url);
    }
    // ...
    HTTP http_;
};
class Http;
typedef PlaceDescriptionServiceTemplate<Http> PlaceDescriptionService;
```

In the test fixture, we declare the service to be of type PlaceDescriptionServiceTemplate bound to the mock type, HttpStub:

c5/19/PlaceDescriptionServiceTest.cpp
```
class APlaceDescriptionService_WithHttpMock: public APlaceDescriptionService {
public:
    PlaceDescriptionServiceTemplate<HttpStub> service;
};
```

The test doesn't provide PlaceDescriptionService with an instance of the mock; it supplies the mock's *type*. PlaceDescriptionService creates its own instance of this type (as the member variable http_). Since Google Mock will be looking to verify interaction expectations on the template object's instance, we need to provide the test with access to it. We change the test to obtain the stub instance via an accessor function on PlaceDescriptionServiceTemplate named http().

c5/19/PlaceDescriptionServiceTest.cpp
```
TEST_F(APlaceDescriptionService_WithHttpMock, MakesHttpRequestToObtainAddress) {

    string urlStart{
        "http://open.mapquestapi.com/nominatim/v1/reverse?format=json&"};

    auto expectedURL = urlStart +
        "lat=" + APlaceDescriptionService::ValidLatitude + "&" +
        "lon=" + APlaceDescriptionService::ValidLongitude;
    EXPECT_CALL(service.http(), initialize());
    EXPECT_CALL(service.http(), get(expectedURL));

    service.summaryDescription(ValidLatitude, ValidLongitude);
}
```

You can support introducing a mock via a template parameter in a number of ways, some even more clever than this implementation (which is based on the Template Redefinition pattern in *Working Effectively with Legacy Code [Fea04]*).

Injection Tools

Tools to handle injecting collaborators as dependent objects are known as *dependency injection* (DI) tools. Two known C++ examples are Autumn Framework[14] and Qt IoC Container.[15] Michael Feathers weighs in on the state of DI frameworks in C++: "It seems that to do DI in C++, you have to place constraints on the classes you create...you have to make them inherit from some other class, use macro preregistration or a metaobject library."[16] You should first master the manual injection techniques described here and then investigate the tools to see whether they improve things. DI tools are generally much more effective in languages that support full reflective capabilities.

---

14. http://code.google.com/p/autumnframework
15. http://sourceforge.net/projects/qtioccontainer
16. http://michaelfeathers.typepad.com/michael_feathers_blog/2006/10/dependency_inje.html

5.8   Design Will Change

Your first reaction to test doubles may be that using them will change your approach to design. You might find that prospect unsettling. Don't worry, it's a natural response.

Cohesion and Coupling

When faced with a troublesome dependency (such as a slow or volatile collaborator), the best option is to isolate it to a separate class. Granted, making an HTTP request isn't very involved. Putting the logic in a small, separate Http class might not seem worth the effort, but you'll have more potential for reuse and more design flexibility (the ability to replace it with a polymorphic substitute, for example). You'll also have a few more options when it comes to creating a test double.

The alternative is to create more procedural, less cohesive code. Take a look at a more typical solution for the PlaceDescriptionService, created in the world of test-after:

```
c5/17/PlaceDescriptionService.cpp
string PlaceDescriptionService::summaryDescription(
      const string& latitude, const string& longitude) const {
   // retrieve JSON response via API
   response_ = "";
   auto url = createGetRequestUrl(latitude, longitude);
   curl_easy_setopt(curl, CURLOPT_URL, url.c_str());
   curl_easy_perform(curl);
   curl_easy_cleanup(curl);

   // parse json response
   Value location;
   Reader reader;
   reader.parse(response_, location);
   auto jsonAddress = location.get("address", Value::null);

   // populate address from json
   Address address;
   address.road = jsonAddress.get("road", "").asString();
   address.city = jsonAddress.get("hamlet", "").asString();
   address.state = jsonAddress.get("state", "").asString();
   address.country = jsonAddress.get("country", "").asString();

   return address.road + ", " + address.city + ", " +
         address.state + ", " + address.country;
}
```

The implementation is but twenty lines that read fairly well, particularly with the guiding comments. It's typical of most test-after code. While it could be broken into several smaller functions, like we did earlier, developers often don't bother. Test-after developers aren't as habituated to regular refactoring, and they don't usually have the fast tests needed to make it quick and safe. So what? Is there anything wrong with code that looks like this? We could refactor it if and when we needed.

From a design stance, the twenty lines violate the SRP—many reasons exist for summaryDescription() to change. The function is tightly coupled to cURL. Further, the twenty lines represent the code smell known as Long Method, making for code that requires too much time to fully understand.

Longer functions like this promote unnecessary duplication. Other services are likely to need some of the same cURL logic, for example. Developers will often re-code the three lines related to cURL rather than try to reuse them. Reuse begins with isolation of reusable constructs that other programmers can readily identify. As long as the potentially reusable chunks of code lay buried in a Long Method, reuse won't happen.

Build a system this way, and you'll create double the lines of code.

You can still test the twenty lines. You can use link substitution to support writing a fast unit test (see Section 8.9, *Creating a Test Double for rlog*, on page 207). Or you can write an integration test that generates a live call to the REST service. But both types of test will be larger, with more setup and verification in a single test (though, overall, the amount of initial test coding effort isn't much different). The integration test will be slow and brittle.

The bulk of code in the world looks even worse than these twenty lines. Your code will look better, because you will seek cohesive, decoupled designs as you practice TDD. You'll start to realize the benefit of a more flexible design. You'll quickly discover how these better designs align with tests that are much smaller and easier to write, read, and maintain.

Shifting Private Dependencies

If you weren't concerned about testing, the HTTP call in the PlaceDescription-Service could remain a *private dependency*, meaning that clients of PlaceDescriptionService would be oblivious to the existence of the HTTP call. When you use setter or constructor injection, however, clients take on the responsibility of creating Http objects and passing them in. You shift the dependency of PlaceDescriptionService to the client.

Developers can be concerned about the ramifications of this choice.

Q.: *Doesn't setter or constructor injection violate the notion of information hiding?*

A.: *From the stance of the client, yes. You can use an alternate form of dependency injection (see Section 5.7, Getting Test Doubles in Place, on page 123). The information you're exposing is unlikely to cause future grief if someone takes advantage of it.*

You also have the option of providing a default instance. We can configure PlaceDescriptionService to contain a CurlHttp instance that gets replaced when the test provides an HttpStub. The production client need not change.

Q.: *But what if a nefarious developer chooses to pass in a destructive Http instance?*

A.: *Choose an alternate injection form if clients are outside your team. If you're worried about developers within the team deliberately taking advantage of the injection point to do evil things, you have bigger problems.*

Q.: *TDD is growing on me, but I'm concerned about changing how I design solely for purposes of testing. My teammates probably feel the same way.*

A.: *Knowing that software works as expected is a great reason to change the way you design code. Have this conversation with your teammates: "I'm more concerned about whether the code works. Allowing this small concession means we can more easily test our code, and getting more tests in place can help us shape the design more easily and trust the code more. Can we rethink our standards?"*

5.9 Strategies for Using Test Doubles

Test doubles are like any tool; the bigger challenge is not in learning how to use them but in knowing when to use them. This section describes a few schools of thought and provides some recommendations for appropriate use of test doubles.

Exploring Design

Suppose AddressExtractor does not exist. When you test-drive summaryDescription(), you'll of course recognize the need for logic that takes a JSON response and ultimately returns a formatted string. You could code the entire implementation for that in the PlaceDescriptionService. It's not much code (a little more than a dozen lines, based on the code in AddressExtractor as it exists).

Some programmers always wear the designer hat, seeking designs that exhibit the potential for reuse, increased flexibility, and improved ease of understanding the code. To adhere to the SRP, they might break the required logic into two needs: parsing the JSON response and formatting the output.

TDD allows you...no, it *requires* you to make conscious design choices at all times. You have the option of implementing the summaryDescription() logic in an infinite number of ways. TDD helps you explore that design. Often that's done by coding something that works and then refactoring to an appropriate solution.

Or, you could first write a test that describes how summaryDescription() should interact with a collaborator. The job of this collaborator is to take a JSON response and return a corresponding address data structure. For the time being, you ignore the details of how to implement the collaborator. You focus instead on test-driving the implementation of summaryDescription() using mocks, just as we did for interactions with the Http object.

When test-driving in this manner, you introduce mocks to supply otherwise-missing collaborator behavior. You design interfaces for the collaborators based on the interests and needs of the client.

At some point, you or someone else will implement the collaborator. You have a choice: remove the mocks so that the code under test uses the production collaborator or keep the mocks in place.

The issue may already be decided for you. If the collaborator introduces troublesome dependencies, you'll need to retain the mock. If it does not, removing the mock means removing a bit of extra complexity in your tests. However, you might choose to retain the mocks, particularly if interactions with the collaborator are an important aspect of design that you should describe.

The best guideline probably takes into account the effort required to maintain and understand the tests. It can be simpler without mocks in place, but that's not always the case. It can require a lot of setup code to initialize some collaborators, which can increase your effort to maintain the tests.

Too Much Mocking?

For seven months in 2003, I worked as a programmer on a large Java development team doing XP. On arrival, I was enthusiastic about seeing a large number of unit tests but not quite so enthusiastic about the test quality or production code quality. None of it was terrible, but I noted too much duplication, methods and tests longer than necessary, and heavy use of mocks. The system worked, though, exhibiting very few defects.

Months later, attempts to scale the system from eleven to more than fifty users resulted in performance issues. All signs pointed to suboptimal use of the middleware framework as the culprit. A team of high-dollar middleware framework experts worked closely with our team to rework the code.

Many of the mocks for controller-level code verified sequences of events by expecting that methods were called in a certain order. (Worse, the tool they used required method expectations to be represented as strings. Renaming a method meant you had to remember to update the string literals used by the mocks.) But these methods were not as abstract as they might have been. When the optimizing team started reworking the code to improve performance, they often changed the underlying design of a given message flow through the system. That meant moving methods around, renaming methods, compressing two methods into one, deleting others, and so on. Every time they made such a change...uh oh! Tests broke, sometimes more than a dozen at once.

Since the tests were tightly coupled to the target implementation, transforming the code went very slowly. Yelling by the VPs and other hostilities commenced. All programmers and TDD itself were called into question.

Having tests highly dependent on implementation specifics—which methods are called in which order—created significant problems. But in hindsight, the far larger problem was our inadequate system design. We might have had an easier time had we factored away duplication across tests. Another significant problem was not having appropriate performance/scaling tests.

Schools of Mock

Practitioners who view TDD primarily as a design exploration tool fall into what's sometimes called the *London school*. Founders of this school include Tim MacKinnon, Steve Freeman, and Philip Craig, authors of the original paper on mocks, *Endo-Testing: Unit Testing with Mock Objects [MFC01]*. The highly regarded book *Growing Object-Oriented Software, Guided by Tests [FP09]*, by Freeman and Nat Pryce, focuses on using TDD to grow out a system in this manner.

Because of its emphasis on object interactions, the London school approach promotes the notion of *Tell-Don't-Ask*. In an object-oriented system, you (a client object) want to *tell* an object to do something by sending it a message and letting it go do its work. You don't want to *ask* an object for information and then do work that could be the responsibility of that object. Tell-Don't-Ask promotes a more decoupled design.

The *classic school* (sometimes called the Cleveland school) emphasizes verification of behavior by inspecting state. Kent Beck's book *Test Driven Development: By Example [Bec02]* focuses almost entirely on this approach to TDD. Folks in this camp avoid introducing mocks until a dependency concern forces the issue.

Introducing a mock creates a dependency of the tests on the implementation details of the target. If you employ a tool, you also create a dependency on that tool. Both dependencies can make your designs more rigid and your tests more fragile if you're not careful. The best defense against challenges created by dependencies is good design: isolate and minimize them.

Using mocks also generates additional complexity that you'll pay for (as I just did, wasting several minutes with my mock declaration mistake).

As a professional, you owe it to yourself to learn about both approaches. While you might choose to follow one school or another, it's possible to incorporate elements of both London and classic schools into your TDD practice.

Using Test Doubles Wisely

If you want a fully test-driven system with fast tests, the predominance of systems will require you to use test doubles. When you use test doubles, consider the following recommendations:

Reconsider the design. Does your compulsion to mock exist in order to simplify creation of dependent objects? Revisit your dependency structure. Are you mocking the same thing in multiple places? Restructure the design to eliminate this duplication.

Recognize the concession to unit testing coverage. A test double represents a hole of sorts in your system's coverage. The lines of logic that your test double supplants is code that your unit tests will not execute. You *must* ensure that other tests cover that logic.

Refactor your tests. Don't let your increased dependency on a third-party tool create a problem. A haphazard approach can quickly generate rampant mocking, resulting in lots of duplication and otherwise difficult tests. Refactor your tests as much as you refactor your production code! Encapsulate expectation declarations in common helper methods to improve abstraction, reduce the extent of the dependency, and minimize duplicate code. When you later want to upgrade to a newer, better tool than Google Mock, you won't be faced with quite as devastating a change.

Question overly complex use of test doubles. If you're struggling with mocks, it could be because either you're trying to test too much or your design is deficient. Having multiple levels of mocks is usually a recipe for headaches. Using fakes, as discussed in Section 5.10, *Miscellaneous Test Double Topics*, on page 136, usually leads to more struggle. If stuck, simplify what you're trying to do by breaking things into smaller tests. Look also at the potential of splitting apart the code you are testing.

Choose expressiveness over power. Choose your mock tool because it helps you create highly abstract tests that document behaviors and design, not because it has cool features and can do clever, esoteric things. Use those clever, esoteric features only when you must.

5.10 Miscellaneous Test Double Topics

In this final section, you'll learn a few odds and ends about using test doubles, including generally accepted terminology, where to define them, whether to mock concrete classes, and their potential impact on performance.

What Do You Call Them?

So far, this chapter has used the terms *test double*, *mock*, and *stub*. Most of the TDD community has accepted common definitions for these terms plus a few others that you might find useful. You will often hear the word *mock* used in place of *test double*. Most of the time, that's appropriate, since most developers use mock tools. Still, if you want to communicate more effectively, use the term most appropriate to your circumstance. *xUnit Test Patterns* [Mes07] acts as the definitive guide for these definitions.

Test double: An element that emulates a production element for testing purposes

Stub: A test double that returns hard-coded values

Spy: A test double that captures information sent to it for later verification

Mock: A test double that self-verifies based on expectations sent to it

Fake: A test double that provides a light-weight implementation of a production class

Our handcrafted test double implementation for get() acted as both a stub and a spy. It acted as a spy by verifying that the URL sent to it contained an accurate HTTP GET request URL. It acted as a stub by returning hard-coded JSON text. We turned it into a mock by using Google Mock to capture expectations and automatically verify whether they were met.

The canonical example for a fake is an in-memory database. Since interacting with file-system-based databases is inherently slow, many teams have implemented a test double class to emulate much of the interaction with the database. The underlying implementation is typically a hash-based structure that provides simple and rapid key-based lookup.

The challenge with fakes is that they become first-rate classes, often growing into complex implementations that contain their own defects. With a database fake, for example, you must properly replicate all the semantics of database interaction using a hash table implementation. It's not impossible, but there are many easy mistakes to make.

Avoid fakes. You will otherwise undoubtedly waste half an afternoon at some point fixing a problem caused by a subtle defect in the fake. (I've wasted several such hours.) Your test suite exists to simplify and speed up development, not to waste time by creating problems of its own.

If you do employ fakes, you'll want to ensure that they are themselves unit tested. Tests for the fake will need to prove that the logic matches behavior in the emulated object.

Where Do They Go?

Start by defining your test double within the same file as the tests that use it. Developers can then readily see the test double declaration that the tests use. Once multiple fixtures use the same test double, you will want to move the declaration to a separate header file. You should move your test doubles out of sight once they become so dumb that you never need to look at them again.

Remember that changes to the production interface will break tests that use derived test doubles. If you're all on the same team and following *collective code ownership* guidelines (everyone has to right to change any code), the developer changing the production interface is responsible for running all tests and fixing any that break. In other circumstances, sending out a message that clearly communicates the change (and implications) is prudent.

Vtables and Performance

You introduce test doubles to support test-driving a class with a problematic dependency. Many techniques for creating test doubles involve creating derived types that override virtual member functions. If the production class previously contained no virtual methods, it now does and thus now contains a vtable. The vtable carries the overhead of an extra level of indirection.

The introduction of a vtable represents a performance concern, since C++ now requires an additional lookup into the vtable (instead of simply calling a function). Also, the compiler can no longer inline a virtual function.

But in most cases, the performance impact of vtables is negligible or even nonexistent. The compiler is able to optimize away some of the cost in certain cases. You'll want the better, polymorphic design most of the time.

However, if you must call the mocked production function extensively, you will want to first profile performance. If the measured degradation is unacceptable, consider a different mocking form (perhaps a template-based solution), rework the design (and possibly recoup the performance loss by optimizing elsewhere), or introduce integration tests to compensate for the loss of the ability to unit test. Visit Section 10.2, *TDD and Performance*, on page 269 for more discussion.

Mocking Concrete Classes

We created a mock by implementing the pure virtual Http interface. Many systems predominantly consist of concrete classes with few such interfaces. From a design stance, introducing interfaces can start to provide you with means of isolating one part of the system from another. The *Dependency Inversion Principle* (DIP)[17] promotes breaking dependencies by having clients depend on abstractions, not concrete implementations. Introducing these abstractions in the form of pure virtual classes can improve build times and isolate complexity. More importantly, they can make testing simpler.

You can, if you must, create a mock that derives from a concrete class. The problem is that the resulting class represents a mix of production and mocked behavior, a beast referred to as a *partial mock*. First, a partial mock is usually a sign that the class you're mocking is too large—if you need to stub some of its elements but not all, you can likely split the class into two around these boundaries. Second, you will likely get into trouble when working with partial mocks. You can quickly end up in "mock hell."

For example, if you were to mock CurlHttp directly by defining a derived class for it, you'd invoke its destructor by default. Is that a problem? Maybe, because it happens to directly interact with the cURL library. That's probably not behavior you want your test to be exercising. In some cases, you can end up with devious defects: "Aha! I thought the code was interacting with the mock method at this point, but it looks like it's interacting with the real method." You don't want to waste the kind of time often needed to get to the "aha!"

When you reach for a clever tool like a partial mock, your design is giving off smells. A cleaner design might, for example, adapt the concrete class with a class that derives from an interface. Tests would no longer require a partial mock, instead creating a test double for the interface.

5.11 Teardown

This chapter provided you with techniques for breaking collaborator dependencies when test-driving. You'll want to review the documentation for your mock tool to fully understand its additional features and nuances. Otherwise,

---

17. *Agile Software Development, Principles, Patterns, and Practices [Mar02]*

you now have a basic understanding of the core TDD mechanisms you'll need to build a production system.

That doesn't mean you can stop reading, particularly not if you want to succeed in the long run. You're just starting to get to the good stuff. Now that you can test-drive all your code, how can you take advantage of it so that your design stays clean and simple? And how can you ensure that your tests, too, stay clean and simple? The next two chapters focus on improving the design of both your production code and tests so that your maintenance efforts remain minimal over time.

## CHAPTER 6

Incremental Design

6.1 Setup

You've learned the core fundamentals of TDD, from mechanics to preferred practices to techniques for dealing with dependencies. You've also refactored along the way, incrementally shaping your code with each change—but to what end?

The primary reason to practice TDD is to support the ability to add or change features at a sustained, stable maintenance cost. TDD provides this support by letting you continually refine the design as you drive changes into your system. The tests produced by practicing TDD demonstrate that your system logic behaves as expected, which allows you to clean up new code as soon as you add it. The implication is momentous. Without TDD, you don't have the rapid feedback to allow you to safely and easily make incremental code changes. Without making incremental code changes, your codebase will steadily degrade.

In this chapter, you'll learn what sorts of things you want to do when in the refactoring step. We'll focus primarily on Kent Beck's concept of *simple design* (see *Extreme Programming Explained: Embrace Change [Bec00]*), a great starter set of rules for keeping your code clean.

6.2 Simple Design

If you knew nothing whatsoever about design, you might consider following three simple rules when practicing TDD.

- Ensure your code is always highly readable and expressive.

- Eliminate all duplication, as long as doing so doesn't interfere with the first rule.

- Ensure that you don't introduce unnecessary complexity into your system. Avoid speculative constructs ("I just know we're gonna have to support many-to-many someday") and abstractions that don't add to your system's expressiveness.

The final rule is important, but the other two hold slightly higher priority. In other words, prefer introducing an abstraction such as a new member function or class if it improves expressiveness.

Following these rules can give you an eminently maintainable system.

The Cost of Duplication

In our coding exercises, we've focused a lot on eliminating duplication. But why?

Duplication is perhaps the biggest cost in maintaining a codebase over time. Imagine your system requires two lines of code to audit important events. Sure, they could go into a helper member function, but it's just two lines of code, right? When you need to add an audit event, it's simple enough to find another audit point and then copy and paste the two lines.

Two lines duplicated doesn't sound bad, but now visualize those two lines of audit code repeated one hundred times throughout your codebase. And then imagine that the auditing requirements change ever so slightly and you need to add a third line of logic. Uh-oh. You'll have to find all one hundred change points, add the missing line, and retest everything, all at considerably higher cost than if there were a single place to do so. What if one of the duplicate pair of lines is slightly different? You may have to spend additional analysis time to determine whether the variation is deliberate. What if you find only ninety-nine of the duplicates but neglect to find and fix the hundredth? You've shipped defective code.

Most developers are lazy about creating new member functions, and sometimes they resist doing so because of dubious claims about degrading performance. But ultimately they are only creating more future work for themselves.

That's not the only way duplicate code emerges. Imagine you've been told to add a variant to an existing feature. Your changes require a half-dozen lines of code executed if some condition exists, else execute a half-dozen lines of existing code.

You discover that the existing feature is implemented in an untested 200-line member function. The right thing would be a design that extracts the 195 or so lines of commonality and allows you to introduce your variant as an extension. Perhaps the template method or strategy design pattern would provide the basis for an appropriate solution.

Most programmers don't do the right thing, not because they don't know how but because they are lazy and fearful. "If I change the existing code and it breaks, I'll get blamed for breaking something that I shouldn't have been messing with in the first place." It's easier to copy the 200 lines, make the changes needed, and move on.

Because of this somewhat natural tendency toward duplication, most large systems contain substantially more code than required. The extra code dramatically increases maintenance costs and risks.

You have the potential to stave off this systematic degradation by incrementally refactoring as part of the TDD cycle.

The Portfolio Manager

Let's take a look at how Beck's notion of simple design plays out in developing a small subsystem.

Story: Portfolio Manager
Investors want to track stock purchases and sales to provide the basis for financial analysis.

In test-driving the portfolio manager, we've ended up with the following effort. (Note: Much of the code for this example will be built behind the scenes. I'll present only the code that's relevant to our design discussions. Refer to the source code download for full listings.)

c6/1/PortfolioTest.cpp
```cpp
#include "gmock/gmock.h"
#include "Portfolio.h"

using namespace ::testing;

class APortfolio: public Test {
public:
   Portfolio portfolio_;
};

TEST_F(APortfolio, IsEmptyWhenCreated) {
   ASSERT_TRUE(portfolio_.IsEmpty());
}

TEST_F(APortfolio, IsNotEmptyAfterPurchase) {
   portfolio_.Purchase("IBM", 1);

   ASSERT_FALSE(portfolio_.IsEmpty());
}
```

```
TEST_F(APortfolio, AnswersZeroForShareCountOfUnpurchasedSymbol) {
    ASSERT_THAT(portfolio_.ShareCount("AAPL"), Eq(0u));
}

TEST_F(APortfolio, AnswersShareCountForPurchasedSymbol) {
    portfolio_.Purchase("IBM", 2);
    ASSERT_THAT(portfolio_.ShareCount("IBM"), Eq(2u));
}
```

c6/1/Portfolio.h
```
#ifndef Portfolio_h
#define Portfolio_h

#include <string>

class Portfolio {
public:
    Portfolio();
    bool IsEmpty() const;
    void Purchase(const std::string& symbol, unsigned int shareCount);
    unsigned int ShareCount(const std::string& symbol) const;

private:
    bool isEmpty_;
    unsigned int shareCount_;
};

#endif
```

c6/1/Portfolio.cpp
```
#include "Portfolio.h"
using namespace std;
Portfolio::Portfolio()
    : isEmpty_{true}
    , shareCount_{0u} {
}
bool Portfolio::IsEmpty() const {
    return isEmpty_;
}

void Portfolio::Purchase(const string& symbol, unsigned int shareCount) {
    isEmpty_ = false;
    shareCount_ = shareCount;
}

unsigned int Portfolio::ShareCount(const string& symbol) const {
    return shareCount_;
}
```

Were you able to understand what the Portfolio class does by reading the tests? You should be building the habit of reading test names as your first understanding of what a class has been designed to do. The tests are your gateway to understanding.

Simple Duplication in the Portfolio Manager

We have duplication in both our tests and our production code. The string literal "IBM" repeats three times across two tests: it appears once in IsNotEmptyAfterPurchase and twice in AnswersShareCountForPurchasedSymbol. Extracting the literal to a constant makes reading things a little easier, it reduces the risk of mistyping the literal in the future, and it makes new tests a little easier to write. Further, if the symbol for IBM needs to change, we can make that change in one place.

c6/2/PortfolioTest.cpp
```cpp
#include "gmock/gmock.h"
#include "Portfolio.h"

using namespace ::testing;
using namespace std;

class APortfolio: public Test {
public:
    static const string IBM;
    Portfolio portfolio_;
};
const string APortfolio::IBM("IBM");
// ...
TEST_F(APortfolio, IsEmptyWhenCreated) {
    ASSERT_TRUE(portfolio_.IsEmpty());
}

TEST_F(APortfolio, IsNotEmptyAfterPurchase) {
    portfolio_.Purchase(IBM, 1);
    ASSERT_FALSE(portfolio_.IsEmpty());
}
// ...
TEST_F(APortfolio, AnswersZeroForShareCountOfUnpurchasedSymbol) {
    ASSERT_THAT(portfolio_.ShareCount("AAPL"), Eq(0u));
}
TEST_F(APortfolio, AnswersShareCountForPurchasedSymbol) {
    portfolio_.Purchase(IBM, 2);

    ASSERT_THAT(portfolio_.ShareCount(IBM), Eq(2u));
}

TEST_F(APortfolio, ThrowsOnPurchaseOfZeroShares) {
    ASSERT_THROW(portfolio_.Purchase(IBM, 0), InvalidPurchaseException);
}
```

Does that mean you should always extract common literals to a variable? Suppose AnswersShareCountForPurchasedSymbol was the only test in which we needed the "IBM" literal. Creating a local variable IBM would have given us the benefits as claimed before. But the value of the variable in this case seems to be less. We can easily see all uses of the literal in a two-line test, so it's trivial and safe to change both if needed.

Design choices are often judgment calls. Strive to adhere to the design principles set out in this chapter to better understand how they benefit your system. With that experience, when you encounter code that requires a judgment call, you'll understand the implication of forgoing a design rule.

Take a look at the production code and see whether you can spot the duplication:

c6/1/Portfolio.cpp
```cpp
#include "Portfolio.h"
using namespace std;
Portfolio::Portfolio()
   : isEmpty_{true}
   , shareCount_{0u} {
}
bool Portfolio::IsEmpty() const {
   return isEmpty_;
}

void Portfolio::Purchase(const string& symbol, unsigned int shareCount) {
   isEmpty_ = false;
   shareCount_ = shareCount;
}

unsigned int Portfolio::ShareCount(const string& symbol) const {
   return shareCount_;
}
```

The code doesn't exhibit visibly obvious line-for-line (or expression-for-expression) duplication. Instead, it contains algorithmic duplication. The IsEmpty() member function returns the value of a bool that changes when Purchase() gets called. Yet the notion of emptiness is directly tied to the number of shares, stored also when Purchase() gets called. We can eliminate this conceptual duplication by eliminating the isEmpty_ variable and instead having IsEmpty() ask about the number of shares.

c6/2/Portfolio.cpp
```cpp
bool Portfolio::IsEmpty() const {
   return 0 == shareCount_;
}
```

(Yes, it's slightly awkward to ask for the number of shares overall in order to determine emptiness, but it's correct for now, in other words, in the incremental sense. Writing what you know to be short-term code should trigger interesting thoughts, which might in turn translate to new tests. The problem with our implementation is that the portfolio will return empty if someone purchases zero shares of a symbol. Our definition of empty is whether the portfolio contains any symbols. So, is that empty? Or should we disallow such purchases? For the purposes of moving forward, we choose the latter and write a test named ThrowsOnPurchaseOfZeroShares.)

Algorithmic duplication—different ways of solving the same problem, or pieces of a problem—becomes a significant problem as your system grows. More often than not, the duplication morphs into unintentional variance, as changes to one implementation don't get rolled into the other implementations.

Can We Really Stick to an Incremental Approach?

A bit of coding later, and we have the following tests written (just the test signature now, as you should be able to imagine what these tests look like)...

c6/3/PortfolioTest.cpp
```
TEST_F(APortfolio, IsEmptyWhenCreated) {
TEST_F(APortfolio, IsNotEmptyAfterPurchase) {
TEST_F(APortfolio, AnswersZeroForShareCountOfUnpurchasedSymbol) {
TEST_F(APortfolio, AnswersShareCountForPurchasedSymbol) {
TEST_F(APortfolio, ThrowsOnPurchaseOfZeroShares) {
TEST_F(APortfolio, AnswersShareCountForAppropriateSymbol) {
TEST_F(APortfolio, ShareCountReflectsAccumulatedPurchasesOfSameSymbol) {
TEST_F(APortfolio, ReducesShareCountOfSymbolOnSell) {
TEST_F(APortfolio, ThrowsWhenSellingMoreSharesThanPurchased) {
```

with the following implementation:

c6/3/Portfolio.cpp
```
#include "Portfolio.h"
using namespace std;
bool Portfolio::IsEmpty() const {
   return 0 == holdings_.size();
}
void Portfolio::Purchase(const string& symbol, unsigned int shareCount) {
   if (0 == shareCount) throw InvalidPurchaseException();
   holdings_[symbol] = shareCount + ShareCount(symbol);
}
void Portfolio::Sell(const std::string& symbol, unsigned int shareCount) {
   if (shareCount > ShareCount(symbol)) throw InvalidSellException();
   holdings_[symbol] = ShareCount(symbol) - shareCount;
}
```

```
unsigned int Portfolio::ShareCount(const string& symbol) const {
    auto it = holdings_.find(symbol);
    if (it == holdings_.end()) return 0;
    return it->second;
}
```

We're told a new story.

Story: Show Purchase History

Investors want to see a list of purchase records for a given symbol, with each record showing the date of purchase and number of shares.

The story throws a wrench into our implementation—we're not tracking individual purchases, and we're not capturing the date on our signatures. This is where many developers question the wisdom of TDD. Had we spent additional time up front vetting the requirements, we might have figured out that we need to track the date of purchase. Our initial design could have incorporated that need.

The story seems to represent a good-sized change, one that might take a bit more than ten minutes. We must define a data structure to represent a purchase, change the signature on the method, supply a date from client code (right now, just our tests), populate the data structure appropriately, and store it.

Nah, let's not do that...at least not all at once. Let's see if we can proceed incrementally, seeking positive feedback every few minutes. One way to do that is to make assumptions. Let's create a test that makes one purchase and then demonstrates that a corresponding record exists in the retrieved list of purchase records. Our assumption is that purchases are always made on a specific date. That makes our current task simpler because we can ignore the need to pass a date to Purchase().

c6/4/PortfolioTest.cpp

```
TEST_F(APortfolio, AnswersThePurchaseRecordForASinglePurchase) {
    portfolio_.Purchase(SAMSUNG, 5);
    auto purchases = portfolio_.Purchases(SAMSUNG);

    auto purchase = purchases[0];
    ASSERT_THAT(purchase.ShareCount, Eq(5u));
    ASSERT_THAT(purchase.Date, Eq(Portfolio::FIXED_PURCHASE_DATE));
}
```

To get this test to pass, we don't even need to associate the purchase record with the holdings_ data structure. Since our current assumption is that this works for only a single purchase, we can define a "global" purchase record collection for Portfolio.

```
c6/4/Portfolio.h
struct PurchaseRecord {
   PurchaseRecord(unsigned int shareCount, const boost::gregorian::date& date)
   : ShareCount(shareCount)
   , Date(date) {
   }

   unsigned int ShareCount;
   boost::gregorian::date Date;
};

class Portfolio {
public:
➤   static const boost::gregorian::date FIXED_PURCHASE_DATE;

   bool IsEmpty() const;

   void Purchase(const std::string& symbol, unsigned int shareCount);
   void Sell(const std::string& symbol, unsigned int shareCount);

   unsigned int ShareCount(const std::string& symbol) const;
➤   std::vector<PurchaseRecord> Purchases(const std::string& symbol) const;

private:
   std::unordered_map<std::string, unsigned int> holdings_;
➤   std::vector<PurchaseRecord> purchases_;
};
```

```
c6/4/Portfolio.cpp
➤ const date Portfolio::FIXED_PURCHASE_DATE(date(2014, Jan, 1));

void Portfolio::Purchase(const string& symbol, unsigned int shareCount) {
   if (0 == shareCount) throw InvalidPurchaseException();
   holdings_[symbol] = shareCount + ShareCount(symbol);
➤   purchases_.push_back(PurchaseRecord(shareCount, FIXED_PURCHASE_DATE));
}

vector<PurchaseRecord> Portfolio::Purchases(const string& symbol) const {
   return purchases_;
}
```

That's simple code, but it takes a few minutes to put into place, each minute
inviting more possibilities for making dumb mistakes. It's nice to get positive
feedback that we've entered code correctly before moving on.

We created a production constant, FIXED_PURCHASE_DATE, to allow us to make
quick, demonstrable progress. We know it's bogus. Let's get rid of it by
removing our temporary but useful assumption that all purchases are on the
same date.

```
c6/5/PortfolioTest.cpp
TEST_F(APortfolio, AnswersThePurchaseRecordForASinglePurchase) {
➤    date dateOfPurchase(2014, Mar, 17);
➤    portfolio_.Purchase(SAMSUNG, 5, dateOfPurchase);

    auto purchases = portfolio_.Purchases(SAMSUNG);

    auto purchase = purchases[0];
    ASSERT_THAT(purchase.ShareCount, Eq(5u));
    ASSERT_THAT(purchase.Date, Eq(dateOfPurchase));
}
```

Rather than having to fix all the other tests that call the Purchase() member function, we can take a smaller step and default the date parameter.

```
c6/5/Portfolio.h
void Purchase(
        const std::string& symbol,

        unsigned int shareCount,

        const boost::gregorian::date& transactionDate=
➤            Portfolio::FIXED_PURCHASE_DATE);
```

```
c6/5/Portfolio.cpp
➤ void Portfolio::Purchase(
➤        const string& symbol, unsigned int shareCount, const date& transactionDate) {
    if (0 == shareCount) throw InvalidPurchaseException();

    holdings_[symbol] = shareCount + ShareCount(symbol);
➤    purchases_.push_back(PurchaseRecord(shareCount, transactionDate));
}
```

Using a fixed date isn't a valid long-term requirement (although defaulting to the current time *might* be), so we now want to eliminate the default parameter on Purchase(). Unfortunately, we have at least a handful of tests that call Purchase() without passing a date.

One solution is to add a date argument to the calls in all of the affected tests. That seems tedious. It also might violate the principle of test abstraction (see Section 7.4, *Test Abstraction*, on page 181) for those tests—none of them cares about the purchase date.

That we need to change many tests at once, without changing the behavior they describe, tells us they contain duplication that we should have eliminated. What if we supply a fixture helper method that handles the call to Purchase() and provides a default value for the date so that the tests need not specify it?

```
c6/6/PortfolioTest.cpp
class APortfolio: public Test {
public:
    static const string IBM;
    static const string SAMSUNG;
    Portfolio portfolio_;
    static const date ArbitraryDate;

    void Purchase(
            const string& symbol,
            unsigned int shareCount,
            const date& transactionDate=APortfolio::ArbitraryDate) {
        portfolio_.Purchase(symbol, shareCount, transactionDate);
    }
};

TEST_F(APortfolio, ReducesShareCountOfSymbolOnSell)  {
    Purchase(SAMSUNG, 30);

    portfolio_.Sell(SAMSUNG, 13);

    ASSERT_THAT(portfolio_.ShareCount(SAMSUNG), Eq(30u - 13));
}

TEST_F(APortfolio, AnswersThePurchaseRecordForASinglePurchase) {
    date dateOfPurchase(2014, Mar, 17);
    Purchase(SAMSUNG, 5, dateOfPurchase);

    auto purchases = portfolio_.Purchases(SAMSUNG);

    auto purchase = purchases[0];
    ASSERT_THAT(purchase.ShareCount, Eq(5u));
    ASSERT_THAT(purchase.Date, Eq(dateOfPurchase));
}
```

One point of potential debate is that the helper function Purchase() removes a bit of information from the tests—specifically, that it's delegating to the portfolio_ instance. A first-time reader must navigate into the helper method to see just what it's doing. But it's a simple function and doesn't bury key information that the reader will have a hard time remembering.

As a rule of thumb, avoid hiding Act (see *Arrange-Act-Assert/Given-When-Then*, on page 84) specifics. We can use the helper method when we need to make a purchase as part of setting up a test. But for tests where we're specifically testing Purchase() behavior, we should directly invoke it. Thus, ReducesShareCountOfSymbolOnSell can use the helper, since it makes a purchase as part of *arranging* the test. AnswersShareCountForPurchasedSymbol verifies purchase behavior, so it retains the direct call to portfolio_.Purchase().

```
c6/7/PortfolioTest.cpp
TEST_F(APortfolio, AnswersShareCountForPurchasedSymbol) {
    portfolio_.Purchase(IBM, 2);
    ASSERT_THAT(portfolio_.ShareCount(IBM), Eq(2u));
}

TEST_F(APortfolio, ReducesShareCountOfSymbolOnSell)  {
    Purchase(SAMSUNG, 30);

    portfolio_.Sell(SAMSUNG, 13);
    ASSERT_THAT(portfolio_.ShareCount(SAMSUNG), Eq(30u - 13));
}
```

Personally, I don't like the inconsistencies this creates in the way the tests
look. I'm OK with running *everything* through the helper method, as long as
it's a simple one-liner delegation, as it is in this case. If that bothers you,
another solution is to simply include the date parameter in each of the tests
and use a constant with a name like ArbitraryPurchaseDate.

We've been taking an incremental approach with very small steps. Does it
cost us? You betcha! It often requires introducing small bits of code that we
later remove—tiny bits of waste product.

In return, we get the much more valuable ability to make continual forward
progress on creating well-designed, correct code. We don't worry about tackling
new, never-before-considered features—we use TDD to incorporate them as
a similar series of small steps. The more we keep our code clean, the easier
it is to make our changes.

More Duplication

After a bit of test and production code cleanup, our tests around the purchase
record are short and sweet.

```
c6/8/PortfolioTest.cpp
TEST_F(APortfolio, AnswersThePurchaseRecordForASinglePurchase) {
    Purchase(SAMSUNG, 5, ArbitraryDate);

    auto purchases = portfolio_.Purchases(SAMSUNG);
    ASSERT_PURCHASE(purchases[0], 5, ArbitraryDate);
}

TEST_F(APortfolio, IncludesSalesInPurchaseRecords) {
    Purchase(SAMSUNG, 10);
    Sell(SAMSUNG, 5, ArbitraryDate);

    auto sales = portfolio_.Purchases(SAMSUNG);
    ASSERT_PURCHASE(sales[1], -5, ArbitraryDate);
}
```

To support the negative amounts in the purchase record, we changed the ShareCount member to a signed integer.

c6/8/Portfolio.h
```
struct PurchaseRecord {
    PurchaseRecord(int shareCount, const boost::gregorian::date& date)
        : ShareCount(shareCount)
        , Date(date) {}
    int ShareCount;
    boost::gregorian::date Date;
};
```

c6/8/PortfolioTest.cpp
```
void ASSERT_PURCHASE(
        PurchaseRecord& purchase, int shareCount, const date& date) {
    ASSERT_THAT(purchase.ShareCount, Eq(shareCount));
    ASSERT_THAT(purchase.Date, Eq(date));
}
```

The production code for the two transaction functions, Purchase() and Sell(), is already looking a bit dense in just three lines each.

c6/8/Portfolio.cpp
```
void Portfolio::Purchase(
        const string& symbol, unsigned int shareCount, const date& transactionDate) {
    if (0 == shareCount) throw InvalidPurchaseException();
    holdings_[symbol] = shareCount + ShareCount(symbol);
    purchases_.push_back(PurchaseRecord(shareCount, transactionDate));
}

void Portfolio::Sell(
        const string& symbol, unsigned int shareCount, const date& transactionDate) {
    if (shareCount > ShareCount(symbol)) throw InvalidSellException();
    holdings_[symbol] = ShareCount(symbol) - shareCount;
    purchases_.push_back(PurchaseRecord(-shareCount, transactionDate));
}
```

Further, they're fairly similar in nature. We haven't yet coded the proper logic to associate the purchase records with the appropriate symbol (perhaps using a hash table), and when we do, we don't want to have to code it twice. Let's see what duplication we can eliminate.

The Purchase() and Sell() functions have small variances between each of the three lines. Let's take a look at each line in turn and see whether we can make them similar. The first line in each is a guard clause that enforces a constraint: sales cannot be for more shares than held, and purchases cannot be for zero shares. But shouldn't sales have the same constraint—that you cannot sell zero shares? Our customer says yes.

A slight problem is that the exception type name InvalidPurchaseException is inappropriate for use in the Sell() function. Let's make it something more specific that both functions can use—ShareCountCannotBeZeroException.

```
c6/9/PortfolioTest.cpp
TEST_F(APortfolio, ThrowsOnPurchaseOfZeroShares) {
    ASSERT_THROW(Purchase(IBM, 0), ShareCountCannotBeZeroException);
}
// ...
TEST_F(APortfolio, ThrowsOnSellOfZeroShares) {
    ASSERT_THROW(Sell(IBM, 0), ShareCountCannotBeZeroException);
}
```

Both transaction methods end up with the same guard clause.

```
c6/9/Portfolio.cpp
void Portfolio::Purchase(
        const string& symbol, unsigned int shareCount, const date& transactionDate) {
➤   if (0 == shareCount) throw ShareCountCannotBeZeroException();
    holdings_[symbol] = shareCount + ShareCount(symbol);
    purchases_.push_back(PurchaseRecord(shareCount, transactionDate));
}

void Portfolio::Sell(
        const string& symbol, unsigned int shareCount, const date& transactionDate) {
    if (shareCount > ShareCount(symbol)) throw InvalidSellException();
➤   if (0 == shareCount) throw ShareCountCannotBeZeroException();
    holdings_[symbol] = ShareCount(symbol) - shareCount;
    purchases_.push_back(PurchaseRecord(-shareCount, transactionDate));
}
```

Moving on to the next line in each transaction method, we update the holdings entry for the appropriate symbol, by either adding to or subtracting from the existing shares for the symbol. But subtraction is the same as adding the inverse.

Let's introduce a signed variable called shareChange to capture the inverse. Note that we can also use it in the final line of code (where we add the purchase record).

```
c6/10/Portfolio.cpp
void Portfolio::Sell(
        const string& symbol, unsigned int shareCount, const date& transactionDate) {
    if (shareCount > ShareCount(symbol)) throw InvalidSellException();
    if (0 == shareCount) throw ShareCountCannotBeZeroException();
➤   int shareChange = -shareCount;
➤   holdings_[symbol] = ShareCount(symbol) + shareChange;
➤   purchases_.push_back(PurchaseRecord(shareChange, transactionDate));
}
```

Now we bounce back to Purchase() and try to make it look more like Sell().

```
c6/11/Portfolio.cpp
void Portfolio::Purchase(
      const string& symbol, unsigned int shareCount, const date& transactionDate) {
   if (0 == shareCount) throw ShareCountCannotBeZeroException();
➤   int shareChange = shareCount;
➤   holdings_[symbol] = ShareCount(symbol) + shareChange;
➤   purchases_.push_back(PurchaseRecord(shareChange, transactionDate));
}
```

We now have two lines of code at the end of each function that duplicate each other, plus the same guard clause in each. Let's move the initialization of shareChange up a line to above the guard clause. Our tests will ensure that it's a safe move, since moving lines up or down is highly risky.

We end up with three common lines at the end of each function. We also rename the use of shareCount in the guard clause to shareChange so that all three to-be-extracted lines use a common variable.

```
c6/12/Portfolio.cpp
void Portfolio::Purchase(
      const string& symbol, unsigned int shareCount, const date& transactionDate) {
   int shareChange = shareCount;
➤   if (0 == shareChange) throw ShareCountCannotBeZeroException();
➤   holdings_[symbol] = ShareCount(symbol) + shareChange;
➤   purchases_.push_back(PurchaseRecord(shareChange, transactionDate));
}

void Portfolio::Sell(
      const string& symbol, unsigned int shareCount, const date& transactionDate) {
   if (shareCount > ShareCount(symbol)) throw InvalidSellException();
   int shareChange = -shareCount;
➤   if (0 == shareChange) throw ShareCountCannotBeZeroException();
➤   holdings_[symbol] = ShareCount(symbol) + shareChange;
➤   purchases_.push_back(PurchaseRecord(shareChange, transactionDate));
}
```

Finally, we extract.

```
c6/13/Portfolio.cpp
void Portfolio::Purchase(
      const string& symbol, unsigned int shareCount, const date& transactionDate) {
   Transact(symbol, shareCount, transactionDate);
}

void Portfolio::Sell(
      const string& symbol, unsigned int shareCount, const date& transactionDate) {
   if (shareCount > ShareCount(symbol)) throw InvalidSellException();
   Transact(symbol, -shareCount, transactionDate);
}
```

```
void Portfolio::Transact(
      const string& symbol, int shareChange, const date& transactionDate) {
   if (0 == shareChange) throw ShareCountCannotBeZeroException();
   holdings_[symbol] = ShareCount(symbol) + shareChange;
   purchases_.push_back(PurchaseRecord(shareChange, transactionDate));
}
```

One more little expressiveness thing is that the name of our exception type InvalidSellException is not very good. Let's change it to InsufficientSharesException.

c6/14/PortfolioTest.cpp
```
TEST_F(APortfolio, ThrowsWhenSellingMoreSharesThanPurchased) {
   ASSERT_THROW(Sell(SAMSUNG, 1), InsufficientSharesException);
}
```

c6/14/Portfolio.cpp
```
void Portfolio::Sell(
      const string& symbol, unsigned int shareCount, const date& transactionDate) {
   if (shareCount > ShareCount(symbol)) throw InsufficientSharesException();
   Transact(symbol, -shareCount, transactionDate);
}
```

Is there anything else we could do from the stance of our two simple design rules? It appears that we've squashed all the duplication. What of readability? Purchase() does nothing other than delegate, so it's clear, and Sell() simply adds a constraint and reverses the shares, so it too makes immediate sense. Transact() doesn't quite have the immediacy we want.

Benefits of Small Methods

To read Transact(), we must slow down and carefully pick out what each line is really trying to accomplish. The first line throws an exception if the change in the number of shares is zero. The second line obtains the shares for the symbol, adds the share change, and assigns it to an appropriate entry in the hashtable. The third line creates a purchase record and adds it to the overall list of purchases.

Transact() consists of three simple one-liners. But if all one-liners require that sort of meticulous reading, then your system overall will be all that more difficult to navigate. It's simply not expressive enough. Let's fix that.

c6/15/Portfolio.cpp
```
void Portfolio::Transact(
      const string& symbol, int shareChange, const date& transactionDate) {
   ThrowIfShareCountIsZero(shareChange);
   UpdateShareCount(symbol, shareChange);
   AddPurchaseRecord(shareChange, transactionDate);
}
```

```
void Portfolio::ThrowIfShareCountIsZero(int shareChange) const {
   if (0 == shareChange) throw ShareCountCannotBeZeroException();
}

void Portfolio::UpdateShareCount(const string& symbol, int shareChange) {
   holdings_[symbol] = ShareCount(symbol) + shareChange;
}

void Portfolio::AddPurchaseRecord(int shareChange, const date& date) {
   purchases_.push_back(PurchaseRecord(shareChange, date));
}
```

I have amazing extra-sensory powers. Back in time, in early 2013 as I write this chapter, I can see the future faces of many readers. I sense consternation. And I understand it.

Here are the reasons you might offer for not doing what we just did:

- It's extra effort. Creating new functions is a pain.

- Creating a function for a one-liner used in only one place seems ridiculous.

- The additional function calls incur performance overhead.

- It's harder to follow the entire flow through all the code.

- You'll end up with tens of thousands of little crummy methods, each with horribly long names.

And here are some reasons why you should consider moving your code in this direction:

- It adheres to the simple design rule of expressiveness. The code requires no explanatory comments. Its functions, each consisting of either one detailed line or a few declarative statements, are immediately understood. Problems stand out like sore thumbs in such small functions.

  In contrast, most systems have lots of dense, long functions that take far too long to comprehend. Defects hide easily in these functions.

- It adheres to the design concept of cohesion and the SRP. All lines of code in a given function are at the same level of abstraction. Each function has one reason to change.

- It paves the way for simpler future design changes. We still need to associate purchase records with the proper symbol. We can now do that in one place, as opposed to two. If we need to specialize AddPurchaseRecord(), we're ready to go. If we need to create a more sophisticated purchase record subsystem, we can quickly move the existing logic to a new class.

If we need to support undo and redo or additional sophistications around purchasing and selling, we're poised to factor into a command pattern with a base class of Transaction.

- Following the flow of code is more easily done without implementation details in the way. Transact() acts as a declaration of policy. The helper methods—ThrowIfShareCountIsZero(), UpdateShareCount(), and AddPurchaseRecord() —are implementation details you don't need to know most of the time. Think about the notion of separating interface from implementation or separating abstractions from concrete details.

- The performance overhead of extract methods in this fashion is almost never a problem. See Section 10.2, *TDD and Performance*, on page 269.

- Small functions represent the start of real reuse. As you extract more similarly small functions, you will begin to more readily spot duplicate concepts and constructs in your development efforts. You won't end up with an unmanageable mass of tiny methods. You will instead shrink your production code size dramatically.

Enough preaching. While you might not be ready to embrace this drastic change in style, you should be willing to at least give it an honest effort as you practice TDD more. Be willing to move in the direction of smaller functions and see what happens.

Finishing the Functionality

We're not done. A portfolio can return a list of purchase records, but only for a single symbol. Our next test requires the portfolio to answer the correct set of purchase records when multiple symbols have been purchased.

```
c6/16/PortfolioTest.cpp
bool operator==(const PurchaseRecord& lhs, const PurchaseRecord& rhs) {
   return lhs.ShareCount == rhs.ShareCount && lhs.Date == rhs.Date;
}

TEST_F(APortfolio, SeparatesPurchaseRecordsBySymbol) {
   Purchase(SAMSUNG, 5, ArbitraryDate);
   Purchase(IBM, 1, ArbitraryDate);

   auto sales = portfolio_.Purchases(SAMSUNG);
   ASSERT_THAT(sales, ElementsAre(PurchaseRecord(5, ArbitraryDate)));
}
```

Google Mock provides the ElementsAre() matcher for verifying explicit elements in a collection. The comparison requires the ability to compare two PurchaseRecord objects, so we add an appropriate implementation for operator==(). (We might also have chosen to implement operator==() as a member function on PurchaseRecord, but currently we only have need for it in a test.) The test initially fails, since the purchases_ vector holds onto two purchase records—one for Samsung, one for IBM.

To get the test to pass, we first declare the purchaseRecords_ member variable in Portfolio.h, an unordered map that stores a vector of PurchaseRecord objects for each symbol. We also change the signature of AddPurchaseRecord() to take a symbol.

```
c6/16/Portfolio.h
class Portfolio {

public:
    bool IsEmpty() const;
    void Purchase(
        const std::string& symbol,
        unsigned int shareCount,
        const boost::gregorian::date& transactionDate);
    void Sell(const std::string& symbol,
        unsigned int shareCount,
        const boost::gregorian::date& transactionDate);
    unsigned int ShareCount(const std::string& symbol) const;
    std::vector<PurchaseRecord> Purchases(const std::string& symbol) const;

private:
    void Transact(const std::string& symbol,
        int shareChange,
        const boost::gregorian::date&);
    void UpdateShareCount(const std::string& symbol, int shareChange);
    void AddPurchaseRecord(
        const std::string& symbol,
        int shareCount,
        const boost::gregorian::date&);
    void ThrowIfShareCountIsZero(int shareChange) const;

    std::unordered_map<std::string, unsigned int> holdings_;
    std::vector<PurchaseRecord> purchases_;
    std::unordered_map<std::string, std::vector<PurchaseRecord>> purchaseRecords_;
};
```

We correspondingly update the implementation of Transact() to pass the symbol to AddPurchaseRecord(). In AddPurchaseRecord(), we write new code that adds a PurchaseRecord to the purchaseRecords_ map (first inserting an empty vector if needed). We leave the existing logic that adds to the purchases_ vector untouched—we want to get our new code working before we worry about cleaning up old code.

```
c6/16/Portfolio.cpp
void Portfolio::Transact(
      const string& symbol, int shareChange, const date& transactionDate) {
   ThrowIfShareCountIsZero(shareChange);
   UpdateShareCount(symbol, shareChange);
➤  AddPurchaseRecord(symbol, shareChange, transactionDate);
}


void Portfolio::AddPurchaseRecord(
      const string& symbol, int shareChange, const date& date) {
   purchases_.push_back(PurchaseRecord(shareChange, date));
➤  auto it = purchaseRecords_.find(symbol);
➤  if (it == purchaseRecords_.end())
➤     purchaseRecords_[symbol] = vector<PurchaseRecord>();
➤  purchaseRecords_[symbol].push_back(PurchaseRecord(shareChange, date));
}

unsigned int Portfolio::ShareCount(const string& symbol) const {
   auto it = holdings_.find(symbol);
   if (it == holdings_.end()) return 0;
   return it->second;
}
vector<PurchaseRecord> Portfolio::Purchases(const string& symbol) const {
➤  // return purchases_;
➤  return purchaseRecords_.find(symbol)->second;
}
```

In the Purchases() function, we return the vector of purchase records corresponding to the symbol. We write just enough code, not worrying yet about the possibility that the symbol is not found. Instead of worrying, we add an entry ("deal with symbol not found in Purchases") to our test list.

Once our tests all pass, we clean up our code by removing references to purchases_. We write the test we just added to our test lists. We clean things up a bit more. Expressiveness-wise, AddPurchaseRecord() is a bit dense. Duplication-wise, ShareCount() and Purchases() contain redundant code around finding elements from a map. We fix both problems.

```
c6/17/PortfolioTest.cpp
TEST_F(APortfolio, AnswersEmptyPurchaseRecordVectorWhenSymbolNotFound) {
   ASSERT_THAT(portfolio_.Purchases(SAMSUNG), Eq(vector<PurchaseRecord>()));
}
```

```
c6/17/Portfolio.h
template<typename T>
T Find(std::unordered_map<std::string, T> map, const std::string& key) const {
   auto it = map.find(key);
   return it == map.end() ? T{} : it->second;
}
```

c6/17/Portfolio.cpp

```cpp
#include "Portfolio.h"
#include "PurchaseRecord.h"
using namespace std;
using namespace boost::gregorian;

bool Portfolio::IsEmpty() const {
   return 0 == holdings_.size();
}

void Portfolio::Purchase(
      const string& symbol,
      unsigned int shareCount,
      const date& transactionDate) {
   Transact(symbol, shareCount, transactionDate);
}

void Portfolio::Sell(
      const string& symbol,
      unsigned int shareCount,
      const date& transactionDate) {
   if (shareCount > ShareCount(symbol)) throw InvalidSellException();
   Transact(symbol, -shareCount, transactionDate);
}

void Portfolio::Transact(
      const string& symbol, int shareChange, const date& transactionDate) {
   ThrowIfShareCountIsZero(shareChange);
   UpdateShareCount(symbol, shareChange);
   AddPurchaseRecord(symbol, shareChange, transactionDate);
}

void Portfolio::ThrowIfShareCountIsZero(int shareChange) const {
   if (0 == shareChange) throw ShareCountCannotBeZeroException();
}

void Portfolio::UpdateShareCount(const string& symbol, int shareChange) {
   holdings_[symbol] = ShareCount(symbol) + shareChange;
}

void Portfolio::AddPurchaseRecord(
      const string& symbol, int shareChange, const date& date) {
   if (!ContainsSymbol(symbol))
      InitializePurchaseRecords(symbol);
   Add(symbol, {shareChange, date});
}

void Portfolio::InitializePurchaseRecords(const string& symbol) {
   purchaseRecords_[symbol] = vector<PurchaseRecord>();
}
```

```
void Portfolio::Add(const string& symbol, PurchaseRecord&& record) {
   purchaseRecords_[symbol].push_back(record);
}

bool Portfolio::ContainsSymbol(const string& symbol) const {
   return purchaseRecords_.find(symbol) != purchaseRecords_.end();
}

unsigned int Portfolio::ShareCount(const string& symbol) const {
   return Find<unsigned int>(holdings_, symbol);
}

vector<PurchaseRecord> Portfolio::Purchases(const string& symbol) const {
   return Find<vector<PurchaseRecord>>(purchaseRecords_, symbol);
}
```

Well, we didn't clean things up just a "bit," did we? We once again did dramatic, lots-of-small-functions refactoring. AddPurchaseRecord() now declares high-level policy, and each of the three functions representing steps in that policy encapsulates details. Overkill? Perhaps. Benefits? Immediacy of comprehension, certainly. The isolation of implementation details also means that if we wanted to use a different data structure, our changes would be easier to spot and also isolated, thus diminishing risk. Also, we can clearly spot each of the steps that alters the state of the Portfolio because of our use of const on appropriate member functions.

Finally, we poised ourselves for a better design. In the next section, our collection of purchase records ends up a first-level class on its own. Our current cleanup of encapsulating all operations on this collection provides for an easier transition to that new design.

To be clear, we aren't prethinking our design. Instead, we get an increment of code to work and then seek to optimize the design of the current solution. The side effect is that subsequent changes are easier.

Incremental Design Made Simple

Our Portfolio contains two collections that parallel each other: holdings_ maps the symbol to a total of shares, and purchaseRecords_ maps the symbol to a list of purchase records. We could eliminate holdings_ and instead calculate the total of shares for a given symbol on demand.

Keeping two collections represents a performance optimization. It results in slightly more complex code, and we need to ensure that the two collections always match each other. That's ultimately your call. If you think you need the performance, keep things the way they are. We don't need it yet, so we'll factor out the common code.

The first step is to change the ShareCount() function to dynamically calculate the number of shares for a given symbol.

```
c6/18/Portfolio.cpp
unsigned int Portfolio::ShareCount(const string& symbol) const {
    auto records = Find<vector<PurchaseRecord>>(purchaseRecords_, symbol);
    return accumulate(records.begin(), records.end(), 0,
        [] (int total, PurchaseRecord record) {
            return total + record.ShareCount; });
}
```

We no longer need to make a call to UpdateShareCount() from Transact(). We can safely delete UpdateShareCount()! We then change IsEmpty() to refer to purchaseRecords_ instead of holdings_, which allows us to finally delete the declaration for holdings_.

```
c6/18/Portfolio.cpp
bool Portfolio::IsEmpty() const {
    return 0 == purchaseRecords_.size();
}

void Portfolio::Transact(
        const string& symbol, int shareChange, const date& transactionDate) {
    ThrowIfShareCountIsZero(shareChange);
    AddPurchaseRecord(symbol, shareChange, transactionDate);
}
```

That was easy enough.

The final effort is to move all code related to the collection of purchase records to a separate class. Why? The Portfolio class is violating the SRP. Its primary reason to change is any modification to the policy of how we manage the portfolio. But it has an additional reason to change—implementation specifics around the collection of purchase records.

So what? Well, we just made a design change that simplifies our code, but that change could also represent an unacceptable performance degradation. Isolating the purchase record code would represent an SRP-compliant design. It would allow us to more easily pinpoint where our performance change should go. Extracting the code would decrease our chance of accidentally breaking something else in Portfolio.

We can once again make this change incrementally, adding a bit of new code and running our tests to ensure things still work. The first step is to introduce a new member variable that maps symbols to holdings. We can name it holdings_ (hey, that sounds familiar!).

```
c6/19/Portfolio.h
```
➤ `std::unordered_map<std::string, Holding> holdings_;`

Next, we incrementally start adding parallel support to update the holdings_ map, starting first in InitializePurchaseRecords().

```
c6/19/Portfolio.cpp
```
```
void Portfolio::InitializePurchaseRecords(const string& symbol) {
    purchaseRecords_[symbol] = vector<PurchaseRecord>();
    holdings_[symbol] = Holding();
}
```
➤

In the Add() function, we delegate to a function with the same name in the Holding class. We obtain the code for the Holding class by copying it over from Portfolio and simplifying it appropriately.

```
c6/19/Portfolio.cpp
```
```
void Portfolio::Add(const string& symbol, PurchaseRecord&& record) {
    purchaseRecords_[symbol].push_back(record);
    holdings_[symbol].Add(record);
}
```
➤

```
c6/19/Holding.h
```
```
void Add(PurchaseRecord& record) {
    purchaseRecords_.push_back(record);
}
std::vector<PurchaseRecord> purchaseRecords_;
```

On to the Purchases() function. We replace the existing code (now commented out—don't worry, these commented lines won't stick around in our code) with a simpler version, again delegating to a new function defined on Holding.

```
c6/19/Portfolio.cpp
```
```
vector<PurchaseRecord> Portfolio::Purchases(const string& symbol) const {
//    return Find<vector<PurchaseRecord>>(purchaseRecords_, symbol);
    return Find<Holding>(holdings_, symbol).Purchases();
}
```

```
c6/19/Holding.h
```
```
std::vector<PurchaseRecord> Purchases() const {
    return purchaseRecords_;
}
```

We update ContainsSymbol() by asking the same question of holdings_ as we previously did of the purchaseRecords_ collection.

```
c6/19/Portfolio.cpp
```
```
bool Portfolio::ContainsSymbol(const string& symbol) const {
//    return purchaseRecords_.find(symbol) != purchaseRecords_.end();
    return holdings_.find(symbol) != holdings_.end();
}
```

Changing ShareCount() is another delegation effort.

```
c6/19/Portfolio.cpp
unsigned int Portfolio::ShareCount(const string& symbol) const {
//    auto records = Find<vector<PurchaseRecord>>(purchaseRecords_, symbol);
//    return accumulate(records.begin(), records.end(), 0,
//        [] (int total, PurchaseRecord record) {
//            return total + record.ShareCount; });
    return Find<Holding>(holdings_, symbol).ShareCount();
}
```

```
c6/19/Holding.h
unsigned int ShareCount() const {
    return accumulate(purchaseRecords_.begin(), purchaseRecords_.end(), 0,
        [] (int total, PurchaseRecord record) {
            return total + record.ShareCount; });
}
```

Last, we try to remove the purchaseRecords_ member variable. The compiler tells us which code still references the variable. We delete those references and make sure our tests still run. (They do!)

```
c6/19/Portfolio.h
// no longer needed!
std::unordered_map<std::string, std::vector<PurchaseRecord>> purchaseRecords_;
```

We're almost done. The last job is to ensure that we've written tests for the Holding class. The code is already tested, in the context of Portfolio, so why add tests? The reason is that we also want the documentation value that tests can provide. If a developer wants to use the Holding class, they should be able to understand how it's used by reading tests that directly document its behavior.

When extracting a new class in this fashion, you'll sometimes be able to move tests directly across (for example, from PortfolioTest to HoldingTest). The tests often simplify, and you'll likely need to reconsider their name. (Look at the source download to see the final tests.)

The end result is that the code in Holding is excruciatingly simple, all one-liners, and immediately understood. The code in Portfolio is also fairly simple, all one- or two-liners, each immediately understood.

Another beautiful thing throughout this whole process is that we were able to make dramatic changes to our design, bit by bit, without worrying. I'll be honest, while initially coding this example for the book, I made at least one dumb mistake and was happy to have tests that immediately let me know.

As far as performance goes, getting back the original performance would be straightforward. If needed, we could cache the share total in a member variable defined on Holding, add to that total on each call to Add(), and simply return that value from ShareCount().

6.3 Where Is the Up-Front Design?

If you were building code in the 1990s, odds are good that your team expended a considerable amount of up-front effort to produce design models. You might have worked with use cases to understand the requirements and subsequently created class diagrams, state models, sequence diagrams, collaboration diagrams, component models, and so on.

Chances are that you create few of these models today. The interest in Agile has led to teams abandoning the production of detailed design models. "Agile says we don't have to do design," or so I've heard.

Just what *does* Agile say about design? The Agile principles (part of the Agile Manifesto; see http://agilemanifesto.org/principles.html) suggest that the software must be valuable to the customer, that it can accommodate changing requirements at any time, that it works, that it has a good design, and that it is no more complex than need be. There's no definition for "good" and no notion of when design actually occurs.

The challenge with Agile is that you are expected to respond to change. A new feature is requested, one that you might not have ever before imagined. You must figure out how to code support for the feature into a system that wasn't explicitly designed to accommodate it.

Suppose you spend a lot of time determining what an "entire" new system must do. You derive the perfect set of corresponding design models and then build out the system. Your team is fast (or so they think) because they're not spending time doing TDD. Each of the analysis, design, and implementation steps take two months, meaning you ship after six months.

Any new requirement cropping up thereafter isn't covered by your extensive up-front design. Sometimes that's OK, but more often than not, this is where your system starts the faster path to degradation. You're able to work in some of the new feature requests simply, but you notice that many other changes are difficult. Some changes require bad hacks, as your system's design can't accommodate them otherwise. Many of the new feature requests require widespread changes throughout the system. The time to analyze the system to know where the changes must go increases.

The speed of building continues to slow as the system's dependency structure degrades. Your team slows down even further as the new changes introduce difficult-to-fix and sometimes seemingly unrelated defects. You wish you had better control over your system in the form of fast unit tests.

It's still worthwhile to sketch an initial design, given what you know about what the system must do. But it's not worthwhile to expend substantial effort in detailing the initial design. Concern yourself with high-level structure: what are the key classes and dependencies in the system, what are interfaces between subsystems and to external systems, and what are some of the core message flows? You can derive a good high-level, starter design in a small fraction of the two months that you might have otherwise taken.

TDD is a means of addressing design on a continual basis. Consider that you are taking all the time saved in initial detailed design efforts and spreading it out across the rest of the product's life span. The studies (*Research on TDD*, on page 303) show that TDD initially takes more development effort but results in higher-quality code. What the studies *don't* discuss is the amount of time you save by minimizing up-front design efforts.

You should certainly invest in up-front design, but accept that your models will almost always be wrong. Once you start coding, many changes can occur: the customer changes their mind, the marketplace changes, you learn more and discover better ways to address the design, or someone realizes requirements are missing or incorrect.

An up-front design is a good starting road map. Discussions around the design help uncover key elements about what the software must do and how you might initially lay it out. But the vast amount of detail required to build out your system will change. A class diagram is a fine thing to create, for example, but don't sweat the low-level details: private vs. public, attribute detail, aggregation vs. composition, and so on. These will come out in the test-driving. Instead, focus on class names, dependencies, and maybe a few key public behaviors.

TDD allows you to retain the simplest possible design for a model based on the current business needs. If you keep your design as clean as possible over time, you have the best chance to incorporate new, never-before-conceived features. If you instead allow your system to degrade (and exhibit lots of duplication and difficult-to-understand code), you'll have a tough time with any new feature request that comes along.

But Where's the Real Meaty Design Talk?

We just had it. Reread the portfolio example. Granted, it's a simple piece of an application, but the concepts all scale up to very large systems.

"No, I mean, where's all that stuff about coupling, cohesion, single responsibility principle and the other SOLID design principles, dependency structures, code smells, law of Demeter, patterns, encapsulation, composition vs. inheritance, and so on?" Good question. First, this isn't a book on classic OO design concepts. This is a book on TDD, and the goal of this chapter was to demonstrate how you can incrementally deal with a continually evolving design.

Second, regarding all those classic design concepts, you should really know all of that. You should also always be seeking to learn more about design. It's all good as long as it makes incremental change easier. If you don't know it all now, don't worry. The simple design concepts will get you a large portion of the way there. But keep digging.

When you're in the refactoring step of TDD, you want to have all the knowledge you possibly can about what constitutes a good design. You'll also want to have all the knowledge possible about what your team thinks. You're in a shared codebase, and you need to agree as a team on what is acceptable and what is not regarding design.

Most of the time, the classic design concepts are in alignment with the notion of simple design. Design patterns, for example, are primarily about the expressiveness of a solution. Some, such as Template Method, are explicitly about eliminating duplication.

Where Do Simple Design and Classic Design Concepts Clash?

There are a few places where you should supplant classic (*aka* old) concepts about design with modern, incremental design ideas. The following list covers some of the common clashes between old-school design and incremental design via TDD:

- *Accessibility*: You still should prefer keeping members as private as possible. It makes some changes easier (for example, safely renaming a public member function requires a lot more work than renaming a private function). Though unlikely, exposing members unnecessarily might open you up to harm from nefarious or stupid clients.

  However, if you need to relax access to allow tests to verify that things actually work as intended, you shouldn't worry most of the time. If everything is tested, the tests will likely protect your system against stupidity. Knowing the system works is far more compelling than over-doting on a vague concern about future abuse. If you're still worried, there are clever but safe means that should relax everyone. Just remember that clever is often a glittery cousin of stupid.

In tests, absolutely stop sweating unnecessary design clutter such as private vs. public. No one is calling your tests. Access specifiers in tests only serve to detract from readability.

- *Timeliness*: Old-school design told you that you needed to try to derive a design as close to perfect as possible. With simple design, that's simply not true. In fact, the more you come up with a design that accommodates every last possible forthcoming feature, the more you'll pay in the meantime, and odds are also that you'll still have substantial rework when the feature does arrive. It's better to learn how to continually accommodate changes via simple, incremental design.

6.4 Refactoring Inhibitors

With the notion of using simple, incremental design as your primary design driver, the refactoring step is where much of the real work gets done. Anything that keeps you from refactoring easily, or even from wanting to refactor, is bad. Very bad. When you stop refactoring incrementally, your system will start degrading quickly.

Be on guard for the following inhibitors to refactoring:

- *Insufficient tests*: Following TDD provides you with fast tests for every small bit of discrete logic you build into your system. These tests provide you with high confidence to change the code for the better. In contrast, when you have fewer fast unit tests and thus lower test coverage, your interest and ability to refactor shrinks dramatically. Your approach to coding becomes fear-based: "If it ain't broke, don't fix it!" You may well know that the right thing to do, for example, is to factor common code into a helper function. But you don't, because those changes involve touching other code—not "yours"—that's already working.

- *Long-lived branches*: Anyone who's had to merge code from a separate branch with lots of activity knows that extensive refactoring makes for merge hell. Developers working on a branch may be asked to minimize the scope of their changes. Doing so might make merges easier but will also make the source base suffer forever. If you must sustain branches over long periods of time, seek to continually integrate from mainline. Otherwise, avoid long-lived branches.

- *Implementation-specific tests*: When test-driving, you specify the behavior of a class through its public interface. By definition, refactoring is changing design without changing externally recognized (public) behavior. Tests that have an awareness of what would otherwise be private details run the risk of breaking when those private details change. You want the ability to change the underlying structure of your code as needed, extracting or inlining methods at will.

  Heavy mocking or stubbing of collaborators can expose information to tests that otherwise would remain private. Done judiciously, using test doubles won't cause problems. With careless use of test doubles, however, you may find yourself breaking lots of tests when you want to refactor your code. That's a good enough reason for many developers to not want to bother refactoring.

- *Crushing technical debt*: The sheer volume of difficult code may be enough to cause many developers to give up. "Where do I start?" The worse you let your code get, the harder it will be to do anything about it. Make sure you always take advantage of the refactoring step.

- *No know-how*: Anything you don't know can and will be used against you. You probably know a bit about design, and you learned about simple design in this chapter, but learn more. If you don't have a solid grounding in design, odds are you won't refactor enough.

- *Premature performance obsession*: Many of the ideas promoted in this book about design center around small classes and functions, which incurs the overhead of creating additional objects and calling extra methods. Many developers resist such changes and are content with longer functions and classes.

  Ensure you first create a clean, maintainable design. Profile the proper design to determine whether it exhibits performance deficiencies. Optimize the code *only* if absolutely necessary. Most optimizations increase the difficulty of understanding and maintaining the code.

- *Management metric mandates*: If their standing in the company or considerable money (in the form of salaries or bonuses) is tied to specific goals, smart employees will do whatever it takes to meet the goal. If the goal is represented by a singular metric, chances are that sharp developers will find a way to more easily achieve that number, whether or not doing so serves the real business need.

As an example, consider the defect density metric, defined as defects per kilo lines of code (KLOC). (Note: You can also capture defect density as defects per function point, but the effort to calculate function points is not trivial. Most shops go with the simpler measure, defects/KLOC.) If your manager heavily emphasizes shrinking defect density, the team will react accordingly. Ensuring the code exhibits fewer defects is harder than "gaming" the metric. The easier route is to increase the lines of code.

Perhaps you believe most programmers aren't that devious. Perhaps not. But when you ask them to factor two near-duplicate 1,000+ line functions into a single function, they're thinking about the loss of a KLOC and the accordant increase in defect density. Good luck convincing them that eliminating the duplication is important.

- *Short-sighted infatuation with speed*: "Just ship it. Stop spending time on refactoring." Can you blame a project manager for not understanding the importance of keeping your system's design clean? Sure, it might look like you're speedy for a while, but you'll eventually suffer dramatically (sometimes devastatingly) for letting your system's quality slide.

Just say no, and otherwise keep your refactoring to yourself. Work to keep your code clean every few minutes as part of the TDD cycle. If asked, you can say "This is how I work as a responsible professional."

You must take advantage of the opportunity that each passing test provides you; otherwise, code cruft will build up quickly and begin to slow the rate of development. You might even feel compelled to ask for a *refactoring iteration*. Don't! Nontechnical folks have no idea what refactoring is. They will simply translate your request as "The programmers just want to play around with the software, and I won't get any business value this iteration."

Unfortunately, no matter how hard you try, you will inevitably have iterations where a new feature doesn't fit easily into the code, causing you to deliver the feature later than expected. When this occurs, ask for forgiveness, and run an honest investigation into how you might have prevented the additional effort. Don't let it happen habitually.

6.5 Teardown

In this chapter, you learned how to ensure your software retains a quality design so that you can easily maintain it over time. You learned how to apply the concepts of simple design during the refactoring step in the TDD cycle.

You also learned about the importance of continual, incremental refactoring and how certain factors can result in insufficient refactoring efforts.

Don't stop here. You'll want to ensure that you apply similar design concepts to your tests, a topic you'll read about in more detail in the next chapter. You'll also want to read more about object-oriented design from other sources. Everything you learn about good design will help you succeed with growing your system.

## CHAPTER 7

Quality Tests

7.1 Setup

You've learned how to test-drive, and more importantly, you learned in the *Incremental Design* chapter how to use TDD to shape your system's design. Safe, continual refactoring sustains the life of your production code. In this chapter, you'll learn how to design your *tests* well to extend their return on value and keep them from becoming a maintenance burden.

You'll learn about quality tests using a few core concepts.

- The FIRST mnemonic, a great way to vet your tests
- One Assert per Test, a guideline to help constrain the size of your tests
- Test Abstraction, a core principle for readable tests

7.2 Tests Come FIRST

Wondering if you've built a good unit test? Vet it against the *FIRST* mnemonic, devised by Brett Schuchert and Tim Ottinger. The mnemonic reminds you of a key part of TDD's definition: tests come *first*.

FIRST breaks down into the following:

- *F* for Fast
- *I* for Isolated
- *R* for Repeatable
- *S* for Self-verifying
- *T* for Timely

Fast

TDD supports incremental and iterative development through its core cycle of specify, build, and refactor. How long should a cycle take? The shorter, the better. You want to know as soon as your code either doesn't work or breaks something else. The more code you grow between introducing a defect and discovering it, the more time you stand to waste in pinpointing and fixing the problem. You want ultra-rapid feedback!

We all make mistakes as we code. We all also initially craft code that exhibits less-than-ideal design characteristics. Much as writers create rough drafts, we create rough code for our first pass. But code gets harder to change as we build slop upon slop. Our best hope for sanity? Continually examine and clean up each small bit of code.

Not only must you ensure your changed or new unit test runs, you must ensure your small change doesn't break something in a far-slung corner of your system. You want to run all existing unit tests with each small change.

Ideally, you want to code a tiny bit of logic, perhaps a line or two, before getting feedback. But doing so incurs the cost of compiling, linking, and running your test suite.

How important is it to keep this cycle cost low? If it takes on average three or four seconds to compile, link, and run your tests, your code increments can be small and your feedback high. But imagine your suite takes two minutes to build and run. How often will you run it? Perhaps once every ten to fifteen minutes? If your tests take twenty minutes to run, you might run a couple times a day.

In the absence of rapid feedback, you will write fewer tests, refactor your code less, and increase the time between introducing a problem and discovering it. Falling back to these old results means that you'll likely see few of the potential benefits of TDD. You might choose to abandon TDD at this point. Don't be that guy!

The Cost of Building

Build times in C++ present a hefty challenge. A compile and link in a sizeable system can require several minutes and sometimes much more.

The lion's share of the build time directly relates to the dependency structure of your code. Code dependent on a change must be rebuilt.

Part of doing TDD well requires crafting a design that minimizes rampant rebuilds. If your heavily used class exposes a large interface, clients must rebuild when it changes, even if your changes have little to do with their interests in your class. Per the Interface Segregation Principle (ISP) (*Agile Software Development, Principles, Patterns, and Practices [Mar02]*), forcing clients to depend upon interfaces they don't use indicates a design deficiency.

Similarly, abusing other principles can result in longer build times. The Dependency Inversion Principle (DIP) tells you to depend upon abstractions, not details (*Agile Software Development, Principles, Patterns, and Practices* [*Mar02*]). If you change details of a concrete class, all its clients must rebuild.

You can introduce an interface—a pure virtual void class—that your concrete class realizes. Client code interacts through the abstraction provided by the interface and isn't triggered to recompile if the implementation details of the concrete class change.

If you're introducing new private methods as part of refactoring, you can find yourself waiting impatiently on long rebuilds. You might consider using the "pointer to implementation" (PIMPL) idiom. To use PIMPL, extract your concrete details to a separate *impl*ementation class. Delegate to the implementation as needed from the interface functions. You're then free to change the implementation all you want, creating new functions at will, without triggering recompiles on the code dependent on the public interface.

With TDD, your design choices no longer represent nebulous concerns; they directly relate to your ability to succeed. Success in TDD is a matter of keeping things clean and fast.

Dependencies on Collaborators

Dependencies on what you're changing increases build time. For running tests, the concern about dependencies moves in the other direction: dependencies from what you're testing on other code increases test execution time.

If you test code that interacts with another class that in turn must invoke an external API (for example, a database call), the tests must wait on the API call. (They're now integration tests, not unit tests.) A few milliseconds to establish a connection and execute a query might not seem like much. But if most tests in your suite of thousands must incur this overhead, the suite will take several minutes or more to complete.

Running a Subset of the Tests

Most unit testing tools allow you to run a subset of the entire test suite. Google Test, for example, allows you to specify a filter. For example, passing the following filter to your test executable will run all tests whose fixture name starts with *Holding* and whose test name includes the word *Avail*. Running a smaller subset of tests might save you a bit of execution time.

```
./test --gtest_filter=Holding*.*Avail*
```

Just because you can doesn't mean that you should...at least not habitually. Regularly filtering your test run suggests you have a bigger problem—your tests have too many dependencies on slower things. Fix the real problem first!

When you aren't able to easily run all your tests, don't immediately jump to running a single unit test at a time. Find a way to run as many tests as possible. At least try to run all of the tests in a given fixture (for example, Holding*.*) before giving up and running only a single test at a time.

Running a subset of the tests might save you time up front, but remember that the fewer tests you run, the more likely you will find problems later. The more you find problems later, the more likely they'll take longer to fix.

Isolated

If you're doing TDD, each of your tests should always fail at least once. When you're creating a new test, you'll know the reason it fails. But what about three days or three months down the road? Will the reason a test fails be clear? Creating tests that can fail for several reasons can waste time for you or someone else needing to pinpoint the cause.

You want your tests to be isolated—failing for a single reason. Small and focused tests, each driving in the existence of a small bit of behavior, increase isolation.

Also, each test should verify a small bit of logic independent from external concerns. If the code it tests interacts with a database, file system, or other API, a failure could be because of one of many reasons. Introducing test doubles (see Chapter 5, *Test Doubles*, on page 105) can create isolation.

Not only should tests be independent from external production system factors, they should also be independent from other tests. Any test that uses static data runs the risk of failing because of stale data.

If your test requires extensive setup or if the production code could be holding on to stale data, you might find yourself digging to find out that a subtle system change broke the test. You might introduce a *precondition assertion* that verifies any assumptions your test makes in its *Arrange* portion.

```
c7/2/libraryTest/HoldingTest.cpp
TEST_F(ACheckedInHolding, UpdatesDateDueOnCheckout)
{
    ASSERT_TRUE(IsAvailableAt(holding, *arbitraryBranch));
    holding->CheckOut(ArbitraryDate);
    ASSERT_THAT(holding->DueDate(),
      Eq(ArbitraryDate + date_duration(Book::BOOK_CHECKOUT_PERIOD)));
}
```

The Library Application

Code examples in this chapter come from a small demo library system. Definitions for a few key terms may help you better understand the examples. A *patron* is a person who *checks out*, or borrows, holdings from *branches*—physical locations in the library system. A *holding* is a single copy of a book at the library.

When a precondition assertion fails, you'll waste less time finding and fixing the problem. If you find yourself employing this technique often, though, find a way to simplify your design instead—precondition asserts suggest that the level of understanding you have about your system is insufficient. They might also suggest you're burying too much information in setup.

Repeatable

Quality unit tests are *repeatable*—you can run them time after time and always obtain the same results, regardless of which other tests (if any) ran first. I appreciate the rapid feedback my test suite provides so much that I'll sometimes run it a second time, just to get the gratification of seeing the tests all pass. Every once in a while, though, my subsequent test run will fail when the previous run succeeded.

Intermittent test failures are bad news. They indicate some level of nondeterministic or otherwise varying behavior in your test runs. Pinpointing the cause of variant behavior can require considerable effort.

Your tests might fail intermittently for one of the following reasons:

- *Static data*: A good unit test doesn't depend upon the side effects of other tests and similarly doesn't let these remnants cause problems. If your test can potentially fail because of lingering static data, you might not see it fail until you add new tests or remove others. In some unit testing frameworks, tests are added to a hash-based collection, meaning that their order of execution can change as the number of tests changes.

- *Volatility of external services*: Avoid writing unit tests that depend on external forces out of your control, such as the current time, file system, databases, and other API calls. Introduce test doubles (Chapter 5, *Test Doubles*, on page 105) as needed to break the dependency.

- *Concurrency*: Threaded or other multiprocessing execution will introduce nondeterministic behavior that can be exceptionally challenging for unit tests. Refer to *TDD and Threading* for a few suggestions on how to test-drive multithreaded code.

Self-Verifying

You automate tests to get your human self out of the picture—to eliminate slow and risky manual testing. A unit test must execute code and verify that it worked without involving you. A unit test must have at least one assertion; it must have failed at least once in the course of its existence, and there must be some way for it to fail sometime in the future.

Avoid any concessions to this guideline. Don't add cout statements to your tests as substitutes for assertions. Manually verifying console or log file output wastes time and increases risk.

Devious programmers looking to bump up their code coverage numbers (a goal sometimes demanded by misguided managers) quickly figure out that they can write tests without assertions. These nontests are a complete waste of effort, but executing a broad swath of code without asserting anything does improve the metrics.

Timely

When do you write tests? In a timely fashion, meaning that you write them first. Why? Because you're doing TDD, of course, and you're doing TDD because it's the best way to sustain a high-quality codebase.

You also don't write a bunch of tests in advance of any code. Instead, you write one test at a time, and even within that one test you write one assertion at a time. Your approach is as incremental as it can be, viewing each test as a small bit of specification that you use to immediately drive in accordant behavior.

7.3   One Assert per Test

You test-drive small, discrete bits of behavior into your system. With each pass through the TDD cycle, you specify behavior plus a way to verify that the behavior actually works—an assertion.

To allow a future programmer to understand the behavior you designed into the system, your test must clearly state intent. The most important declaration of intent is the test's name, which should clarify the context and goal.

The more behavior you drive from a single test, the less your test name can concisely describe the behavior.

In the library system, a holding is unavailable when a patron has checked it out and is available once a patron has checked it in. We might design a single test focused on availability.

```
c7/3/libraryTest/HoldingTest.cpp
TEST_F(HoldingTest, Availability)
{
    holding->Transfer(EAST_BRANCH);
    holding->CheckOut(ArbitraryDate);
    EXPECT_FALSE(holding->IsAvailable());

    date nextDay = ArbitraryDate + date_duration(1);
    holding->CheckIn(nextDay, EAST_BRANCH);
    EXPECT_TRUE(holding->IsAvailable());
}
```

Combining behaviors into a single test puts them all into the same place—sort of. You'll likely find that many of your methods work in concert with other methods, meaning that it can be a real challenge to figure out to which method-focused test the test code belongs. The downside is that it will take additional time for a reader to understand what's going on, particularly as you add a third, fourth, or umpteenth behavior to the test.

Splitting into multiple tests allows you to derive names that clearly state what happens under what conditions. It also allows you to take advantage of *Arrange-Act-Assert/Given-When-Then* for increased clarity.

```
c7/3/libraryTest/HoldingTest.cpp
TEST_F(AHolding, IsNotAvailableAfterCheckout)
{
    holding->Transfer(EAST_BRANCH);

    holding->CheckOut(ArbitraryDate);

    EXPECT_THAT(holding->IsAvailable(), Eq(false));
}

TEST_F(AHolding, IsAvailableAfterCheckin)
{
    holding->Transfer(EAST_BRANCH);
    holding->CheckOut(ArbitraryDate);

    holding->CheckIn(ArbitraryDate + date_duration(1), EAST_BRANCH);

    EXPECT_THAT(holding->IsAvailable(), Eq(true));
}
```

The names of single-purpose tests stand on their own—you don't have to read a test to understand what it does. The complete set of such test names acts as a concordance of system capabilities. You start to view test names as related groupings of behaviors, not just discrete verifications.

Looking at test names holistically can trigger thoughts about missing tests. "We have library tests that describe availability on checkout and check-in. What holds true about availability when we've added a new book to the system through an inventory process? We'd better write that test!"

Should you ever have more than one assert per test? Strive hard to have only one. Sometimes it makes sense to have more, though.

Assertions are postconditions. If multiple assertions are required to describe a single behavior, you can justify a second assertion in a test. Consider the method IsEmpty(), often added to increase expressiveness beyond what a function like Size() produces. You might choose to involve both functions as postcondition tests around emptiness of a new collection.

You might also choose to have multiple assertions to verify a bunch of data elements.

`c7/3/libraryTest/HoldingTest.cpp`
```
TEST_F(AHolding, CanBeCreatedFromAnother)
{
   Holding holding(THE_TRIAL_CLASSIFICATION, 1);
   holding.Transfer(EAST_BRANCH);

   Holding copy(holding, 2);

   ASSERT_THAT(copy.Classification(), Eq(THE_TRIAL_CLASSIFICATION));
   ASSERT_THAT(copy.CopyNumber(), Eq(2));
   ASSERT_THAT(copy.CurrentBranch(), Eq(EAST_BRANCH));
   ASSERT_TRUE(copy.LastCheckedOutOn().is_not_a_date());
}
```

Finally, you might combine assertions where the description of behavior doesn't vary but the implementation is getting more specialized as more data variants are added. For example, this utility converts Arabic numbers to Roman numbers:

`c7/3/libraryTest/RomanTest.cpp`
```
TEST(ARomanConverter, AnswersArabicEquivalents)
{
   RomanConverter converter;
   ASSERT_EQ("I", converter.convert(1));
   ASSERT_EQ("II", converter.convert(2));
   ASSERT_EQ("III", converter.convert(3));
   ASSERT_EQ("IV", converter.convert(4));
   ASSERT_EQ("V", converter.convert(5));
   // ...
}
```

You could choose to split tests in either of these cases. But having separate tests doesn't appear to have as much value, evidenced by the names you might come up with: ConvertsRomanIIToArabic, ConvertsRomanIIIToArabic, and so on. Or CopyPopulatesClassification, CopyPopulatesCopyNumber, and so on.

The key thing to remember is to have one behavior per test. And in case it's not obvious, any test with conditional logic (for example, if statements) is almost certainly violating this guideline.

One Assert per Test isn't a hard rule, but it's usually a better choice. Head in the direction of fewer assertions per test, not more. The more you do it, the more you'll find the value. For now, strive for a single assert per test and contemplate the results.

7.4 Test Abstraction

Uncle Bob defines abstraction as "amplification of the essential and elimination of the irrelevant." Abstraction is as important in your tests as it is in object-oriented design. Since you want to be able to read your tests as documentation, they must cut to the chase, declaring their intent as clearly and simply as possible.

From a simplistic stance, you can increase abstraction in your tests by making them more cohesive (One Assert per Test), focusing on better naming (for the test itself as well as the code within), and abstracting away the rest of the cruft (using perhaps fixture helper functions or SetUp()).

We'll work through identifying nine different test smells and cleaning up test code accordingly.

Bloated Construction

Let's start with one of the tests for a LineReader class. The test names don't tell us much about how LineReader works. We hope that cleaning up the tests will help.

c7/3/linereader/LineReaderTest.cpp
```
TEST(LineReaderTest, OneLine) {
    const int fd = TemporaryFile();
    write(fd, "a", 1);
    lseek(fd, 0, SEEK_SET);
    LineReader reader(fd);

    const char *line;
    unsigned len;
    ASSERT_TRUE(reader.GetNextLine(&line, &len));
```

```
    ASSERT_EQ(len, (unsigned)1);
    ASSERT_EQ(line[0], 'a');
    ASSERT_EQ(line[1], 0);
    reader.PopLine(len);

    ASSERT_FALSE(reader.GetNextLine(&line, &len));

    close(fd);
}
```

The highlighted three lines appear to create a temporary file, populate it with a single character ("a"), and reset the file pointer to its beginning. This *bloated construction* requires the reader to wade through unnecessary test setup details. We can replace the bloat with a single-line abstraction.

`c7/4/linereader/LineReaderTest.cpp`
```
TEST(LineReaderTest, OneLine) {
➤   const int fd = WriteTemporaryFile("a");
    LineReader reader(fd);

    const char *line;
    unsigned len;
    ASSERT_TRUE(reader.GetNextLine(&line, &len));
    ASSERT_EQ(len, (unsigned)1);
    ASSERT_EQ(line[0], 'a');
    ASSERT_EQ(line[1], 0);
    reader.PopLine(len);

    ASSERT_FALSE(reader.GetNextLine(&line, &len));

    close(fd);
}
```

The test is a couple lines shorter and hides the implementation details required to create a file with a small amount of data. We won't usually care, and in the rare case we do, we can simply navigate to see what WriteTemporaryFile() really does.

Irrelevant Details

The test first creates a temporary file. The original programmer, being a good coding citizen, made sure the file was closed at the end of the test.

`c7/5/linereader/LineReaderTest.cpp`
```
TEST(LineReaderTest, OneLine) {
➤   const int fd = WriteTemporaryFile("a");
    LineReader reader(fd);

    const char *line;
    unsigned len;
```

```
    ASSERT_TRUE(reader.GetNextLine(&line, &len));
    ASSERT_EQ(len, (unsigned)1);
    ASSERT_EQ(line[0], 'a');
    ASSERT_EQ(line[1], 0);
    reader.PopLine(len);

    ASSERT_FALSE(reader.GetNextLine(&line, &len));

➤    close(fd);
  }
```

The call to close() is clutter, another detail that distracts from understanding the test. We can take advantage of the TearDown() hook to ensure the file gets closed. We can also eliminate the type information from the variable declaration for fd (file descriptor, presumably), moving it too into the fixture.

c7/6/linereader/LineReaderTest.cpp
```
class LineReaderTest: public testing::Test {
public:
➤    int fd;
    void TearDown() {
➤        close(fd);
    }
};

TEST_F(LineReaderTest, OneLine) {
➤    fd = WriteTemporaryFile("a");
    LineReader reader(fd);

    const char *line;
    unsigned len;
    ASSERT_TRUE(reader.GetNextLine(&line, &len));
    ASSERT_EQ(len, (unsigned)1);
    ASSERT_EQ(line[0], 'a');
    ASSERT_EQ(line[1], 0);
    reader.PopLine(len);

    ASSERT_FALSE(reader.GetNextLine(&line, &len));
}
```

The temporary now seems of little use. We collapse the creation of the LineReader into a single line.

c7/7/linereader/LineReaderTest.cpp
```
TEST_F(LineReaderTest, OneLine) {
➤    LineReader reader(WriteTemporaryFile("a"));

    const char *line;
    unsigned len;
    ASSERT_TRUE(reader.GetNextLine(&line, &len));
```

```
    ASSERT_EQ(len, (unsigned)1);
    ASSERT_EQ(line[0], 'a');
    ASSERT_EQ(line[1], 0);
    reader.PopLine(len);

    ASSERT_FALSE(reader.GetNextLine(&line, &len));
}
```

Hmm…there's a slight problem. We're no longer closing the temporary file in TearDown() (we're instead attempting to close using the uninitialized file descriptor fd). We choose to improve the design of the LineReader by supporting RAII and closing the file itself on destruction. (See http://en.wikipedia.org/wiki/ Resource_Acquisition_Is_Initialization for further information about the RAII idiom.) Code details left to the reader! (Or, you can look at the supplied source.)

The test still contains details we don't need to see most of the time—two lines declare the line and len variables. They're also replicated throughout several other LineReader tests. Let's get rid of the clutter and duplication.

c7/8/linereader/LineReaderTest.cpp

```
class LineReaderTest: public testing::Test {
public:
    int fd;
➤   const char *line;
➤   unsigned len;
};

TEST_F(LineReaderTest, OneLine) {
    LineReader reader(WriteTemporaryFile("a"));

    ASSERT_TRUE(reader.GetNextLine(&line, &len));
    ASSERT_EQ(len, (unsigned)1);
    ASSERT_EQ(line[0], 'a');
    ASSERT_EQ(line[1], 0);
    reader.PopLine(len);

    ASSERT_FALSE(reader.GetNextLine(&line, &len));
}
```

Missing Abstractions

Many developers too often overlook the opportunity to create simple abstractions. Despite seeming like extra effort for questionable gain, extracting small chunks of code to helper methods and classes is win-win-win. First, it amplifies your code's expressiveness, potentially eliminating the need for an explanatory comment. Second, it promotes reuse of those small chunks of code, which in turn can help you eliminate sizeable amounts of duplicative code. Third, it makes subsequent tests easier to write.

Our test currently requires three lines of code to verify the results of getting the next line from the reader.

c7/9/linereader/LineReaderTest.cpp
```cpp
TEST_F(LineReaderTest, OneLine) {
  LineReader reader(WriteTemporaryFile("a"));

  ASSERT_TRUE(reader.GetNextLine(&line, &len));
➤  ASSERT_EQ(len, (unsigned)1);
➤  ASSERT_EQ(line[0], 'a');
➤  ASSERT_EQ(line[1], 0);
  reader.PopLine(len);

  ASSERT_FALSE(reader.GetNextLine(&line, &len));
}
```

A helper function reduces the three assertions to a single, more abstract declaration. (You could also introduce a custom assertion on the matcher if your unit testing tool supports it.)

c7/10/linereader/LineReaderTest.cpp
```cpp
void ASSERT_EQ_WITH_LENGTH(
    const char* expected, const char* actual, unsigned length) {
  ASSERT_EQ(length, strlen(actual));
  ASSERT_STREQ(expected, actual);
}

TEST_F(LineReaderTest, OneLine) {
  LineReader reader(WriteTemporaryFile("a"));

  ASSERT_TRUE(reader.GetNextLine(&line, &len));
➤  ASSERT_EQ_WITH_LENGTH("a", line, len);
  reader.PopLine(len);

  ASSERT_FALSE(reader.GetNextLine(&line, &len));
}
```

Multiple Assertions

We've whittled down the test to a couple statements and three assertions. We take advantage of *One Assert per Test*, creating three tests, each with a clear name that summarizes its one goal.

c7/11/linereader/LineReaderTest.cpp
```cpp
TEST_F(GetNextLinefromLineReader, UpdatesLineAndLenOnRead) {
  LineReader reader(WriteTemporaryFile("a"));
  reader.GetNextLine(&line, &len);
  ASSERT_EQ_WITH_LENGTH("a", line, len);
}
```

```
TEST_F(GetNextLinefromLineReader, AnswersTrueWhenLineAvailable) {
  LineReader reader(WriteTemporaryFile("a"));
  bool wasLineRead = reader.GetNextLine(&line, &len);
  ASSERT_TRUE(wasLineRead);
}

TEST_F(GetNextLinefromLineReader, AnswersFalseWhenAtEOF) {
  LineReader reader(WriteTemporaryFile("a"));
  reader.GetNextLine(&line, &len);
  reader.PopLine(len);
  bool wasLineRead = reader.GetNextLine(&line, &len);
  ASSERT_FALSE(wasLineRead);
}
```

Reviewing the new tests and their names, it should be apparent that we are missing tests. The behavior of PopLine() isn't adequately explained without some analysis and intuition, and we wonder what happens when GetNextLine() gets called twice in succession. We can add the missing tests AdvancesToNextLineAfterPop and RepeatedlyReturnsCurrentRecord (an exercise again left to the reader).

Continually reviewing your whole set of test names will help you find the holes in your specifications.

Irrelevant Data

Data used in a test should help tell its story. Embedded literals are otherwise a distraction or, worse, a puzzle. If a function call requires arguments but they have no relevance to the test at hand, you can often get away with passing 0 or similar values indicating emptiness (such as "" for string literals). To a reader, these literals should suggest "nothing interesting to see here." (If zero *is* a meaningful value, introduce a constant to help explain why.)

Sometimes you'll have no choice but to pass a nonzero or nonempty value. A simple constant can quickly tell a reader all they need to know. In the test AnswersTrueWhenLineAvailable, we don't care about the file contents, so we replace the literal "a" passed to WriteTemporaryFile() with an intention-revealing name.

`c7/12/linereader/LineReaderTest.cpp`
```
TEST_F(GetNextLinefromLineReader, AnswersTrueWhenLineAvailable) {
  LineReader reader(WriteTemporaryFile(ArbitraryText));

  bool wasLineRead = reader.GetNextLine(&line, &len);

  ASSERT_TRUE(wasLineRead);
}
```

After a few passes through an overblown test, we've ended up with three concise tests, each a handful of lines or less. We clearly understand what each test does in a matter of seconds. And we now better understand the behaviors LineReader supports.

To sniff out a few more smells, we'll take a look at some other not-so-clean tests—the LineReader tests are good enough for now.

Unnecessary Test Code

Some elements don't belong in tests at all. This section discusses a few code constructs you can remove outright from your tests.

Assert Not Null

Seg faults are no fun. If you dereference a null pointer, you're going have a bad time as the rest of your test run crashes. Coding defensively is an understandable reaction.

`c7/12/libraryTest/PersistenceTest.cpp`
```
TEST_P(PersistenceTest, AddedItemCanBeRetrievedById)
{
    persister->Add(*objectWithId1);

    auto found = persister->Get("1");

    ASSERT_THAT(found, NotNull());
    ASSERT_THAT(*found, Eq(*objectWithId1));
}
```

But remember, you are designing tests either to drive happy-path behavior or to generate and expect failure. For the persister code, a test already exists that demonstrates when the Get() call can return null.

`c7/12/libraryTest/PersistenceTest.cpp`
```
TEST_P(PersistenceTest, ReturnsNullPointerWhenItemNotFound)
{
    ASSERT_THAT(persister->Get("no id there"), IsNull());
}
```

AddedItemCanBeRetrievedById is a happy-path test. Once we get it working, it should always work...barring a defect that someone codes in the future or a failure to allocate memory. As such, the null check (ASSERT_THAT(found, NotNull())) will unlikely ever fail for this happy-path test.

We'll eliminate the assert not null statement. (We should really avoid raw pointers at all to make this a nonissue.) It adds no documentation value to the test and acts only as a safeguard. The downside is if we remove the guard clause and the pointer ends up null, we get a seg fault. We're willing to take that trade-off—in the worst, very unlikely case, we acknowledge the seg fault, add a null check, and rerun the test to verify our assumption. If our tests are fast, it's not a big deal.

If you're reluctant to let an occasional test run crash with a seg fault, some unit test frameworks provide alternate solutions that don't require an entire additional line to verify each pointer. Google Test, for example, supplies the Pointee() matcher.

```
c7/13/libraryTest/PersistenceTest.cpp
TEST_P(PersistenceTest, AddedItemCanBeRetrievedById)
{
    persister->Add(*objectWithId1);

    auto found = persister->Get("1");

    ASSERT_THAT(found, Pointee(*objectWithId1));
}
```

When doing TDD, it's conceivable you coded an assertion for a null check as an incremental step. It's OK to take that small step. However, once you think a test is complete, take a look back and eliminate any elements that don't add documentation value. Usually, not null assertions fall into this category.

Exception Handling

If the code you're test-driving can generate an exception, you need to test-drive a case that documents how that happens. In the library system, the function to add a branch can throw an exception in at least one case.

```
c7/13/libraryTest/BranchServiceTest.cpp
TEST_F(BranchServiceTest, AddThrowsWhenNameNotUnique)
{
    service.Add("samename", "");

    ASSERT_THROW(service.Add("samename", ""), DuplicateBranchNameException);
}
```

Since the add() function can throw an exception, some programmers want to protect themselves in *other* tests that call add().

```
c7/13/libraryTest/BranchServiceTest.cpp
TEST_F(BranchServiceTest, AddGeneratesUniqueId)
{
    // Don't do this!
    // Eliminate try/catch in tests that should
    // not generate exceptions
```

```
try
{
    string id1 = service.Add("name1", "");
    string id2 = service.Add("name2", "");
    ASSERT_THAT(id1, Ne(id2));
}
catch (...) {
    FAIL();
}
}
```

You design most of your tests for the happy path that should never generate an exception. If you similarly add a try/catch block to ten other tests that call add(), you've added sixty lines of exception handling code. The unnecessary exception handling code only detracts from readability and increases maintenance cost.

The relevant test code is so much clearer when it's not buried amid exception handling clutter.

c7/14/libraryTest/BranchServiceTest.cpp
```
TEST_F(BranchServiceTest, AddGeneratesUniqueId)
{
    string id1 = service.Add("name1", "");
    string id2 = service.Add("name2", "");

    ASSERT_THAT(id1, Ne(id2));
}
```

Assertion Failure Comments

Not all unit test frameworks support Hamcrest-style notation (ASSERT_THAT). Or your codebase may be a little older, still using classic form assertions (ASSERT_TRUE, for example; see *Classic Form Assertions*, on page 90). (Or you might not find much value in Hamcrest.)

Hamcrest-style assertions have a bonus benefit of improved failure messages. In contrast, when a simple ASSERT_TRUE fails, the resulting failure message may not instantly tell you all you want to know. Some frameworks, such as CppUnit, let you provide an additional argument representing a message to display if the assertion fails.

```
CPPUNIT_ASSERT_MESSAGE(service.Find(*eastBranch),
    "unable to find the east branch");
```

My recommendation is to omit such assertion failure comments. If added to every assertion, they result in considerable clutter that detracts from the ability to easily read the test and increases the amount of code that must be maintained. The assertion without the message reads well.

```
CPPUNIT_ASSERT(service.Find(*eastBranch));
```

The assertion with the message doesn't add anything useful. Like normal code comments, you should strive to obviate the need for them. If your assertion doesn't make sense without an assertion failure comment, address the other problems in your test first.

If a test unexpectedly fails in the midst of a suite run, the reason might not be immediately clear from the failure output. Usually you'll get the information you need, though, to be able to pinpoint the failing line of test code. If necessary, add a temporary failure message and run again.

Comments

If you must add comments to explain what your test does, you've missed the point of using tests as documentation. Rework your test, focusing on better naming and improved cohesion.

You might at times see test code that looks like this:

`c7/15/libraryTest/BranchServiceTest.cpp`
```
// test that adding a branch increments the count
TEST_F(BranchServiceTest, AddBranchIncrementsCount)
{
   // first branch
   service.Add(*eastBranch); // East
   ASSERT_THAT(service.BranchCount(), Eq(1));

   // second branch
   service.Add(*westBranch); // West
   ASSERT_THAT(service.BranchCount(), Eq(2)); // count now 2
}
```

Some folks find it helpful, but comments shouldn't restate what code already clearly states—or could clearly state if it was better structured. Find a way to eliminate comments while retaining test expressiveness. You can lose all of the comments in the prior example without losing any meaning.

`c7/16/libraryTest/BranchServiceTest.cpp`
```
TEST_F(BranchServiceTest, AddBranchIncrementsCount)
{
   service.Add(*eastBranch);
   ASSERT_THAT(service.BranchCount(), Eq(1));
   service.Add(*westBranch);
   ASSERT_THAT(service.BranchCount(), Eq(2));
}
```

Implicit Meaning

"Why does this test assert what it does?" You want readers of your tests to be able to answer that question without wasting time on careful analysis of the test or production code.

You will often move details from the test into SetUp() or another helper method. But be careful not to hide too much; otherwise, you'll make test readers dig about for answers. Proper function and variable naming can go a long way toward keeping the test's meaning explicit.

The following test requires a little bit of reading between the lines:

c7/16/libraryTest/BranchServiceTest.cpp
```cpp
TEST_F(ABranchService, ThrowsWhenDuplicateBranchAdded)
{
    ASSERT_THROW(service.Add("east", ""), DuplicateBranchNameException);
}
```

We might surmise that code in SetUp() inserts the East branch into the system. Perhaps all of the tests in the fixture require the existence of one branch, so eliminating the duplication of adding East in SetUp() is a good idea. But why require readers to make the extra effort?

We can clarify the test by changing its name and introducing a fixture variable with a meaningful name.

c7/17/libraryTest/BranchServiceTest.cpp
```cpp
TEST_F(ABranchServiceWithOneBranchAdded, ThrowsWhenDuplicateBranchAdded)
{
    ASSERT_THROW(service.Add(alreadyAddedBranch->Name(), ""),
        DuplicateBranchNameException);
}
```

Here's a simple example of a test that requires the reader to dig deep into detail and count the number of days between two dates:

c7/17/libraryTest/HoldingTest.cpp
```cpp
TEST_F(AMovieHolding, AnswersDateDueWhenCheckedOut)
{
    movie->CheckOut(date(2013, Mar, 1));

    date due = movie->DueDate();

    ASSERT_THAT(due, Eq(date(2013, Mar, 8)));
}
```

Asserting against a simple expression can dramatically increase understanding.

```
c7/18/libraryTest/HoldingTest.cpp
TEST_F(AMovieHolding, AnswersDateDueWhenCheckedOut)
{
    date checkoutDate(2013, Mar, 1);
    movie->CheckOut(checkoutDate);
    date due = movie->DueDate();
    ASSERT_THAT(due, Eq(checkoutDate + date_duration(Book::MOVIE_CHECKOUT_PERIOD)));
}
```

Correlating expected output with test context is a bit of an art. You'll need to be creative from time to time. You'll also need to remind yourself that you know the intimate details of what's going on in the test you just designed, but others wom't.

Misleading Organization

Once you get into the habit of organizing your tests using *Arrange-Act-Assert/Given-When-Then* and expecting to see it in other tests, you slow down a little when you encounter a noncompliant test. Immediate understanding disappears because you must work a little harder to figure out what's test setup and what's actual functionality. How long does it take you to discern the goal of the following test (with a deliberately useless name)?

```
c7/18/libraryTest/HoldingServiceTest.cpp
TEST_F(HoldingServiceTest, X)
{
    HoldingBarcode barcode(THE_TRIAL_CLASSIFICATION, 1);
    string patronCardNumber("p5");
    CheckOut(barcode, branch1, patronCardNumber);
    date_duration oneDayLate(Book::BOOK_CHECKOUT_PERIOD + 1);
    holdingService.CheckIn(barcode.AsString(),
        *arbitraryDate + oneDayLate, branch2->Id());
    ASSERT_THAT(FindPatronWithId(patronCardNumber).FineBalance(),
        Eq(Book::BOOK_DAILY_FINE));
}
```

Here is the code reworked using AAA to emphasize what's relevant:

```
c7/19/libraryTest/HoldingServiceTest.cpp
TEST_F(HoldingServiceTest, X)
{
    HoldingBarcode barcode(THE_TRIAL_CLASSIFICATION, 1);
    string patronCardNumber("p5");
    CheckOut(barcode, branch1, patronCardNumber);
    date_duration oneDayLate(Book::BOOK_CHECKOUT_PERIOD + 1);
    holdingService.CheckIn(barcode.AsString(),
            *arbitraryDate + oneDayLate, branch2->Id());
    ASSERT_THAT(FindPatronWithId(patronCardNumber).FineBalance(),
            Eq(Book::BOOK_DAILY_FINE));
}
```

With the execution statement isolated, it's immediately clear that the test focuses on check-ins. Further reading across the execution line adds the suggestion that the test is concerned with late check-ins. With that understanding of what gets invoked in the system, you can quickly move to the assert portion of the test and determine that the behavior being verified is that a patron's fine balance has been updated accordingly.

Your time to understand existing code is one of the larger expenses in software development. Every little thing you do can help diminish some of that effort, and the beauty of AAA is that it costs almost nothing.

Obscure or Missing Name

Naming things well is one of the most important things you can do in software design. A good name is often the solution to a test correlation problem (see *Implicit Meaning*, on page 191). You'll also find that the inability to derive a concise name indicates a possible design problem.

Tests are no different. A test exhibiting confusing names, or lacking a name where one is needed to explain, does not provide useful documentation.

c7/19/libraryTest/PersistenceTest.cpp
```
TEST_P(PersistenceTest, RetrievedItemIsNewInstance)
{
    persister->Add(*obj);

    ASSERT_FALSE(obj == persister->Get("1").get());
}
```

The simple change that makes all the difference for the reader is as follows:

c7/20/libraryTest/PersistenceTest.cpp
```
TEST_P(PersistenceTest, RetrievedItemIsNewInstance)
{
    persister->Add(*objectWithId1);

    ASSERT_FALSE(objectWithId1 == persister->Get("1").get());
}
```

You don't need to name every relevant piece of data, as long as it can be readily correlated to something else. Here's an example:

c7/19/libraryTest/PatronTest.cpp
```
TEST_F(PatronTest, AddFineUpdatesFineBalance)
{
    jane->AddFine(10);

    ASSERT_THAT(jane->FineBalance(), Eq(10));
}
```

It's obvious that the argument 10 passed to AddFine() corresponds to the expected fine balance of 10.

7.5 Teardown

Keeping your tests clean and direct will promote your regular use of them as documentation artifacts. The more you seek to actively read tests and to always reach for the tests first, the more likely you will invest the effort needed to sustain them long-term. Use the guidelines provided in this chapter to help you recognize and correct problems with your test design.

You've learned a considerable amount about TDD so far. Your production code is clean and well-tested, and your tests are clean and helpful. But what about all the code that you or your test-driving teammates didn't produce? "It was like that when I got here!" You'll next learn a few techniques for dealing with the challenge of legacy code.

## CHAPTER 8

Legacy Challenges

8.1 Setup

You now know how to craft well-designed code using TDD. But the reality for most programmers is that you're not working on new code most of the time. Instead, you're slogging through vast amounts of existing code that was not built using TDD—*legacy code*. And most of that vastness exposes a terrifying wasteland of difficult, poorly designed, hastily constructed code.

How do you begin to deal with this sea of legacy code? Can you still practice TDD in such a codebase, or is TDD applicable only to pristine codebases? In this chapter, you'll learn some techniques that will help you begin to tackle this serious and ever-present challenge.

You'll learn a small set of techniques and thoughts around safe refactoring of code when you don't have tests. You'll add tests to existing code to characterize its behavior, which will allow you to begin test-driving in any changes you need to make. You'll learn how to use linker stubbing to help you quickly dispense with testing headaches that third-party libraries often create. Finally, you'll learn about the Mikado Method, a technique for managing large-scale code refactoring efforts.

We'll use CppUTest as our unit testing tool of choice as we work through the examples in this chapter. The mocking framework built into CppUTest can make it easier to deal with legacy testing challenges. You can continue to follow along with Google Test/Google Mock, if you prefer, with relatively straightforward adaptations to your unit test code.

8.2 Legacy Code

Legacy code challenges tend to induce the strong motivator of fear into even the most senior developers. Consider having to specialize a small part of a longer, untested function. Imagine that getting your feature implemented is a matter of introducing three lines worth of variant behavior in the midst of thirty lines. As an experienced programmer, you know that the right design would involve factoring common behavior to a common place. The template method design pattern represents one acceptable solution.

(Another solution would involve introducing a conditional. But that's often a recipe for gradual decay, as functions become weighted down with flags and nested blocks.)

Yet, also from the stance of experience, many programmers resist doing the right thing, which would involve changing existing, working code. Perhaps they've experienced smackdowns in the past, chastised for breaking something that had worked all along. "It ain't broke—don't fix it!" They instead take the path of least resistance: copy, paste, and change. The end result is sixty lines of code instead of less than thirty-five. Being driven by fear creates rampant duplication in codebases.

The best way to enable doing the right thing is to have tests that provide fast feedback. On most systems, you don't have that luxury. Michael Feathers, in *Working Effectively with Legacy Code [Fea04]*, defines a *legacy* system as one with insufficient tests.

Working on a legacy codebase demands a choice. Are you willing to let the cost of maintenance steadily increase, or are you willing to start fixing the problem? With an incremental approach, using some of the techniques outlined in this chapter, you'll find that it's not an impossible problem to solve. Most of the time, it's probably worth the effort to put a stake in the ground and demand no one allow the system to get worse. About the only time it's not worth it is on a closed system or on one that you will soon sunset.

8.3 Themes

We'll work through an example of incrementally improving a legacy codebase. You'll learn a handful of specific techniques, each tailored to the specific legacy challenge at hand. The approaches you'll learn are a subset of at least a couple dozen such techniques found in *Working Effectively with Legacy Code [Fea04]* and elsewhere. You'll discover that the techniques are simple to learn and that once you've learned a handful, it's pretty easy to figure out many of the rest.

Core themes for approaching legacy challenges include the following:

- Test-drive whenever you can. Test-drive code changes into either new members or even new classes when possible.

- Don't decrease the test coverage. It's very easy to introduce a small amount of code and then dismiss it as "only a few simple lines." Every line of new code for which you don't have a test results in lower coverage.

- You'll have to change existing code to write tests! Legacy code doesn't easily accommodate tests in many circumstances, largely because of dependencies on challenging collaborators. You'll need a way of breaking these dependencies before you can write tests.

- There are a number of small, constrained code changes that entail minimal risk. You can manually make small and safe code transformations using one of a number of techniques.

- Everything you type represents risk. Even a single mistyped character can introduce an insidious defect that can waste hours. Type as little as possible, and *think* every time you press a key.

- Stick to small, incremental changes. It works for TDD; it can also work for legacy code. Taking larger steps will get you in trouble.

- Do one thing at a time. When tackling legacy code, avoid combining steps or goals. For example, don't combine refactoring while at the same time trying to write tests.

- Accept that some incremental changes will make the code uglier. Remember, one thing at a time. You might require a few more hours to do the "right" thing. Don't wait—commit the working solution now, because you might not end up having the full few hours you need.

  And don't be too concerned about offending some design sensibilities in the meantime. You may eventually find the time to return to clean up the code. You may not, but it's still an improvement. You've taken steps in the right direction, and you can prove that everything still works.

- Accommodate incremental improvements to the periphery of your change. Faced with a monstrous codebase, adding tests only when you touch relevant code won't make a terribly large dent. More important is the mentality that everything new going in gets tested.

  With an always-test mentality in place, you can begin to take advantage of the tests you add. With every test you make pass, take a look around the area you just covered with tests. There's almost always an opportunity for a small, safe bit of refactoring. You'll also discover how much easier it is to write a second test once you've written a first. You can accommodate such little bits of improvement here and there without impacting your ability to deliver, and you'll begin to make a larger dent in the challenging codebase.

8.4   The Legacy Application

Story: WAV Snippet Publisher

As a content reseller, I want the WAV Snippet Publisher to extract a short snippet from each WAV file in a source directory and publish it as a new WAV file in a target directory.

The Waveform Audio (WAV) file standard derives from Microsoft and IBM and is based upon their Resource Interchange File Format (RIFF) (http://en.wikipedia.org/wiki/WAV). WAV files contain audio data encoded into a collection of samples, often using the commonly accepted Pulse-Code Modulation (PCM) standard. See http://en.wikipedia.org/wiki/Pulse-code_modulation. You can find a simplified version of the WAV format at https://ccrma.stanford.edu/courses/422/projects/WaveFormat/.

The snippet publisher meets the current but growing needs of the customer, though the implementation contains many limitations. For example, it doesn't handle the rare case where the length of the audio samples is odd. Nor does it handle multiple-channel WAV files. It also does not support all platforms because of little/big endian differences. Our customer has asked us to resolve all of these limitations (leaving the rest to you for future incorporation).

Story: Add Support for Multiple Channels

Currently, the snippet publisher handles only single-channel (mono) WAV files properly. As a content reseller, I want to ensure that stereo WAV snippets do not get chopped in half.

Ahh! Change is here already! Unfortunately, almost no unit tests exist for the WAV Snippet Publisher, though that shouldn't be surprising. (In preparing for this chapter, I built the codebase without employing TDD. It seemed quicker at first, but my lack of tests quickly chewed up more time than saved as I fell into a couple of defect weed patches.)

The open() function represents the bulk of the WAV Snippet Publisher logic. It sprawls across the next few pages.

```
wav/1/WavReader.cpp
void WavReader::open(const std::string& name, bool trace) {
    rLog(channel, "opening %s", name.c_str());

    ifstream file{name, ios::in | ios::binary};
    if (!file.is_open()) {
        rLog(channel, "unable to read %s", name.c_str());
        return;
    }

    ofstream out{dest_ + "/" + name, ios::out | ios::binary};

    RiffHeader header;
    file.read(reinterpret_cast<char*>(&header), sizeof(RiffHeader));
```

```cpp
    if (toString(header.id, 4) != "RIFF") {
        rLog(channel, "ERROR: %s is not a RIFF file",
            name.c_str());
        return;
    }
    if (toString(header.format, 4) != "WAVE") {
        rLog(channel, "ERROR: %s is not a wav file: %s",
            name.c_str(),
            toString(header.format, 4).c_str());
        return;
    }
    out.write(reinterpret_cast<char*>(&header), sizeof(RiffHeader));

    FormatSubchunkHeader formatSubchunkHeader;
    file.read(reinterpret_cast<char*>(&formatSubchunkHeader),
        sizeof(FormatSubchunkHeader));

    if (toString(formatSubchunkHeader.id, 4) != "fmt ") {
        rLog(channel, "ERROR: %s expecting 'fmt' for subchunk header; got '%s'",
            name.c_str(),
            toString(formatSubchunkHeader.id, 4).c_str());
        return;
    }

    out.write(reinterpret_cast<char*>(&formatSubchunkHeader),
        sizeof(FormatSubchunkHeader));

    FormatSubchunk formatSubchunk;
    file.read(reinterpret_cast<char*>(&formatSubchunk), sizeof(FormatSubchunk));

    out.write(reinterpret_cast<char*>(&formatSubchunk), sizeof(FormatSubchunk));

    rLog(channel, "format tag: %u", formatSubchunk.formatTag); // show as hex?
    rLog(channel, "samples per second: %u", formatSubchunk.samplesPerSecond);
    rLog(channel, "channels: %u", formatSubchunk.channels);
    rLog(channel, "bits per sample: %u", formatSubchunk.bitsPerSample);

    auto bytes = formatSubchunkHeader.subchunkSize - sizeof(FormatSubchunk);

    auto additionalBytes = new char[bytes];
    file.read(additionalBytes, bytes);
    out.write(additionalBytes, bytes);

    FactOrData factOrData;
    file.read(reinterpret_cast<char*>(&factOrData), sizeof(FactOrData));
    out.write(reinterpret_cast<char*>(&factOrData), sizeof(FactOrData));

    if (toString(factOrData.tag, 4) == "fact") {
        FactChunk factChunk;
        file.read(reinterpret_cast<char*>(&factChunk), sizeof(FactChunk));
```

```
        out.write(reinterpret_cast<char*>(&factChunk), sizeof(FactChunk));

        file.read(reinterpret_cast<char*>(&factOrData), sizeof(FactOrData));
        out.write(reinterpret_cast<char*>(&factOrData), sizeof(FactOrData));

        rLog(channel, "samples per channel: %u", factChunk.samplesPerChannel);
    }

    if (toString(factOrData.tag, 4) != "data") {
        string tag{toString(factOrData.tag, 4)};
        rLog(channel, "%s ERROR: unknown tag>%s<", name.c_str(), tag.c_str());
        return;
    }

    DataChunk dataChunk;
    file.read(reinterpret_cast<char*>(&dataChunk), sizeof(DataChunk));

    rLog(channel, "riff header size = %u" , sizeof(RiffHeader));
    rLog(channel, "subchunk header size = %u", sizeof(FormatSubchunkHeader));
    rLog(channel, "subchunk size = %u", formatSubchunkHeader.subchunkSize);
    rLog(channel, "data length = %u", dataChunk.length);

    // TODO if odd there is a padding byte!
    auto data = new char[dataChunk.length];
    file.read(data, dataChunk.length);
    file.close();

    // all of it
//    out.write(data, dataChunk.length);
    // TODO: multiple channels
➤    uint32_t secondsDesired{10};
➤    if (formatSubchunk.bitsPerSample == 0) formatSubchunk.bitsPerSample = 8;
➤    uint32_t bytesPerSample{formatSubchunk.bitsPerSample / uint32_t{8}};
➤    uint32_t samplesToWrite{secondsDesired * formatSubchunk.samplesPerSecond};
➤    uint32_t totalSamples{dataChunk.length / bytesPerSample};
➤
➤    samplesToWrite = min(samplesToWrite, totalSamples);
➤
➤    uint32_t totalSeconds{totalSamples / formatSubchunk.samplesPerSecond};
➤    rLog(channel, "total seconds %u ", totalSeconds);
➤
➤    dataChunk.length = samplesToWrite * bytesPerSample;
➤    out.write(reinterpret_cast<char*>(&dataChunk), sizeof(DataChunk));
➤
➤    uint32_t startingSample{
➤        totalSeconds >= 10 ? 10 * formatSubchunk.samplesPerSecond : 0};
➤    rLog(channel, "writing %u samples", samplesToWrite);
➤    for (auto sample = startingSample;
➤        sample < startingSample + samplesToWrite;
➤        sample++) {
```

```
➤          auto byteOffsetForSample = sample * bytesPerSample;
➤          for (uint32_t byte{0}; byte < bytesPerSample; byte++)
➤             out.put(data[byteOffsetForSample + byte]);
➤       }
       rLog(channel, "completed writing %s", name.c_str());
       descriptor_->add(dest_, name,
             totalSeconds, formatSubchunk.samplesPerSecond, formatSubchunk.channels);
       out.close();
   }
```

The open() function contains comments, to-dos, commented-out logic, questionable names, magic numbers, repetition, and a one-stop-shopping collection of code to solve all problems. What's not to like?

Well, we don't like much in this code. The convoluted code provides ample opportunities for us to mess up as we attempt to add support for multiple channels. It would help to have tests in the areas we want to change.

8.5   A Test-Driven Mentality

Tests still come first in your approach to legacy code. You will need to write tests to *characterize* existing behavior, even though these tests cover code already written. You will also test-drive any new code you write.

You'll likely realize that writing tests after the fact (something I refer to as *Test-After Development* [TAD]) requires considerably more effort than had you created the code using TDD. The primary reason is that programmers don't structure their code to be easily tested if they're not worried about testing it. The second reason is that when test-driving, you should be continually factoring toward smaller, more reusable elements that make the crafting of new tests and code easier.

Testing the open() function looks like it will be very time-consuming. We'd have to create or find one or more WAV files that we could test with. We'd need to read the resulting output file and check all of its content. That's a lot of detail that we don't have time for now.

Life can be simpler. You really only need tests around code you will change, a baseline that tells you when you've broken existing behavior. You do not need to test code leading up to that area of change, although you will need to determine what dependent code might break as a result.

You also want to avoid tests that must interact directly with the filesystem in order to keep your test suite fast and to reduce the headaches of managing files. You can partially accomplish that by using in-memory streams where possible instead of file-bound streams.

8.6 Safe Refactoring to Support Testing

So that we can begin to add support for multiple channels, let's figure out where it might be useful to verify functionality in the open() function.

Near its end appears a number of calculations—total seconds, how many samples to write, where to start, and so on. After all these calculations is a for loop that appears to write samples to an output file. (This chunk of code appears highlighted in the earlier listing of open().) We'll need to change a calculation or two plus fix the loop in order to support multiple channels.

The most interesting piece of code is the loop. Let's write tests around that...but how? We'd need to set up lots of information to get that far in the open() function.

Instead, let's isolate the loop code to its own member function and test it directly.

> *Q.: You're going to change the code? Don't you run the risk of breaking things?*
>
> *A.: Yes. This is how we will add a small test increment that covers the code we must change. Extracting a chunk of code into its method is one of the few code transformations that we can do in a very safe manner.*
>
> *Q.: It's a bit of work to extract a function and put the prototype into the header. Isn't there an easier way?*
>
> *A.: Method extract is the simplest approach we have. It would take hours to get the prior part of open() tested.*
>
> *Q.: I now understand and buy into why it's better to have testable code. But you'll have to expose the method as public, a choice that many of my fellow programmers would find contemptible.*
>
> *A.: If absolutely required, you can employ other techniques that result in less-open code. For example, you can define the method as protected and then create a test derivative that exposes it as public. It seems like a lot of extra effort—and maintenance—for little gain. I prefer the simpler approach.*
>
> *Remind your fellows that it's better that we know the code works than worry about the unlikely scenario of exposed code getting abused.*
>
> *You might also appease them by writing a prudent comment that explains why the function is exposed. Exposing a member might also highlight the design flaw that it exhibits feature envy. In turn, that exposure might prod someone to fix the design problem.*

Our approach to extracting a function involves small, rote steps.

1. We type the call to the yet-to-be-extracted function where it belongs.

```
wav/2/WavReader.cpp
uint32_t startingSample{
    totalSeconds >= 10 ? 10 * formatSubchunk.samplesPerSecond : 0};
➤ writeSamples(out, data, startingSample, samplesToWrite, bytesPerSample);

    rLog(channel, "writing %u samples", samplesToWrite);
    for (auto sample = startingSample;
        sample < startingSample + samplesToWrite;
        sample++) {
      auto byteOffsetForSample = sample * bytesPerSample;
      for (uint32_t byte{0}; byte < bytesPerSample; byte++)
        out.put(data[byteOffsetForSample + byte]);
    }
    rLog(channel, "completed writing %s", name.c_str());
    descriptor_->add(dest_, name,
          totalSeconds, formatSubchunk.samplesPerSecond, formatSubchunk.channels);
```

2. We add a corresponding function declaration before the open() function by simply doing a copy/paste of the function call in the code. (We'll move it out of the header once we get it compiling.) We type the function's return type (void) and the braces. We keep it as a free function for now, which will allow us to get the parameter types correct without having to replicate that effort in the prototype.

```
wav/2/WavReader.cpp
void writeSamples(out, data, startingSample, samplesToWrite, bytesPerSample) {
}
```

3. We add type information to the signature for writeSamples(). We use the compiler to let us know if the call to writeSamples() doesn't match the signature, and we fix problems when the compiler points to them. Once we get it right, we add the prototype to WavReader.h, and we scope the implementation of writeSamples() to the class (WavReader::).

```
wav/3/WavReader.cpp
void WavReader::writeSamples(ofstream& out, char* data,
        uint32_t startingSample,
        uint32_t samplesToWrite,
        uint32_t bytesPerSample) {
}
```

```
wav/3/WavReader.h
public:
    // ...
    void writeSamples(std::ofstream& out, char* data,
          uint32_t startingSample,
          uint32_t samplesToWrite,
          uint32_t bytesPerSample);
```

4. We copy the for loop into the body of writeSamples() and ensure it compiles. It might not compile if, for example, we forgot to pass a necessary parameter.

wav/4/WavReader.cpp
```
void WavReader::writeSamples(ofstream& out, char* data,
    uint32_t startingSample,
    uint32_t samplesToWrite,
    uint32_t bytesPerSample) {
  rLog(channel, "writing %i samples", samplesToWrite);

  for (auto sample = startingSample;
      sample < startingSample + samplesToWrite;
      sample++) {
    auto byteOffsetForSample = sample * bytesPerSample;
    for (uint32_t byte{0}; byte < bytesPerSample; byte++)
      out.put(data[byteOffsetForSample + byte]);
  }
}
```

We remove the for loop code from the open() member function.

wav/4/WavReader.cpp
```
uint32_t startingSample{
    totalSeconds >= 10 ? 10 * formatSubchunk.samplesPerSecond : 0};

➤ writeSamples(out, data, startingSample, samplesToWrite, bytesPerSample);

  rLog(channel, "completed writing %s", name.c_str());

  descriptor_->add(dest_, name,
      totalSeconds, formatSubchunk.samplesPerSecond, formatSubchunk.channels);
```

We compile and run any tests we have. We've successfully, and with reasonable safety, extracted a chunk of code to its own function. Extracting writeSamples() has also increased the abstraction level of the open() function.

Sometimes you'll encounter challenging compilation errors in your attempts to extract a function. If you ever feel like you must change lines of code to get your attempt to compile, you've likely extracted the wrong chunk of code. Stop and re-think your approach. Either change the scope of your extract or find a way to write a few more tests first.

Every paste from existing code introduces duplication. For that reason, many test-drivers consider copy/paste an "evil" mechanism. When crafting new code, you should maintain a mental stack of every paste operation and remember to pop off that stack by factoring out any remaining duplication.

Yet with legacy code, copy/paste is often your benevolent friend. Minimizing your actual typing, preferring instead to copy from existing structures, decreases your risk of making a dumb mistake when manipulating existing code. The steps taken here (which represent one possible approach) to extract the writeSamples() member minimize typing and maximize points at which the compiler can help you catch mistakes.

We did *not* change any code within writeSamples(). That means our only risk lies around calling the function properly. (If it had a nonvoid return, we'd also want to ensure the return value was handled appropriately.) If we didn't intend to change any code in writeSamples(), we wouldn't worry about writing tests for it. We'd instead focus on writing tests around the passing of arguments to writeSamples(). We'll give that a shot a bit later.

8.7 Adding Tests to Characterize Existing Behavior

We need to change code in writeSamples(). Let's start with a couple tests!

wav/6/WavReaderTest.cpp
```cpp
#include "CppUTest/TestHarness.h"
#include "WavReader.h"
#include <iostream>
#include <string>
#include <sstream>

using namespace std;

TEST_GROUP(WavReader_WriteSamples)
{
   WavReader reader{"",""};
   ostringstream out;
};

TEST(WavReader_WriteSamples, WritesSingleSample) {
   char data[] { "abcd" };
   uint32_t bytesPerSample { 1 };
   uint32_t startingSample { 0 };
   uint32_t samplesToWrite { 1 };
   reader.writeSamples(&out, data, startingSample, samplesToWrite, bytesPerSample);
   CHECK_EQUAL("a", out.str());
}

TEST(WavReader_WriteSamples, WritesMultibyteSampleFromMiddle) {
   char data[] { "0123456789ABCDEFG" };
   uint32_t bytesPerSample { 2 };
   uint32_t startingSample { 4 };
   uint32_t samplesToWrite { 3 };

   reader.writeSamples(&out, data, startingSample, samplesToWrite, bytesPerSample);
   CHECK_EQUAL("89ABCD", out.str());
}
```

The direct tests against writeSamples() help us understand the looping behavior in isolation. They're not great, though. The test WritesMultibyteSampleFrom-Middle requires careful reading and a little bit of math. How would you make it more directly expressive?

Rather than slow down our tests by using actual files, we use fast, in-memory string objects of type std::ostringstream. Doing so requires changing the interface of writeSamples() to take std::ostream objects, the common type from which both std::ofstream and std::ostringstream derive. More specifically, we alter the interface to take a *pointer* to an std::ostream. Production code can pass the address of a file stream; tests can pass the address of a string stream. We change the dereferencing of the writeSamples() local variable out to use pointer semantics.

```
wav/6/WavReader.cpp
writeSamples(&out, data, startingSample, samplesToWrite, bytesPerSample);
```

```
wav/6/WavReader.cpp
void WavReader::writeSamples(ostream* out, char* data,
    uint32_t startingSample,
    uint32_t samplesToWrite,
    uint32_t bytesPerSample) {
  rLog(channel, "writing %i samples", samplesToWrite);

  for (auto sample = startingSample;
      sample < startingSample + samplesToWrite;
      sample++) {
    auto byteOffsetForSample = sample * bytesPerSample;
    for (uint32_t byte{0}; byte < bytesPerSample; byte++)
      out->put(data[byteOffsetForSample + byte]);
  }
}
```

8.8 Sidetracked by the Reality of Legacy Code

Our test suite fails! For each test, CppUTest compares memory at the start of its execution with memory at its completion and fails if there's a mismatch. With a bit of probing, we discover the leaker culprit to be either the third-party logging library, rlog, or our WavReader application's use of rlog. Dealing with the leak isn't our primary goal. We need a way to move forward.

CppUTest allows us to turn off leak detection, but it's a highly useful feature that we want to keep. Further, even if we turned off leak detection, the logging code—which appears throughout WavReader—spews messages onto the console every time we run tests. It's a nuisance. What might we do other than grin and bear it? It's possible there's a way to turn off logging without changing the code, but we're running out of time and need to move forward.

Third-party libraries can create no end of headaches for testing. They might be slow, they might require extensive configuration, and they might have undesirable side effects. When you first start tackling a legacy codebase, chances are you'll spend a lot of time up front dealing with similar challenges arising from third-party libraries.

One possible solution is to dummy-out a third-party library via *linker substitution*. For the WavReader application, we will create a library of stub functions for each rlog function we use and link against that library when we build our test executable.

Linker-substitution, or link-time substitution, sounds a lot harder than it is, but it's a fairly quick process to set up.

8.9 Creating a Test Double for rlog

We don't have to stub *everything* that rlog defines, only the things our test executable requires. We start by commenting out the line in the makefile that links rlog into the test executable. Here's our update to CMakeLists.txt (we're using CMake):

```
wav/7/CMakeLists.txt
project(SnippetPublisher)
cmake_minimum_required(VERSION 2.6)

include_directories($ENV{BOOST_ROOT}/ $ENV{RLOG_HOME} $ENV{CPPUTEST_HOME}/include)
link_directories($ENV{RLOG_HOME}/rlog/.libs $ENV{CPPUTEST_HOME}/lib)
set(Boost_USE_STATIC_LIBS ON)

add_definitions(-std=c++0x)

set(CMAKE_CXX_FLAGS "${CMAXE_CXX_FLAGS} -DRLOG_COMPONENT=debug -Wall")
set(sources WavReader.cpp WavDescriptor.cpp)
set(testSources WavReaderTest.cpp)
add_executable(utest testmain.cpp ${testSources} ${sources})
add_executable(SnippetPublisher main.cpp ${sources})

find_package(Boost $ENV{BOOST_VERSION} COMPONENTS filesystem system)
target_link_libraries(utest ${Boost_LIBRARIES})
target_link_libraries(utest CppUTest)
target_link_libraries(utest pthread)
target_link_libraries(utest rt)
#target_link_libraries(utest rlog)

target_link_libraries(SnippetPublisher ${Boost_LIBRARIES})
target_link_libraries(SnippetPublisher pthread)
target_link_libraries(SnippetPublisher rlog)
```

Now when we build, we receive numerous link errors.

```
Linking CXX executable utest
CMakeFiles/utest.dir/WavReader.cpp.o: In function `WavReader::WavReader(
    std::string const&, std::string const&)':
WavReader.cpp:(.text+0xef): undefined reference to
    `rlog::StdioNode::StdioNode(int, int)'
WavReader.cpp:(.text+0x158): undefined reference to
    `rlog::GetComponentChannel(char const*, char const*, rlog::LogLevel)'
WavReader.cpp:(.text+0x17c): undefined reference to
    `rlog::GetComponentChannel(char const*, char const*, rlog::LogLevel)'
WavReader.cpp:(.text+0x18e): undefined reference to
    `rlog::StdioNode::subscribeTo(rlog::RLogNode*)'
WavReader.cpp:(.text+0x1e4): undefined reference to
    `rlog::PublishLoc::~PublishLoc()'
...
```

We need to supply stubs for each of those attempts to hook into rlog. Here is one approach:

1. Copy over an rlog header file into a subdirectory, renaming it as a .cpp file.

2. Edit the .cpp file, converting prototypes into stubs that do nothing other than return a default value if required.

3. Compile and repeat the prior steps until no link errors exist.

Since StdioNode appears at the top of our link error list, we start there.

wav/8/rlog/StdioNode.cpp
```
#include <rlog/StdioNode.h>

class RLogNode;
class RLogData;

using namespace std;

namespace rlog {
    StdioNode::StdioNode(int _fdOut, int flags)
        : RLogNode() {}
    StdioNode::StdioNode(int _fdOut, bool colorizeIfTTY)
        : RLogNode(), fdOut( _fdOut ) { }
    StdioNode::~StdioNode() { }
    void StdioNode::subscribeTo( RLogNode *node ) { }
    void StdioNode::publish( const RLogData &data ) { }
}
```

That's not too tough, but converting headers into implementation files can get a bit tedious and tricky at times. (Maybe there's a magic tool out there that can do this for you!) Here are a few things (and not everything) to consider:

- As the very first thing you do, #include the header from whence you created the implementation file.

- You may need to wrap the implementations in a namespace.

- Remove virtual and static keywords.

- Remove public: and other access specifiers.

- Remove member variables and enums.

- Be careful about removing preprocessor defines and typedefs.

- Return the simplest possible type if the function specifies a return value —for example, 0, false, "", a null pointer, or an instance created using a no-arg constructor.

- If you must return a const reference, create a global and return that.

- Don't forget to scope the function to the appropriate class.

- Don't sweat the way it looks when done; the important thing is that it compiles.

We add a makefile that builds our new stub library.

`wav/8/rlog/CMakeLists.txt`
```
project(rlogStub)
cmake_minimum_required(VERSION 2.6)

include_directories($ENV{RLOG_HOME})

add_definitions(-std=c++0x)

set(CMAKE_CXX_FLAGS "${CMAXE_CXX_FLAGS} -DRLOG_COMPONENT=debug -Wall")
set(sources StdioNode.cpp)

add_library(rlogStub ${sources})

target_link_libraries(rlogStub pthread)
```

We update our test build to incorporate the stub library. The production app, SnippetPublisher, continues to use the production rlog library.

`wav/8/CMakeLists.txt`
```
project(SnippetPublisher)
cmake_minimum_required(VERSION 2.6)

include_directories($ENV{BOOST_ROOT}/ $ENV{RLOG_HOME} $ENV{CPPUTEST_HOME}/include)
link_directories($ENV{RLOG_HOME}/rlog/.libs $ENV{CPPUTEST_HOME}/lib)
set(Boost_USE_STATIC_LIBS ON)
```

```
➤ add_subdirectory(rlog)
  add_definitions(-std=c++0x)

  set(CMAKE_CXX_FLAGS "${CMAXE_CXX_FLAGS} -DRLOG_COMPONENT=debug -Wall")
  set(sources WavReader.cpp WavDescriptor.cpp)
  set(testSources WavReaderTest.cpp)
  add_executable(utest testmain.cpp ${testSources} ${sources})
  add_executable(SnippetPublisher main.cpp ${sources})

  find_package(Boost $ENV{BOOST_VERSION} COMPONENTS filesystem system)
  target_link_libraries(utest ${Boost_LIBRARIES})
  target_link_libraries(utest CppUTest)
  target_link_libraries(utest pthread)
➤ target_link_libraries(utest rlogStub)

  target_link_libraries(SnippetPublisher ${Boost_LIBRARIES})
  target_link_libraries(SnippetPublisher pthread)
  target_link_libraries(SnippetPublisher rlog)
```

An attempt to build with the StdioNode.h stub fails. We add stubs for RLogChannel.h, RLogNode.h, and rlog.h, each an implementation of the actual rlog header file. Here's the implementation for RLogChannel.h, slightly more interesting because of the need to supply return values:

wav/9/rlog/RLogChannel.cpp
```cpp
#include "rlog/RLogChannel.h"
#include <string>
#include <iostream>

namespace rlog
{
RLogChannel::RLogChannel( const std::string &name, LogLevel level ){ }
RLogChannel::~RLogChannel(){}
void RLogChannel::publish(const RLogData &data){}

std::string nameReturn("");
const std::string &RLogChannel::name() const { return nameReturn; }

LogLevel RLogChannel::logLevel() const { return LogLevel(); }
void RLogChannel::setLogLevel(LogLevel level) {}
RLogChannel *getComponent(RLogChannel *componentParent,
                     const char *component){ return 0; }
}
```

We work on creating one stub at a time, remembering to update our makefile for each.

wav/9/rlog/CMakeLists.txt
```cmake
set(sources rlog.cpp RLogChannel.cpp RLogNode.cpp StdioNode.cpp)
```

We attempt a build with each new stub we put in place. After getting all four stubs in place, we experience the exhilaration of link and test success! Yay. Elapsed time: perhaps twenty minutes. Staving off continual future headaches seems well worth the effort.

8.10 Test-Driving Changes

We can now test-drive our changes to writeData() to incorporate the number of channels. The channel count represents the number of tracks (sound from separate sources) to play simultaneously. For monaural (mono) output, the channel count is one. For stereo, it is two. Playback of the WAV requires iterating through all the samples in order. A given sample is comprised of a series of subsamples, one per channel. Monaural representation for a four-sample audio clip, where a sample is a single byte, might look like this:

```
AA BB CC DD
```

Suppose there is a second channel with the following sample sequence:

```
01 02 03 04
```

The resulting WAV stream should appear like this:

```
AA 01 BB 02 CC 03 DD 04
```

Here's a test showing how increasing the channel requires more bytes in the data stream:

```
wav/10/WavReaderTest.cpp
#include "CppUTest/TestHarness.h"
#include "WavReader.h"
#include <iostream>
#include <string>
#include <sstream>

using namespace std;

TEST_GROUP(WavReader) {
};

TEST(WavReader_WriteSamples, IncorporatesChannelCount) {
    char data[] { "0123456789ABCDEFG" };
    uint32_t bytesPerSample { 2 };
    uint32_t startingSample { 0 };
    uint32_t samplesToWrite { 2 };
    uint32_t channels { 2 };
    reader.writeSamples(
        &out, data, startingSample, samplesToWrite, bytesPerSample, channels);
    CHECK_EQUAL("01234567", out.str());
}
```

To avoid having to change a number of other tests right now, we can default the channels parameter. As usual, our goal is to get tests passing and then clean up.

```
wav/10/WavReader.h
void writeSamples(std::ostream* out, char* data,
     uint32_t startingSample,
     uint32_t samplesToWrite,
     uint32_t bytesPerSample,
     uint32_t channels=1);
```

We now implement the code that makes the new test pass.

```
wav/10/WavReader.cpp
void WavReader::writeSamples(ostream* out, char* data,
     uint32_t startingSample,
     uint32_t samplesToWrite,
     uint32_t bytesPerSample,
     uint32_t channels) {
   rLog(channel, "writing %i samples", samplesToWrite);

   for (auto sample = startingSample;
       sample < startingSample + samplesToWrite;
       sample++) {
     auto byteOffsetForSample = sample * bytesPerSample * channels;

     for (uint32_t channel{0}; channel < channels; channel++) {
       auto byteOffsetForChannel =
         byteOffsetForSample + (channel * bytesPerSample);
       for (uint32_t byte{0}; byte < bytesPerSample; byte++)
         out->put(data[byteOffsetForChannel + byte]);
     }
   }
}
```

There's one more thing to correct. When we write the new ten-second WAV, we update the data chunk's length. The length is currently incorrect since it does not factor in the number of channels. It's a one-liner, but we'll happily extract it to a function we can test and correct. We follow the same pattern. We write a test to characterize existing behavior, alter the test to specify new behavior, and change the production code. Here are the resulting test, extracted function, and client code in open() that calls the new function:

```
wav/11/WavReaderTest.cpp
TEST_GROUP(WavReader_DataLength) {
   WavReader reader{"",""};
};

TEST(WavReader_DataLength, IsProductOfChannels_BytesPerSample_and_Samples) {
   uint32_t bytesPerSample{ 2 };
```

```
    uint32_t samples { 5 };
    uint32_t channels { 4 };

    uint32_t length { reader.dataLength(bytesPerSample, samples, channels) };

    CHECK_EQUAL(2 * 5 * 4, length);
}
```

wav/11/WavReader.cpp

```
    // ...
    rLog(channel, "total seconds %u ", totalSeconds);

➤   dataChunk.length = dataLength(
➤       samplesToWrite,
➤       bytesPerSample,
➤       formatSubchunk.channels);

    out.write(reinterpret_cast<char*>(&dataChunk), sizeof(DataChunk));
    // ...

uint32_t WavReader::dataLength(
    uint32_t samples,
    uint32_t bytesPerSample,
    uint32_t channels
    ) const {
  return samples * bytesPerSample * channels;
}
```

8.11 A New Story

Story: Enhance the Descriptor

Background: In its penultimate step, the open() function sends a message to a WavDescriptor object, whose job is to append a formatted data record to a descriptor file. The WAV publisher user interface uses the descriptor file's contents to display available WAVs.

The descriptor accepts the WAV filename, total seconds (before snipping), samples per second, and number of channels.

Story: As a content reseller, I want the descriptors for WAV files to also include the new snippet file length. Alter the descriptor object to accept the length.

Someone else will change the implementation of WavDescriptor to include the snippet file length in each record (let's hope they're using TDD!). Our job will involve only making changes to WavReader.

Our effort to complete this task involves two things. First, calculate or obtain the file size. Second, prove that we pass this value across to the WavDescriptor.

When adding new functionality, your best bet is to first seek to test-drive it into a new method or even a new class. This ensures that code coverage does not decrease as your codebase grows. It also better helps you adhere to the SRP and reap all the benefits of small functions and classes.

We need a function that returns a file's size given its name. For our test-driven new functionality, do this:

`wav/12/FileUtilTest.cpp`
```cpp
// slow tests that must interact with the filesystem
TEST_GROUP_BASE(FileUtil_Size, FileUtilTests) {
};


TEST(FileUtil_Size, AnswersFileContentSize) {
    string content("12345");
    createTempFile(content);

    size_t expectedSize { content.length() + sizeof('\0') };
    LONGS_EQUAL(expectedSize, (unsigned)util.size(TempFileName));
}
```

`wav/12/FileUtil.h`
```cpp
class FileUtil {
public:
    std::streamsize size(const std::string& name) {
        std::ifstream stream{name, std::ios::in | std::ios::binary};
        stream.seekg(0, std::ios::end);
        return stream.tellg();
    }
};
```

What stinks about this test? It's not fast (see Section 4.3, *Fast Tests, Slow Tests, Filters, and Suites*, on page 86).

You might end up with a small number of slow tests that you arrive at by test-driving. Perhaps that's OK, but strive to make their number *very* small—as close to zero as possible. More importantly, designate such tests as slow and ensure that you have a way to run fast, slow, or fast and slow suites.

8.12 A Brief Exploration in Seeking Faster Tests

Right now, we have exactly one slow test for the WAV Snippet Publisher codebase. We'll strive to keep it that way. But if you need another file-based utility, you'd want to ensure you don't add a second slow test. Once you allow them, slow tests add up quickly.

One possible solution is to separate out the portion of the functionality that deals only with the stream and test-drive it. For the size() function, we could create an even smaller method.

wav/12/StreamUtilTest.cpp
```
TEST(StreamUtil_Size, AnswersNumberOfBytesWrittenToStream) {
    istringstream readFrom{"abcdefg"};

    CHECK_EQUAL(7, StreamUtil::size(readFrom));
}
```

wav/12/StreamUtil.cpp
```
std::streamsize size(std::istream& stream) {
    stream.seekg(0, std::ios::end);
    return stream.tellg();
}
```

FileUtil's size() function would simply delegate work to StreamUtil's size() function, passing it the ifstream. We might consider the resulting FileUtil function to be so small as to not break and consider not writing a unit test for it.

We could also create a FileUtil function, execute(), whose sole job is to create an ifstream and pass it to a function that operates on that stream. Client code would pass a function pointer to execute().

wav/12/FileUtilTest.cpp
```
streamsize size = util.execute(TempFileName,
             [&](istream& s) { return StreamUtil::size(s); });
```

wav/12/FileUtil.h
```
std::streamsize execute(
      const std::string& name,
      std::function<std::streamsize (std::istream&)> func) {
    std::ifstream stream{name, std::ios::in | std::ios::binary};
    return func(stream);
}
```

The benefit is that we'd need only one test—for the execute() function—that handled files. All other tests would be fast, stream-only tests.

8.13 Mondo Extracto

We need to figure out where within the open() function to call size(). Our call could go near the end of open(), immediately before the code sends a message to the descriptor object. But since size() re-opens a file, we need to ensure that the new WAV file gets closed first.

Unfortunately, the structure of open() presents quite a challenge. Code all the way up to the call to the descriptor is riddled with file reads and writes. Writing a test able to execute the entire function remains fairly challenging. (We could pass a real, vetted WAV file to open(), but that would net us a slow and dependent test.)

Instead, we refactor open() with the goal of deriving some functions that we might stub or mock. After about a dozen minutes of generally safe function extract operations, our code looks much healthier. They still contain ugly spots, but our functions are getting close to being readily digestible.

wav/13/WavReader.cpp

```cpp
void WavReader::open(const std::string& name, bool trace) {
    rLog(channel, "opening %s", name.c_str());

    ifstream file{name, ios::in | ios::binary};
    if (!file.is_open()) {
        rLog(channel, "unable to read %s", name.c_str());
        return;
    }

    ofstream out{dest_ + "/" + name, ios::out | ios::binary};

    FormatSubchunk formatSubchunk;
    FormatSubchunkHeader formatSubchunkHeader;
    readAndWriteHeaders(name, file, out, formatSubchunk, formatSubchunkHeader);

    DataChunk dataChunk;
    read(file, dataChunk);

    rLog(channel, "riff header size = %i" , sizeof(RiffHeader));
    rLog(channel, "subchunk header size = %i", sizeof(FormatSubchunkHeader));
    rLog(channel, "subchunk size = %i", formatSubchunkHeader.subchunkSize);
    rLog(channel, "data length = %i", dataChunk.length);

    auto data = readData(file, dataChunk.length); // leak!

    writeSnippet(name, file, out, formatSubchunk, dataChunk, data);
}

void WavReader::read(istream& file, DataChunk& dataChunk) {
    file.read(reinterpret_cast<char*>(&dataChunk), sizeof(DataChunk));
}

char* WavReader::readData(istream& file, int32_t length) {
    auto data = new char[length];
    file.read(data, length);
    //file.close(); // istreams are RAII
    return data;
}

void WavReader::readAndWriteHeaders(
        const std::string& name,
        istream& file,
        ostream& out,
        FormatSubchunk& formatSubchunk,
```

```
        FormatSubchunkHeader& formatSubchunkHeader) {
    RiffHeader header;
    file.read(reinterpret_cast<char*>(&header), sizeof(RiffHeader));
    // ...
}

void WavReader::writeSnippet(
        const string& name, istream& file, ostream& out,
        FormatSubchunk& formatSubchunk,
        DataChunk& dataChunk,
        char* data
        ) {
    uint32_t secondsDesired{10};
    if (formatSubchunk.bitsPerSample == 0) formatSubchunk.bitsPerSample = 8;
    uint32_t bytesPerSample{formatSubchunk.bitsPerSample / uint32_t{8}};

    uint32_t samplesToWrite{secondsDesired * formatSubchunk.samplesPerSecond};
    uint32_t totalSamples{dataChunk.length / bytesPerSample};

    samplesToWrite = min(samplesToWrite, totalSamples);

    uint32_t totalSeconds{totalSamples / formatSubchunk.samplesPerSecond};

    rLog(channel, "total seconds %u ", totalSeconds);

    dataChunk.length = dataLength(
            samplesToWrite,
            bytesPerSample,
            formatSubchunk.channels);
    out.write(reinterpret_cast<char*>(&dataChunk), sizeof(DataChunk));

    uint32_t startingSample{
        totalSeconds >= 10 ? 10 * formatSubchunk.samplesPerSecond : 0};

    writeSamples(&out, data, startingSample, samplesToWrite, bytesPerSample);

    rLog(channel, "completed writing %s", name.c_str());

    descriptor_->add(dest_, name,
            totalSeconds, formatSubchunk.samplesPerSecond, formatSubchunk.channels);

    //out.close(); // ostreams are RAII
}
```

Since writeSnippet() now takes an input stream and an output stream, it no longer depends upon the file system. Writing a test for it, and perhaps also for read() and readData(), now seems reasonable. We'd want to refactor readAndWriteHeaders() (not fully shown) into more manageable chunks before writing tests, but doing so wouldn't take long.

We even uncovered a likely memory leak. Breaking code into smaller functions can make defects obvious.

As we refactored, we deleted the "to-do" comments and commented-out calls to close the streams. We'll need to revisit our choice shortly, but it is not necessary to explicitly close a file (std::ofstream supports RAII), and close() is not part of the std::ostream interface. While our analysis is probably sufficient, now is the time to run whatever other tests we have, manual or automated.

Are we ready yet to add code to support our file size story? A little more refactoring might make it even simpler, but let's see what we can do to test writeSnippet() now that it's a small, focused function. We'll write a few tests that characterize its various behaviors.

8.14 Spying to Sense Using a Member Variable

We decide we want to first ensure that the code properly calculates totalSeconds, a value sent to the descriptor. (We might not need to add this test if we're not going to make changes to writeSnippet(). The test exists here to demonstrate a specific technique.)

```
wav/14/WavReaderTest.cpp
TEST_GROUP(WavReader_WriteSnippet) {
    WavReader reader{"",""};
    istringstream input{""};
    FormatSubchunk formatSubchunk;
    ostringstream output;
    DataChunk dataChunk;
    char* data;
    uint32_t TwoBytesWorthOfBits{2 * 8};

    void setup() override {
        data = new char[4];
    }

    void teardown() override {
        delete[] data;
    }
};

TEST(WavReader_WriteSnippet, UpdatesTotalSeconds) {
    dataChunk.length = 8;
    formatSubchunk.bitsPerSample = TwoBytesWorthOfBits;
    formatSubchunk.samplesPerSecond = 1;

    reader.writeSnippet("any", input, output, formatSubchunk, dataChunk, data);

    CHECK_EQUAL(8 / 2 / 1, reader.totalSeconds);
}
```

We initialize a fair number of things in the test. Since none of them is relevant to the test's expected result, we bury our initialization code in the WavReader _WriteSnippet test group (fixture) definition. We also move the struct definitions from WavReader.cpp into WavReader.h so that the test can access them (not shown).

Wait! How in the world are we verifying the value of totalSeconds, given that it was defined locally to writeSnippet()? Simple: totalSeconds is now a public member variable!

```
wav/14/WavReader.h
public:
    // ...
    uint32_t totalSeconds;
```

```
wav/14/WavReader.cpp
void WavReader::writeSnippet(
        const string& name, istream& file, ostream& out,
        FormatSubchunk& formatSubchunk,
        DataChunk& dataChunk,
        char* data
        ) {
    uint32_t secondsDesired{10};
    if (formatSubchunk.bitsPerSample == 0) formatSubchunk.bitsPerSample = 8;
    uint32_t bytesPerSample{formatSubchunk.bitsPerSample / uint32_t{8}};

    uint32_t samplesToWrite{secondsDesired * formatSubchunk.samplesPerSecond};
    uint32_t totalSamples{dataChunk.length / bytesPerSample};

    samplesToWrite = min(samplesToWrite, totalSamples);

➤    totalSeconds = totalSamples / formatSubchunk.samplesPerSecond;

    rLog(channel, "total seconds %u ", totalSeconds);
    // ...
}
```

Our test *spies* on the otherwise-hidden totalSeconds. Mother of all violations! Chill. Wrestling with a legacy codebase under control sometimes requires getting a little dirty. Remind yourself that it's dirtier still to make changes and not know if you broke something.

Besides, we have a better way that will work for our case.

8.15 Spying to Sense Using a Mock

One of the goals of writeSnippet() is to send the total seconds to the descriptor. In the prior section, we inspected this value by turning it into a member variable. We can instead have the WavReader use a test double of the descriptor that captures the total seconds sent to it.

You learned about how to create test doubles using Google Mock in *Test Doubles*. Since we're using CppUTest for our current example, we'll use its own mock tool, CppUMock. As with Google Mock, we define a derivative of WavDescriptor that will spy on messages sent to its add() function.

```
wav/15/WavReaderTest.cpp
class MockWavDescriptor : public WavDescriptor {
public:
   MockWavDescriptor(): WavDescriptor("") {}
   void add(
      const string&, const string&,
      uint32_t totalSeconds,
      uint32_t, uint32_t) override {
      mock().actualCall("add")
         .withParameter("totalSeconds", (int)totalSeconds);
   }
};
```

The override to add() requires us to make it virtual in WavDescriptor.

```
wav/15/WavDescriptor.h
virtual void add(
   const std::string& dir, const std::string& filename,
   uint32_t totalSeconds, uint32_t samplesPerSecond,
   uint32_t channels) {
   // ...
   WavDescriptorRecord rec;
   cpy(rec.filename, filename.c_str());
   rec.seconds = totalSeconds;
   rec.samplesPerSecond = samplesPerSecond;
   rec.channels = channels;

   outstr->write(reinterpret_cast<char*>(&rec), sizeof(WavDescriptorRecord));
}
```

The highlighted line in MockWavDescriptor tells a global CppUTest MockSupport object (retrieved by a call to mock()) to record an actual call to a function named "add." The MockSupport object also captures the value of a parameter named "totalSeconds." (I quote these names since you get to choose them arbitrarily when you work with CppUMock. It's a cheap form of reflection.)

We inject the test double into the WavReader by passing it as a third argument to its constructor.

```
wav/15/WavReaderTest.cpp
TEST_GROUP(WavReader_WriteSnippet) {
   shared_ptr<MockWavDescriptor> descriptor{new MockWavDescriptor};
   WavReader reader{"", "", descriptor};
   istringstream input{""};
   FormatSubchunk formatSubchunk;
```

```
   ostringstream output;
   DataChunk dataChunk;
   char* data;
   uint32_t TwoBytesWorthOfBits{2 * 8};
   void setup() override {
      data = new char[4];
   }

   void teardown() override {
      mock().clear();
      delete[] data;
   }
};
```

In the test itself, we tell the MockSupport object to expect that a function with name add gets called. We tell it to expect that the call is made with a specific value for its parameter named totalSeconds. This arrangement of the test is known as setting an expectation. Once the actual call to writeSnippet() gets made, the Assert portion of the test verifies that all expectations added to the MockSupport object were met.

wav/15/WavReaderTest.cpp
```
TEST(WavReader_WriteSnippet, UpdatesTotalSeconds) {
   dataChunk.length = 8;
   formatSubchunk.bitsPerSample = TwoBytesWorthOfBits;
   formatSubchunk.samplesPerSecond = 1;
➤  mock().expectOneCall("add").withParameter("totalSeconds", 8 / 2 / 1);
   reader.writeSnippet("any", input, output, formatSubchunk, dataChunk, data);
➤  mock().checkExpectations();
}
```

We correspondingly change the descriptor pointer member to be a shared pointer. Using a shared pointer allows both the test and the production code to properly manage creating and deleting the descriptor object. We also choose to default the descriptor argument to be a null pointer in order to minimize the impact to existing tests.

wav/15/WavReader.h
```
class WavReader {
public:
   WavReader(
         const std::string& source,
         const std::string& dest,
         std::shared_ptr<WavDescriptor> descriptor=0);
   // ...
private:
   // ...
   std::shared_ptr<WavDescriptor> descriptor_;
};
```

wav/15/WavReader.cpp
```
WavReader::WavReader(
      const std::string& source,
      const std::string& dest,
      shared_ptr<WavDescriptor> descriptor)
   : source_(source)
   , dest_(dest)
   , descriptor_(descriptor) {
   if (!descriptor_)
      descriptor_ = make_shared<WavDescriptor>(dest);

   channel = DEF_CHANNEL("info/wav", Log_Debug);
   log.subscribeTo((RLogNode*)RLOG_CHANNEL("info/wav"));

   rLog(channel, "reading from %s writing to %s", source.c_str(), dest.c_str());
}

WavReader::~WavReader() {
   descriptor_.reset();
   delete channel;
}
```

We don't have to change a lick of code in the writeSnippet() function that we're testing! Code in writeSnippet() blissfully continues to call the add() function on the descriptor without knowing whether the descriptor is a production WavDescriptor instance or a test double.

We can finally complete the story by test-driving that writeSnippet() obtains and passes on the file size. In fact, we choose to co-opt the test UpdatesTotalSeconds and update it to verify both arguments. We create a mock for FileUtil in order to support answering a stub value given a request for a file size. We inject the FileUtil mock instance of FileUtil using a setter function instead of the constructor.

wav/16/WavReaderTest.cpp
```
class MockWavDescriptor : public WavDescriptor {
public:
   MockWavDescriptor(): WavDescriptor("") {}
   void add(
      const string&, const string&,
      uint32_t totalSeconds,
      uint32_t, uint32_t,
      uint32_t fileSize) override {
      mock().actualCall("add")
         .withParameter("totalSeconds", (int)totalSeconds)
         .withParameter("fileSize", (int)fileSize);
   }
};
```

```
➤  class MockFileUtil: public FileUtil {
➤  public:
➤      streamsize size(const string& name) override {
➤          return mock().actualCall("size").returnValue().getIntValue();
➤      }
➤  };

   TEST_GROUP(WavReader_WriteSnippet) {
       shared_ptr<MockWavDescriptor> descriptor{new MockWavDescriptor};
       WavReader reader{"", "", descriptor};

➤      shared_ptr<MockFileUtil> fileUtil{make_shared<MockFileUtil>()};

       istringstream input{""};
       FormatSubchunk formatSubchunk;
       ostringstream output;
       DataChunk dataChunk;
       char* data;
       uint32_t TwoBytesWorthOfBits{2 * 8};

       const int ArbitraryFileSize{5};

       void setup() override {
          data = new char[4];
➤         reader.useFileUtil(fileUtil);
       }

       void teardown() override {
          mock().clear();
          delete[] data;
       }
   };

   TEST(WavReader_WriteSnippet, SendsFileLengthAndTotalSecondsToDescriptor) {
       dataChunk.length = 8;
       formatSubchunk.bitsPerSample = TwoBytesWorthOfBits;
       formatSubchunk.samplesPerSecond = 1;

➤      mock().expectOneCall("size").andReturnValue(ArbitraryFileSize);

       mock().expectOneCall("add")
          .withParameter("totalSeconds", 8 / 2 / 1)

➤         .withParameter("fileSize", ArbitraryFileSize);

       reader.writeSnippet("any", input, output, formatSubchunk, dataChunk, data);

       mock().checkExpectations();
   }
```

```
wav/16/WavReader.cpp
void WavReader::writeSnippet(
    const string& name, istream& file, ostream& out,
    FormatSubchunk& formatSubchunk,
    DataChunk& dataChunk,
    char* data
    ) {
// ...
    writeSamples(&out, data, startingSample, samplesToWrite, bytesPerSample);

    rLog(channel, "completed writing %s", name.c_str());

➤   auto fileSize = fileUtil_->size(name);

    descriptor_->add(dest_, name,
        totalSeconds, formatSubchunk.samplesPerSecond, formatSubchunk.channels,
➤       fileSize);

    //out.close(); // ostreams are RAII
}
```

8.16 Alternate Injection Techniques

So far you've seen a few creative techniques to support the ability to test otherwise-difficult-to-reach code. We used constructor injection, setter injection, and a member variable spy. The techniques you learned about in *Test Doubles*, such as Override Factory Method or Introduce via Template Parameter, can apply here. If absolutely necessary, you can look at even more creative approaches, such as using the preprocessor to redefine bits of code.

Avoid falling into the hammer-nail trap of sticking to one dependency-breaking technique. *Working Effectively with Legacy Code [Fea04]* introduces a couple dozen useful patterns. Your job is to familiarize yourself with all of them so that you can choose the most appropriate to your situation.

8.17 Large-Scale Change with the Mikado Method

From time to time, you'll need to make a large-scale change to the codebase. Perhaps the code passes a few discrete variables all over the place and you want to aggregate them into a struct. Or you want to restructure a large class used by many clients. Making these changes might require a few days or weeks of work. You could slog ahead with your changes, but life isn't going to be easy for those few days or weeks.

As you begin to make a sweeping change, you typically uncover more places and things that need to change. You may find that the uncovered changes themselves lead to tangential goals that you must first accomplish. A few days grows into a few weeks or more.

You might even run out of time. The business might bump up the priority of another task, forcing you to abandon your trek toward an improved codebase for the time being. If you were working on the mainline (trunk), you've possibly left the code in a worse state by leaving around an incomplete solution. Worse, even with all the effort to date, you might still not have a firm grasp on how far you got and how much work is outstanding. Meanwhile, you've possibly confused and frustrated the rest of your team as your half-reared solution impinges on the code they're changing. And even if you do eventually return to your refactoring initiative, chances are you'll spend ample time coming up to speed on determining where you were and what work remains outstanding.

If you first make your broad changes on a branch, you find that the merge-hell span increases the longer you take to finish. Even incremental merges into your branch may start frustrating you as other developers (with no apparent concern for your health) change the very things you are altering. "Can you please just wait until I'm done?" No.

The Mikado Method, devised by Daniel Brolund and Ola Ellnestam, provides a disciplined approach. You can read extensively about the technique in *The Mikado Method [EB14]*. The remainder of this chapter will briefly overview the process and take you through a short exercise of applying the technique.

8.18 An Overview of the Mikado Method

The complete process follows an initially daunting nine-step cycle. Once you've worked your way through the cycle a few times, however, it won't be far from second nature. You'll ingrain it even faster than the TDD cycle.

1. Draw the Mikado Goal, an end state you want to reach.

2. Implement the goal in a naive manner.

3. Find any errors.

4. Derive immediate solutions to the errors.

5. Draw the immediate solutions as new prerequisites.

6. Revert code to its initial state if there were errors.

7. Repeat steps 2 through 6 for each immediate solution.

8. Check in code if there were no errors; mark the prerequisite goal complete.

9. Is the Mikado Goal met? If so, you are done!

Most of the days or weeks you end up spending on a large refactoring initiative isn't spent on the actual code changes themselves. The size of each change is usually small (although there might be a large volume of changes). The time is instead spent on the requisite analysis and mental probing that you undertake. "Where are all the clients that call this function? If I change them, what other clients are impacted? What does this code do exactly? How am I going to prove that this still works?"

With the Mikado Method, you separate the analysis from time spent applying code changes based on that analysis. You reduce the code changes to a simple change graph, or *Mikado graph*, a script of sorts. The graph depicts a primary goal—the *Mikado Goal*—and a set additional goals on which the primary goal depends. You repeat, often, attempts to apply portions of the change graph to the codebase. The repetition teaches you to make the correct code changes with high confidence and speed.

Building the Mikado graph leaves you with visual summary of the tasks that you must accomplish. You can optionally farm out pieces to your teammates to expedite completing the Mikado Goal. The graph provides a focal point for cross-team communication and coordination.

8.19 Moving a Method via Mikado

We could consider a WAV snippet, or possibly a WAV snippet writer, as an abstraction of its own. The name of our primary class, WavReader, already suggests that anything to do with *writing* snippets is an inappropriate responsibility. Further, we are making extensive changes to the snippet logic and want to isolate the changes to a class with smaller scope.

As a short-term Mikado Goal, we want to extract the writeSnippet() function into its own class, Snippet. Once we complete the immediate goal, we plan to clean the Snippet code considerably. One goal at a time, however.

Given the space constraints of a book, this is a smaller example, but it's no less real than your regular refactoring challenges. It's also surprising how many discrete steps we'll work through, even in a task this small. The Mikado Method will prevent us from dropping the ball (or missing it entirely) while juggling all those steps.

Following the first step of the Mikado Method, we represent our end goal as a couple concentric ellipses. We prefer a large whiteboard as our tool. We want everyone to see the Mikado graph, so it will likely require a lot of space, and we'll be building it out incrementally, making changes as we go.

extract snippet code
from WavReader

Per the second Mikado step, we run straight to the goal line in an extremely naive manner. We *move* (*cut* and paste) the writeSnippet() function across to a new file, Snippet.h, where we wrap it in a class definition.

wav/17/Snippet.h

```cpp
#ifndef Snippet_h
#define Snippet_h

class Snippet {
public:
  void writeSnippet(
      const string& name, istream& file, ostream& out,
      FormatSubchunk& formatSubchunk,
      DataChunk& dataChunk,
      char* data
      ) {
    // ...
  uint32_t secondsDesired{10};
  if (formatSubchunk.bitsPerSample == 0) formatSubchunk.bitsPerSample = 8;
  uint32_t bytesPerSample{formatSubchunk.bitsPerSample / uint32_t{8}};

  uint32_t samplesToWrite{secondsDesired * formatSubchunk.samplesPerSecond};
  uint32_t totalSamples{dataChunk.length / bytesPerSample};

  samplesToWrite = min(samplesToWrite, totalSamples);

  uint32_t totalSeconds { totalSamples / formatSubchunk.samplesPerSecond };

  rLog(channel, "total seconds %i ", totalSeconds);

  dataChunk.length = dataLength(
      samplesToWrite,
      bytesPerSample,
      formatSubchunk.channels);
  out.write(reinterpret_cast<char*>(&dataChunk), sizeof(DataChunk));

  uint32_t startingSample{
     totalSeconds >= 10 ? 10 * formatSubchunk.samplesPerSecond : 0};

  writeSamples(&out, data, startingSample, samplesToWrite, bytesPerSample);

  rLog(channel, "completed writing %s", name.c_str());

  auto fileSize = fileUtil_->size(name);
```

```
    descriptor_->add(dest_, name,
        totalSeconds, formatSubchunk.samplesPerSecond, formatSubchunk.channels,
        fileSize);
    //out.close(); // ostreams are RAII
    }
};
```

```
#endif
```

From WavReader, we create a Snippet object and then invoke its writeSnippet() member function.

wav/17/WavReader.cpp
```
#include "Snippet.h"
// ...
void WavReader::open(const std::string& name, bool trace) {
    // ...
    auto data = readData(file, dataChunk.length); // leak!
➤   Snippet snippet;
➤   snippet.writeSnippet(name, file, out, formatSubchunk, dataChunk, data);
}
```

We compile (Mikado step 3: find any errors). A quick sift through the many compile errors suggests they are because of missing definitions in Snippet.h, which in turn prevent the call to writeSnippet() from compiling.

We decide that there are two prerequisites to accomplishing our Mikado Goal (step 4: devise immediate solutions to the errors):

1. Get a new Snippet class in place by *copying* code.

2. Change WavReader to use that Snippet object (the code change we already tried).

We reflect our refinement to the plan as prerequisites in our Mikado graph (step 5: add immediate solutions as new prerequisites).

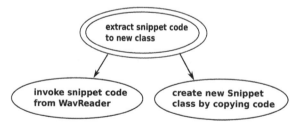

We'll return later to *invoke snippet code from WavReader*. For now let's focus on creating Snippet, an independent class that we can incrementally grow.

Now for the fun part, Mikado step 6. We revert our changes, since we had errors. Yup, we discard the code. We've captured the result of our analysis and attempt in a graph, and it didn't take us long to make the actual changes once we knew what to do. (We'll see how this plays out later.)

If you're using a good source repository tool like git, step 6 can be as simple as this:

```
git reset --hard && git clean -f
```

This is of course potentially data-destroying. <Insert standard legal disclaimer here.>

We move on. Our goal is to successively work our way out toward *leaf* nodes on the graph—goals that we can complete without requiring prerequisite actions—repeating the preceding Mikado steps for each node. We turn our focus to seeing whether *create new Snippet class by copying code* is a leaf. Our first naive attempt is essentially the same code we just tried: copy writeSnippet() to Snippet.h, wrapping it in a class definition and removing WavReader:: from the declaration. We get the compiler to recognize Snippet.h by adding an #include statement to WavReader.

Choosing a naive goal that is likely to fail can be off-putting to some folks. However, it keeps us from endless up-front analysis without any concrete feedback. It also tends to promote building smaller substeps in the Mikado graph.

Again, we receive compiler errors about unrecognized std types, but this time the compiler output is not conflated with problems in WavReader. To expedite getting to the Mikado Goal, we decide to add a using directive to solve the problem. *Yes, this is "bad."* We make a note to clean up the code once we complete the Mikado Goal. (We could add the cleanup as a node on the Mikado graph, but we'll keep this example simple for now.)

Our resolution to the failure becomes a new Mikado Goal.

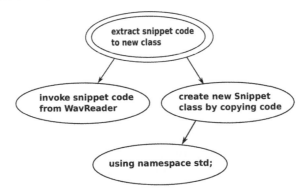

We're being brief on the graph, which suits our needs, though it might not suit yours. Our goal encompasses including the namespace declaration as well as Snippet.h and a class definition.

You might be wondering about the granularity of each step in the Mikado Method. Should you detail every code operation? The answer depends on the size of your challenge, whether you hope to enlist others, and what is implicitly understood by those involved. For most undertakings, you can summarize detailed steps and presume that you'll remember the required specifics or that your teammates will know what to do. If you want someone else to be able to implement the change by reading your graph, you might want to include more detail.

Our graph represents a fairly low-level goal. In the context of a more typically larger Mikado Goal, we might represent our entire goal ("extract snippet code to new class") as but a single node.

We revert once again because of failures that including a using directive should fix. You may still find the notion of reverting code still a bit disturbing, but remember that it's helping you build a very incremental and well-documented road map to a solution.

Reverting will become fairly natural soon. The time it takes you to re-apply code changes will diminish dramatically. Occasionally you'll attempt a naive solution that ends up being a complete dead end. Your comfort level with reverting and starting over will make this a stress-free event.

We now start at the "using namespace std;" goal and attempt to resolve it. We add an #include statement to WavReader. We then add Snippet.h, toss a class shell into it, and add the using directive.

`wav/18/Snippet.h`
```
#ifndef Snippet_h
#define Snippet_h

using namespace std;

class Snippet {
public:
};

#endif
```

That works! Our tests all pass. We have completed the "using namespace std;" goal and could conceivably add it to the codebase without harming anything. It's up to us to decide whether to commit at this point. Since we're using a powerful source versioning tool, we will commit as often as is safe, never mind how small our change is. (Using git, you can squash a bunch of commits into one if having too many creates headaches.)

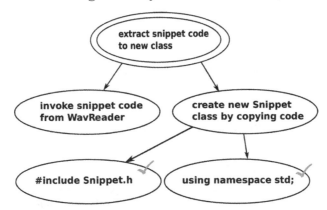

We check the goal off on the Mikado graph. Also, we choose to document adding an #include statement to WavReader on the graph as a completed goal.

We make another attempt to implement the goal "create new Snippet class by copying code." Our errors, smaller now, tell us that several members (both functions and variables) are undefined. We take a look at the functions, dataLength() and writeSamples(), and note that they don't depend upon any member variables. Copying across these functions as the next prerequisite goal makes the most sense.

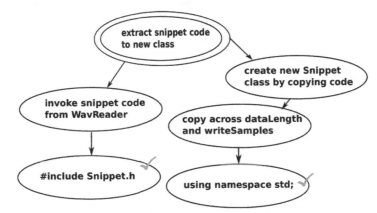

Reverting again and copying across the functions...oops...fails. It turns out there *was* a member variable, channels. (Not only is it missing the trailing underscore that helps us recognize member variables, but the code also reuses the variable for a nested loop. Ugh. We add this to our "fix later" list.)

We revert and shrink our current goal to copying only dataLength().

```
wav/19/Snippet.h
class Snippet {
public:
➤    uint32_t dataLength(
➤          uint32_t samples,
➤          uint32_t bytesPerSample,
➤          uint32_t channels
➤          ) const {
➤        return samples * bytesPerSample * channels;
➤    }
};
```

We commit the code and update the graph.

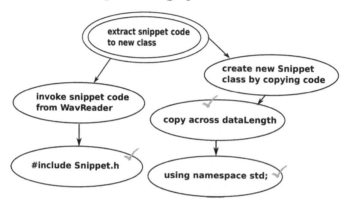

Next, we try copying writeSnippets() and now also writeSamples(). We fail again. The error is undefined member variables. The resolution is to add constructor and member variables to Snippet.h. Can we make the change and commit? You bet! The end result is a checked-off prerequisite goal.

```
wav/20/Snippet.h
class Snippet {
public:
➤    Snippet(shared_ptr<FileUtil> fileUtil,
➤        shared_ptr<WavDescriptor> descriptor,
➤        const std::string& dest,
➤        rlog::RLogChannel* channel)
➤        : fileUtil_(fileUtil)
➤        , descriptor_(descriptor)
➤        , dest_(dest)
➤        , channel_(channel) { }
// ...
➤ private:
➤    shared_ptr<FileUtil> fileUtil_;
➤    shared_ptr<WavDescriptor> descriptor_;
➤    const string dest_;
➤    rlog::RLogChannel* channel_;
};
```

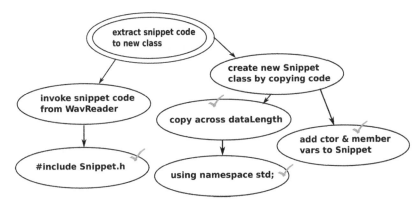

And, yay! After reverting, we're able to successfully copy across writeSnippets() and writeSamples() and then commit. We're also able to check off the final outstanding prerequisite step: "invoke snippet code from WavReader." (The phrasing snippet.writeSnippet is awkward, sure, but we can rename the function once we complete the Mikado Goal.)

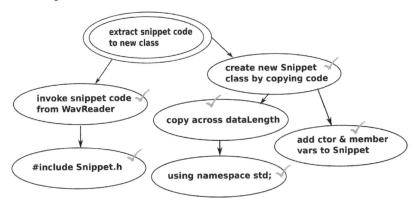

Our code requires a couple small, reasonably safe manual tweaks. We rename the member variable channel to channel_. We also default the channels argument on writeSamples() to 1, replicating its definition from WavReader.h. Despite being small, these changes still contain a small element of risk that we accept (and use to prod ourselves to run a few slower tests).

wav/21/Snippet.h

```
class Snippet {
public:
    // ...
    void writeSnippet(
        const string& name, istream& file, ostream& out,
        FormatSubchunk& formatSubchunk,
        DataChunk& dataChunk,
        char* data
        ) {
```

```
      uint32_t secondsDesired{10};
      if (formatSubchunk.bitsPerSample == 0) formatSubchunk.bitsPerSample = 8;
      uint32_t bytesPerSample{formatSubchunk.bitsPerSample / uint32_t{8}};

      uint32_t samplesToWrite{secondsDesired * formatSubchunk.samplesPerSecond};
      uint32_t totalSamples{dataChunk.length / bytesPerSample};

      samplesToWrite = min(samplesToWrite, totalSamples);

      uint32_t totalSeconds { totalSamples / formatSubchunk.samplesPerSecond };

➤     rLog(channel_, "total seconds %i ", totalSeconds);

      dataChunk.length = dataLength(
            samplesToWrite,
            bytesPerSample,
            formatSubchunk.channels);
      out.write(reinterpret_cast<char*>(&dataChunk), sizeof(DataChunk));

      uint32_t startingSample{
         totalSeconds >= 10 ? 10 * formatSubchunk.samplesPerSecond : 0};

      writeSamples(&out, data, startingSample, samplesToWrite, bytesPerSample);

➤     rLog(channel_, "completed writing %s", name.c_str());

      auto fileSize = fileUtil_->size(name);

      descriptor_->add(dest_, name,
            totalSeconds, formatSubchunk.samplesPerSecond, formatSubchunk.channels,
            fileSize);

      //out.close(); // ostreams are RAII
   }
   void writeSamples(ostream* out, char* data,
         uint32_t startingSample,
         uint32_t samplesToWrite,
         uint32_t bytesPerSample,
➤        uint32_t channels=1) {
➤     rLog(channel_, "writing %i samples", samplesToWrite);
      // ...
   }
};
```

```
wav/21/WavReader.cpp
void WavReader::open(const std::string& name, bool trace) {
   // ...
   auto data = readData(file, dataChunk.length); // leak!

   writeSnippet(name, file, out, formatSubchunk, dataChunk, data);
}
```

Are we done? Not quite. We need to delete the three snippet functions from WavReader. That's a step not yet represented on our Mikado graph. We can add it as a direct prerequisite of the primary goal ("extract snippet code to new class").

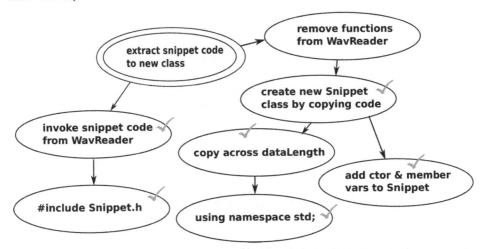

Inserting a new prerequisite without a failure isn't wrong, per se, but it's similar to writing a test that automatically passes. Earlier we chose to copy across functions to Snippet. Perhaps we should have forced the issue and insisted that *moving* the methods was a more direct goal.

No matter, we choose to move forward this time. Our attempt to remove the functions from WavReader fails—this time because of the tests. We add a prerequisite goal, fix the tests, check off the prerequisite, successfully delete the functions from WavReader, and we are done! (We could create a few prerequisite steps for *fix the tests*, but no doubt you get the picture by now.)

You can find the final code in the distribution for the book. But it's always important to see that last check mark applied to the Mikado Goal on the graph! (See Figure 1, *The Mikado Goal with the Last Checkmark*, on page 236.)

From a design stance, we are in a happier place. WavReader worries primarily about reading WAV files, and Snippet worries primarily about writing out snippets from WAV file data. Previously, we had a mild concern about exposing the otherwise-private functions (such as writeSnippet()). They now appear as part of the public interface for Snippet, and our concern diminishes. There's more tweaking we could do, of course, but that's always the case. It's good enough for now, an incremental improvement, and we move on.

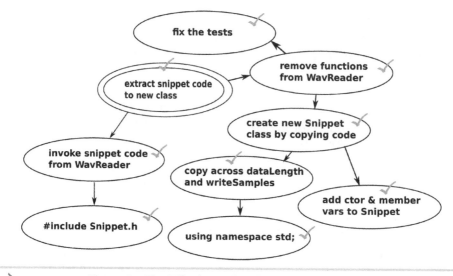

Figure 1—The Mikado Goal with the Last Checkmark

8.20 More Thoughts on the Mikado Method

Even in a small refactoring, as in the previous example, it's easy to get lost and to forget things. Building the Mikado graph helps you track where you've been and where you still need to go.

Working backward is an important part of the Mikado Method. The opposite, typical approach involves taking the code as it is and attempting to refactor toward a somewhat-vague end goal. You have a rough vision of what the solution should look like when you get there.

The forward approach can get you where you want to go, but its haphazard approach creates some problems. It's easy to make a number of code changes that lead nowhere. You resist starting over, because that will require you to decipher all the steps you've made so far. More often than not, you choose to slog forward, potentially leaving some of the less-than-ideal code changes in place.

As mentioned earlier, sometimes you get only halfway to the end goal and are forced to abandon partial solutions. Incomplete refactoring attempts can make the codebase quite confusing.

Where the Mikado Method shines is with a larger refactoring that might take several days or more to accomplish. Since most of that time is exploration and analysis time, you can distill the actual work to a simple script represented by the Mikado graph. Further, the act of repeatedly attempting solutions and reverting when there's a problem means that you will have streamlined the process of reapplying steps in a solution. (You might even keep little snippets of code handy as you build the graph.)

With a complete, well-practiced Mikado graph, you might be able to distill a couple weeks of exploration and analysis into a couple-hour script. You can subsequently apply the script during off-hours in order to effect broad, sweeping changes across your system. You tell your teammates to ensure they've integrated all code before leaving for the day, you apply the script, and worst case you revert it if there are problems. Your team comes in the next morning and pulls your large-scale change. Your work creates minimal impact for them, and vice versa.

You've experienced the core of the Mikado Method. However, I highly recommend exploring the technique in further detail. The Mikado Method book (*Behead Your Legacy Beast: Refactor and Restructure Relentlessly with the Mikado Method [BE12]*) will supply you with everything you'll want to know. It also provides an excellent summary of principles for dealing with legacy systems.

8.21 Is It Worth It?

After working your way through the legacy code examples in this chapter, you might be thinking, "Gee, this is a lot of work. Why bother?"

You already know the cost of not bothering. Your system no doubt reminds you daily of the increasing pain caused by slow and sure degradation. Builds take longer, analysis time takes longer, tests take longer to run, and maintenance takes longer.

Using legacy code management techniques, including the ones overviewed in this chapter, you can turn a system around as long as you have the support and dedication of your entire team. Initial efforts will make only tiny dents in your codebase. But if everyone has the goal of making incremental improvement as they do their "real" work, you'll start to see dramatic payoff in the areas of change. (How long? That depends on your system size, rate of change, difficulty of the code, willingness of the team, and so on.)

Your team must make a choice: either dispense with legacy system salvaging techniques and let the codebase continue to degrade (it will) or put a stake in the ground and decide to change direction for the better. If you choose the latter, help your team derive some ground rules that cover expectations around every bit of code checked in.

8.22 Teardown

Daunting legacy code challenges can scare away the best developers. In this chapter, you've learned that, yet again, an incremental approach works well for tackling the problem. With a modicum of investment around safe code restructuring, you can keep moving forward. You don't need to test everything, just the stuff you need to change!

You've also learned how to make broad, sweeping changes across your system with minimal stress by using the Mikado Method.

In the next chapter, you'll learn how to use TDD to help tackle one of the bigger challenges in software development: how to craft a robust, multithreaded application.

## CHAPTER 9

TDD and Threading

9.1 Setup

The challenge of crafting a solid multithreaded application can eat up hours or days of your time as you struggle to decipher race conditions and deadlocks. Can you test-drive such an application?

Of course, but writing tests that cope with multiple threads isn't easy. The tests themselves must sometimes spawn additional threads and thus can add their own layer of concurrency complexity to the mix.

9.2 Core Concepts for Test-Driving Threads

In this chapter, you'll work through an example that demonstrates a few core concepts around test-driving threads.

Separate threading logic from application logic. The best object-oriented design is one that separates concerns as much as possible. Your design for a multi-threaded application should be no different. Threading is one concern, and your application logic is another. Keep them separate as much as possible and minimize their intermingling. Once again, small methods and classes are a best friend here (see *Benefits of Small Methods*, on page 156).

Sleep is bad, m'kay? Pausing execution in a thread via sleep_for(), in order to wait for a condition to be met, is a poor solution for many reasons. Test runs will be slow and failures sporadic. Often the reaction to a failing "sleeper" test is to increase the wait time, which will increase the average test execution time and, worse, hide any real problems longer.

Throttle down to single-threaded for application-specific tests. Your application code must first work in a single-threaded environment before you introduce threads. Once the threads are in place, you'll still need to demonstrate that the application code performs correctly.

Providing a way to eliminate concurrency concerns for the application-specific unit tests will help you keep your sanity. In a sense, testing multithreaded code moves you into the realm of integration testing. To override threading control, you can either design hooks into your application or introduce test doubles.

Demonstrate concurrency issues before introducing concurrency controls. Throwing concurrency controls (locks and waits) everywhere can severely degrade your application's performance and might not even solve any real concurrency problems. The core theme of the following example involves first writing a test that demonstrates a potential concurrency problem and then exacerbating it to the point where the test fails every time. Demonstrating failure first allows you to remain test-driven. You add only the concurrency control that makes the test pass.

The challenge of test-driving threads still requires careful thought and analysis around how the threads can interleave. Following the previous concepts may minimize the troubles you face and should result in a cleaner solution.

9.3 The GeoServer

The GeoServer provides support for client applications seeking to track the geographic location of large numbers of users (don't worry, it's not for sale to your government, and I'll divulge your location only with your permission). Clients will typically be map-centric phone applications. We'll concentrate only on building parts of the server, so use your imagination as to what the client might look like.

A client registers with the server to begin tracking the location of its user. The client transmits location updates to the server from time to time.

Here's the current code for the GeoServer (including the header file for the Location class):

c9/1/GeoServerTest.cpp
```
#include "CppUTest/TestHarness.h"
#include "CppUTestExtensions.h"
#include "GeoServer.h"

using namespace std;

TEST_GROUP(AGeoServer) {
   GeoServer server;

   const string aUser{"auser"};
   const double LocationTolerance{0.005};
};
```

```
TEST(AGeoServer, TracksAUser) {
    server.track(aUser);

    CHECK_TRUE(server.isTracking(aUser));
}

TEST(AGeoServer, IsNotTrackingAUserNotTracked) {
    CHECK_FALSE(server.isTracking(aUser));
}

TEST(AGeoServer, TracksMultipleUsers) {
    server.track(aUser);
    server.track("anotheruser");

    CHECK_FALSE(server.isTracking("thirduser"));
    CHECK_TRUE(server.isTracking(aUser));
    CHECK_TRUE(server.isTracking("anotheruser"));
}

TEST(AGeoServer, IsTrackingAnswersFalseWhenUserNoLongerTracked) {
    server.track(aUser);
    server.stopTracking(aUser);

    CHECK_FALSE(server.isTracking(aUser));
}

TEST(AGeoServer, UpdatesLocationOfUser) {
    server.track(aUser);
    server.updateLocation(aUser, Location{38, -104});

    auto location = server.locationOf(aUser);
    DOUBLES_EQUAL(38, location.latitude(), LocationTolerance);
    DOUBLES_EQUAL(-104, location.longitude(), LocationTolerance);
}

TEST(AGeoServer, AnswersUnknownLocationForUserNotTracked) {
    CHECK_TRUE(server.locationOf("anAbUser").isUnknown());
}

TEST(AGeoServer, AnswersUnknownLocationForTrackedUserWithNoLocationUpdate) {
    server.track(aUser);
    CHECK_TRUE(server.locationOf(aUser).isUnknown());
}

TEST(AGeoServer, AnswersUnknownLocationForUserNoLongerTracked) {
    server.track(aUser);
    server.updateLocation(aUser, Location(40, 100));
    server.stopTracking(aUser);
    CHECK_TRUE(server.locationOf(aUser).isUnknown());
}
```

c9/1/GeoServer.h

```cpp
#ifndef GeoServer_h
#define GeoServer_h

#include <string>
#include <unordered_map>

#include "Location.h"

class GeoServer {
public:
   void track(const std::string& user);
   void stopTracking(const std::string& user);
   void updateLocation(const std::string& user, const Location& location);

   bool isTracking(const std::string& user) const;
   Location locationOf(const std::string& user) const;

private:
   std::unordered_map<std::string, Location> locations_;

   std::unordered_map<std::string, Location>::const_iterator
      find(const std::string& user) const;
};

#endif
```

c9/1/GeoServer.cpp

```cpp
#include "GeoServer.h"
#include "Location.h"
using namespace std;
void GeoServer::track(const string& user) {
   locations_[user] = Location();
}

void GeoServer::stopTracking(const string& user) {
   locations_.erase(user);
}

bool GeoServer::isTracking(const string& user) const {
   return find(user) != locations_.end();
}

void GeoServer::updateLocation(const string& user, const Location& location) {
   locations_[user] = location;
}
Location GeoServer::locationOf(const string& user) const {
   if (!isTracking(user)) return Location{}; // TODO performance cost?
   return find(user)->second;
}
```

```cpp
std::unordered_map<std::string, Location>::const_iterator
   GeoServer::find(const std::string& user) const {
   return locations_.find(user);
}
```

```cpp
#ifndef Location_h
#define Location_h

#include <limits>
#include <cmath>
#include <ostream>

const double Pi{ 4.0 * atan(1.0) };
const double ToRadiansConversionFactor{ Pi / 180 };
const double RadiusOfEarthInMeters{ 6372000 };
const double MetersPerDegreeAtEquator{ 111111 };

const double North{ 0 };
const double West{ 90 };
const double South{ 180 };
const double East{ 270 };
const double CloseMeters{ 3 };

class Location {
public:
   Location();
   Location(double latitude, double longitude);

   inline double toRadians(double degrees) const {
      return degrees * ToRadiansConversionFactor;
   }

   inline double toCoordinate(double radians) const {
      return radians * (180 / Pi);
   }

   inline double latitudeAsRadians() const {
      return toRadians(latitude_);
   }

   inline double longitudeAsRadians() const {
      return toRadians(longitude_);
   }

   double latitude() const;
   double longitude() const;

   bool operator==(const Location& that);
   bool operator!=(const Location& that);
```

```
    Location go(double meters, double bearing) const;
    double distanceInMeters(const Location& there) const;
    bool isUnknown() const;
    bool isVeryCloseTo(const Location& there) const;

private:
    double latitude_;
    double longitude_;

    double haversineDistance(Location there) const;
};

std::ostream& operator<<(std::ostream& output, const Location& location);

#endif
```

You can refer to the source distribution for other source files not listed here. Hmmm...a comment in GeoServer.cpp! Someone is worried about the potential performance cost of looking up into the locations_ map twice. We'll worry about that later (see Section 10.2, *TDD and Performance*, on page 269).

With the simple stuff out of the way, let's build something meaty into the GeoServer.

Story: Retrieve Nearby Users

As a client user, I want to frequently request a list of all other users (along with their geographic coordinates) whose current position lies within a rectangular map area so that I can represent their positions on a map.

We build an implementation into GeoServer.

c9/2/GeoServerTest.cpp
```cpp
TEST_GROUP(AGeoServer_UsersInBox) {
    GeoServer server;

    const double TenMeters { 10 };
    const double Width { 2000 + TenMeters };
    const double Height { 4000 + TenMeters};
    const string aUser { "auser" };
    const string bUser { "buser" };
    const string cUser { "cuser" };

    Location aUserLocation { 38, -103 };

    void setup() override {
        server.track(aUser);
        server.track(bUser);
        server.track(cUser);
        server.updateLocation(aUser, aUserLocation);
    }
```

```
    vector<string> UserNames(const vector<User>& users) {
        return Collect<User,string>(users, [](User each) { return each.name(); });
    }
};

TEST(AGeoServer_UsersInBox, AnswersUsersInSpecifiedRange) {
    server.updateLocation(
        bUser, Location{aUserLocation.go(Width / 2 - TenMeters, East)});

    auto users = server.usersInBox(aUser, Width, Height);

    CHECK_EQUAL(vector<string> { bUser }, UserNames(users));
}

TEST(AGeoServer_UsersInBox, AnswersOnlyUsersWithinSpecifiedRange) {
    server.updateLocation(
        bUser, Location{aUserLocation.go(Width / 2 + TenMeters, East)});

    server.updateLocation(
        cUser, Location{aUserLocation.go(Width / 2 - TenMeters, East)});

    auto users = server.usersInBox(aUser, Width, Height);

    CHECK_EQUAL(vector<string> { cUser }, UserNames(users));
}
```

c9/2/GeoServer.cpp

```
bool GeoServer::isDifferentUserInBounds(
        const pair<string, Location>& each,
        const string& user,
        const Area& box) const {
    if (each.first == user) return false;
    return box.inBounds(each.second);
}

vector<User> GeoServer::usersInBox(
        const string& user, double widthInMeters, double heightInMeters) const {
    auto location = locations_.find(user)->second;
    Area box { location, widthInMeters, heightInMeters };

    vector<User> users;
    for (auto& each: locations_)
        if (isDifferentUserInBounds(each, user, box))
            users.push_back(User{each.first, each.second});
    return users;
}
```

An Area is a rectangle centered around a Location. It can answer whether it contains a(nother) location. Here's the header file for Area:

```
c9/2/Area.h
#ifndef Area_h
#define Area_h

#include "Location.h"

class Area {
public:
   Area(const Location& location, double width, double height);
   Location upperLeft() const;
   Location upperRight() const;
   Location lowerRight() const;
   Location lowerLeft() const;
   bool inBounds(const Location&) const;

private:
   double left_;
   double right_;
   double top_;
   double bottom_;
};

#endif
```

A User is a container holding the user's name and a location object.

```
c9/2/User.h
#ifndef User_h
#define User_h
#include "Location.h"

class User {
public:
   User(const std::string& name, Location location)
      : name_(name), location_(location) {}
   std::string name() { return name_; }
   Location location() { return location_; }

private:
   std::string name_;
   Location location_;
};
#endif
```

9.4 Performance Requirements

We have a performance challenge. Our product owner indicates that we expect a large volume of users. The initial release should support tracking 50,000 users simultaneously.

We write a test that emulates scaling up to large numbers of users.

```
c9/3/GeoServerTest.cpp
TEST(AGeoServer_UsersInBox, HandlesLargeNumbersOfUsers) {
    Location anotherLocation{aUserLocation.go(10, West)};
    const unsigned int lots {500000};
    for (unsigned int i{0}; i < lots; i++) {
        string user{"user" + to_string(i)};
        server.track(user);
        server.updateLocation(user, anotherLocation);
    }

    auto users = server.usersInBox(aUser, Width, Height);
    CHECK_EQUAL(lots, users.size());
}
```

When we run our tests, we notice a pause while CppUTest executes HandlesLargeNumbersOfUsers, perhaps a second and a half. While that doesn't seem long, that's one test. In a system where you'll eventually have thousands of tests, a measly few dozen slow tests will dissuade you from running them as frequently as you must. We don't want to run the slow HandlesLargeNumbersOfUsers test as part of our fast test suite. Still, we will likely want to run it in the future. When we're done mucking with it, our best bet will be to move HandlesLargeNumbersOfUsers to a different test executable that runs slow tests.

Our code certainly seems slow, but are we certain it's too slow? We rerun our tests using the -v option of CppUTest.

```
build/utest -v
```

Output from the test run confirms that our new test is the culprit.

```
TEST(ALocation, ProvidesPrintableRepresentation) - 0 ms
TEST(ALocation, IsNotVeryCloseToAnotherWhenNotSmallDistanceApart) - 0 ms
TEST(ALocation, IsVeryCloseToAnotherWhenSmallDistanceApart) - 0 ms
TEST(ALocation, CanBeAPole) - 0 ms
TEST(ALocation, AnswersNewLocationGivenDistanceAndBearingVerifiedByHaversine) - 0 ms
TEST(ALocation, AnswersNewLocationGivenDistanceAndBearing) - 0 ms
TEST(ALocation, IsNotEqualToAnotherWhenLatAndLongMatch) - 0 ms
TEST(ALocation, IsNotEqualToAnotherWhenLongDiffers) - 0 ms
TEST(ALocation, IsNotEqualToAnotherWhenLatDiffers) - 0 ms
TEST(ALocation, AnswersDistanceFromAnotherInMeters) - 0 ms
TEST(ALocation, IsUnknownWhenLatitudeAndLongitudeNotProvided) - 0 ms
TEST(ALocation, IsNotUnknownWhenLatitudeAndLongitudeProvided) - 0 ms
TEST(ALocation, AnswersLatitudeAndLongitude) - 0 ms
➤ TEST(AGeoServer_UsersInBox, HandlesLargeNumbersOfUsers) - 1689 ms
TEST(AGeoServer_UsersInBox, AnswersOnlyUsersWithinSpecifiedRange) - 0 ms
# ... (results of other tests omitted)

OK (39 tests, 39 ran, 49 checks, 0 ignored, 0 filtered out, 1798 ms)
```

Still, we don't know that the actual call to usersInBox() is a problem. Perhaps the *Arrange* portion of the test that tracks and updates the location for half a million users is the problem. We need a more granular measurement.

As a temporary probe, we declare an instance of an RAII timer in the test HandlesLargeNumbersOfUsers. Refer to Section 10.2, *TDD and Performance*, on page 269 for further information about the home-grown TestTimer class.

```
c9/4/GeoServerTest.cpp
TEST(AGeoServer_UsersInBox, HandlesLargeNumbersOfUsers) {
   Location anotherLocation{aUserLocation.go(10, West)};
   const unsigned int lots {500000};
   for (unsigned int i{0}; i < lots; i++) {
      string user{"user" + to_string(i)};
      server.track(user);
      server.updateLocation(user, anotherLocation);
   }

   TestTimer timer;
   auto users = server.usersInBox(aUser, Width, Height);

   CHECK_EQUAL(lots, users.size());
}
```

Our probe tells us that the call to usersInBox() takes a bit longer than 200ms on average (we run the tests a few times just to make sure).

```
. . . . . . . . . . . . .
HandlesLargeNumbersOfUsers elapsed time = 219.971ms
. . . . . . . . . . . . . . . . . . . . . . . . .
OK (39 tests, 39 ran, 49 checks, 0 ignored, 0 filtered out, 1823 ms)
```

We remind ourselves that this information is relative and could change dramatically when run on a different machine. But it's enough to suggest there could be a problem.

While 200ms isn't nearly as bad as a second and a half, our product owner is unhappy with the results. We get together with her and discuss options. Together, we derive a new story that should support our need to scale.

Story: Retrieving Nearby Users Is an Asynchronous Request

As a client user, I expect the "retrieve nearby users" request to respond almost immediately. I want to receive each element from the list of nearby users asynchronously so that I can display each on the map as I receive it.

You might have learned that stories shouldn't be technical. That guideline exists to prevent the creation of stories that do not provide verifiable value to the business. Tasks such as "creating the database tables" or "upgrading compiler version" might be essential, but you should execute them only in the context of a business need. Our story necessarily discusses a solution in technical terms, but it does represent a feature that delivers demonstrable and verifiable business value.

9.5 Designing an Asynchronous Solution

Test-driving your code will result in a design that usually differs from what you initially conceived. That's not an excuse to abandon up-front design completely, however. You usually want to start with a road map that provides a reasonable direction.

Just don't invest much time adding detail to the road map, because you'll no doubt need to take a few detours as you travel the road ahead. The sections of the road map that detail the road ultimately not traveled represent a waste of your time.

A GeoServer client wants a simple interface—pass the server a user, a width, and a height, and receive a list of users in response. To support an asynchronous experience, however, the client will need to pass a callback function that handles receiving each in-bounds user.

We want to isolate the client from any details of threading. Here's our proposed design:

- For each incoming request, create a work item and add it to a single work queue. The work item contains all the information needed to determine whether a user lies within an area.

- From the GeoServer, start one or more worker threads. When not processing work, each thread waits for an item to become available in the work queue. Once a thread pulls a work item, it tells it to execute.

We could code all of the logic in the GeoServer class directly, but we won't. Conflating threading and application logic can lead to long, ugly debugging sessions when there's a problem. And there's almost always a problem.

Instead, we will separate the three concerns implied into three classes.

- Work, which represents a work item to be queued and executed

- ThreadPool, which creates worker threads to handle the work queue

- GeoServer, which creates a Work object and sends it to the ThreadPool for execution

The Work class is probably the simplest place to start.

```cpp
#include "CppUTest/TestHarness.h"
#include "Work.h"
#include <functional>
#include <vector>
#include <sstream>

using namespace std;

TEST_GROUP(AWorkObject) {
};

TEST(AWorkObject, DefaultsFunctionToNullObject) {
   Work work;
   try {
      work.execute();
   }
   catch(...) {
      FAIL("unable to execute function");
   }
}

TEST(AWorkObject, DefaultsFunctionToNullObjectWhenConstructedWithId) {
   Work work(1);
   try {
      work.execute();
   }
   catch(...) {
      FAIL("unable to execute function");
   }
}

TEST(AWorkObject, CanBeConstructedWithAnId) {
   Work work(1);
   LONGS_EQUAL(1, work.id());
}

TEST(AWorkObject, DefaultsIdTo0) {
   Work work;
   LONGS_EQUAL(0, work.id());
}
TEST(AWorkObject, DefaultsIdTo0WhenFunctionSpecified) {
   Work work{[]{}};
   LONGS_EQUAL(0, work.id());
}

TEST(AWorkObject, CanBeConstructedWithAFunctionAndId) {
   Work work{[]{}, 1};
   LONGS_EQUAL(1, work.id());
}
```

```
TEST(AWorkObject, ExecutesFunctionStored) {
    bool wasExecuted{false};
    auto executeFunction = [&] () { wasExecuted = true; };
    Work work(executeFunction);
    work.execute();
    CHECK_TRUE(wasExecuted);
}

TEST(AWorkObject, CanExecuteOnDataCapturedWithFunction) {
    vector<string> data{"a", "b"};
    string result;
    auto callbackFunction = [&](string s) {
        result.append(s);
    };
    auto executeFunction = [&]() {
        stringstream s;
        s << data[0] << data[1];
        callbackFunction(s.str());
    };
    Work work(executeFunction);
    work.execute();
    CHECK_EQUAL("ab", result);
}
```

`c9/5/Work.h`

```
#ifndef Work_h
#define Work_h
#include <functional>

class Work {
public:
    static const int DefaultId{0};
    Work(int id=DefaultId)
        : id_{id}
        , executeFunction_{[]{}} {}
    Work(std::function<void()> executeFunction, int id=DefaultId)
        : id_{id}
        , executeFunction_{executeFunction}
        {}
    void execute() {
        executeFunction_();
    }
    int id() const {
        return id_;
    }
private:
    int id_;
    std::function<void()> executeFunction_;
};
#endif
```

The Work test CanExecuteOnDataCapturedWithFunction merely shows how lambdas work and is technically not necessary. It passes immediately. The test serves to reinforce our still-growing knowledge of how to use lambdas and demonstrates how client code can take advantage of a Work object. The function stored in executeFunction captures the locally defined data vector and subsequently demonstrates execution on that data. (The capture specification of [&] tells C++ to capture any referenced variable by reference.) The function also captures the locally defined callbackFunction, to which it then sends the result of concatenating elements from the data vector.

We'll eventually delete the CanExecuteOnDataCapturedWithFunction test. When we get to the point of creating a Work object from the GeoServer code, it will provide us with an example of what we'll want to do.

9.6 Still Simply Test-Driving

We move on to designing the ThreadPool class. Before we introduce threads, we test-drive some building blocks for handling requests.

c9/5/ThreadPoolTest.cpp

```cpp
#include "CppUTest/TestHarness.h"
#include "ThreadPool.h"

using namespace std;

TEST_GROUP(AThreadPool) {
   ThreadPool pool;
};

TEST(AThreadPool, HasNoWorkOnCreation) {
   CHECK_FALSE(pool.hasWork());
}

TEST(AThreadPool, HasWorkAfterAdd) {
   pool.add(Work{});
   CHECK_TRUE(pool.hasWork());
}

TEST(AThreadPool, AnswersWorkAddedOnPull) {
   pool.add(Work{1});
   auto work = pool.pullWork();

   LONGS_EQUAL(1, work.id());
}

TEST(AThreadPool, PullsElementsInFIFOOrder) {
   pool.add(Work{1});
   pool.add(Work{2});
```

```
    auto work = pool.pullWork();

    LONGS_EQUAL(1, work.id());
}

TEST(AThreadPool, HasNoWorkAfterLastElementRemoved) {
    pool.add(Work{});
    pool.pullWork();
    CHECK_FALSE(pool.hasWork());
}

TEST(AThreadPool, HasWorkAfterWorkRemovedButWorkRemains) {
    pool.add(Work{});
    pool.add(Work{});
    pool.pullWork();
    CHECK_TRUE(pool.hasWork());
}
```

c9/5/ThreadPool.h

```
#ifndef ThreadPool_h
#define ThreadPool_h

#include <string>
#include <deque>
#include "Work.h"

class ThreadPool {
public:
    bool hasWork() {
        return !workQueue_.empty();
    }

    void add(Work work) {
        workQueue_.push_front(work);
    }

    Work pullWork() {
        auto work = workQueue_.back();
        workQueue_.pop_back();
        return work;
    }

private:
    std::deque<Work> workQueue_;
};
#endif
```

The test AnswersWorkAddedOnPull must verify that work pulled matches the
same work added. We might have compared addresses, but we decide to make
our tests easier by supporting an ID for Work objects.

```
c9/5/Work.h
#ifndef Work_h
#define Work_h
#include <functional>

class Work {
public:
   static const int DefaultId{0};
   Work(int id=DefaultId)
      : id_{id}
      , executeFunction_{[]{}} {}
   Work(std::function<void()> executeFunction, int id=DefaultId)
      : id_{id}
      , executeFunction_{executeFunction}
      {}
   void execute() {
      executeFunction_();
   }
   int id() const {
      return id_;
   }
private:
   int id_;
   std::function<void()> executeFunction_;
};
#endif
```

9.7 Ready for a Thready!

(Note: CppUTest's memory leak detector is not currently thread-safe. You will want to turn it off for this exercise *only*; see http://www.cpputest.org/node/25 for further information. Turning off memory leak detection will cause problems when coding the exercise in *Legacy Challenges*.)

We want ThreadPool to handle pulling and executing work on its own. We'll need a thread. We create a test that shows how we want to send a Work object to the ThreadPool's add() function and let the pool execute the work asynchronously.

```
c9/6/ThreadPoolTest.cpp
TEST(AThreadPool, PullsWorkInAThread) {
   pool.start();
   condition_variable wasExecuted;
   bool wasWorked{0};
   Work work{[&] {
      unique_lock<mutex> lock(m);
      wasWorked = true;
      wasExecuted.notify_all();
   }};
```

```
    pool.add(work);

    unique_lock<mutex> lock(m);
    CHECK_TRUE(wasExecuted.wait_for(lock, chrono::milliseconds(100),
        [&] { return wasWorked; }));
}
```

Our asynchronous approach means that add() can return control to the test
before the work finishes executing. We need a way to verify that the work
actually gets executed. We use a wait/notify scheme. After creating a
ThreadPool instance, the test defines a condition variable named wasExecuted.
We use this semaphore to prevent the test from completing too quickly.

We create a work item with a function callback that sets a flag and notifies
any threads waiting on the wasExecuted condition. Our expectation is that this
work item will get executed by the ThreadPool's worker thread. After the test
calls pool.add(work), it creates a mutex lock and then waits until the flag is set.
The test fails if the condition variable isn't cleared in a timely fashion.

We add a start() function to our ThreadPool class, deciding that clients must
indicate when the ThreadPool should start its worker threads. Since threads
don't start automatically on instantiation of the ThreadPool, the application-
specific ThreadPool tests we wrote earlier need not worry about any threading
concerns. The start() function kicks off a worker thread, which is joined in the
destructor if initialized.

The worker() function waits for work and then pulls and executes it.

c9/6/ThreadPool.h
```
#include <string>
#include <deque>
➤ #include <thread>
➤ #include <memory>

#include "Work.h"

class ThreadPool {
public:
➤    virtual ~ThreadPool() {
➤        if (workThread_)
➤            workThread_->join();
➤    }

➤    void start() {
➤        workThread_ = std::make_shared<std::thread>(&ThreadPool::worker, this);
➤    }
     // ...
private:
```

```
➤     void worker() {
➤         while (!hasWork())
➤             ;
➤         pullWork().execute();
➤     }

      std::deque<Work> workQueue_;
➤     std::shared_ptr<std::thread> workThread_;
    };
```

On first execution of the test, we receive an error message.

```
..terminate called after throwing an instance of 'std::system_error'
  what():  Operation not permitted
```

A quick web search and a Stackoverflow.com page hit later, we eliminate this error by changing CMakeLists.txt to link in pthread.

c9/6/CMakeLists.txt
```
# ...
target_link_libraries(utest CppUTest)
➤ target_link_libraries(utest pthread)
```

Our test runs successfully...sometimes. We need only glance at our deliberately simplistic implementation to know it's a problem. Were you to create a command-line script that repeatedly runs the tests, you would find that our new threaded test crashes every once in a while with a segmentation fault. We'll investigate another approach: forcing failure directly from the test itself.

9.8 Exposing Concurrency Issues

We want to demonstrate that the worker thread can pull and execute multiple work items from the queue.

c9/7/ThreadPoolTest.cpp
```
TEST(AThreadPool, ExecutesAllWork) {
    pool.start();
    unsigned int count{0};
    unsigned int NumberOfWorkItems{3};
    condition_variable wasExecuted;
    Work work{[&] {
        std::unique_lock<std::mutex> lock(m);
        ++count;
        wasExecuted.notify_all();
    }};
    for (unsigned int i{0}; i < NumberOfWorkItems; i++)
        pool.add(work);
    unique_lock<mutex> lock(m);
    CHECK_TRUE(wasExecuted.wait_for(lock, chrono::milliseconds(100),
            [&] { return count == NumberOfWorkItems; }));
}
```

Our implementation introduces a while loop and a boolean flag that tells the loop to stop when the ThreadPool instance destructs.

```
c9/7/ThreadPool.h
#include <string>
#include <deque>
#include <thread>
#include <memory>
#include <atomic>
#include "Work.h"
class ThreadPool {
public:
   virtual ~ThreadPool() {
      done_ = true;
      if (workThread_)
         workThread_->join();
   }
   // ...
private:
   void worker() {
      while (!done_) {
         while (!hasWork())
            ;
         pullWork().execute();
      }
   }
   std::atomic<bool> done_{false};
   std::deque<Work> workQueue_;
   std::shared_ptr<std::thread> workThread_;
};
```

Unfortunately...no, *fortunately*, our lame implementation hangs the test run every time. Consistent failure when dealing with threads is a great step toward a solution. A bit of analysis suggests that once the test completes, the ThreadPool destructor sets the done_ flag to true and then attempts to join the thread. The thread can't complete because it's stuck in the while loop that waits for work to be available.

We add a conditional to our wait-for-work loop and also break out of the loop if the done_ flag turns on.

```
c9/8/ThreadPool.h
void worker() {
   while (!done_) {
      while (!done_ && !hasWork())
         ;
      if (done_) break;
      pullWork().execute();
   }
}
```

Our tests no longer hang and pass on their first run. Once again, however, they fail intermittently. We need to hit things harder from the test so that it fails every time. A quick attempt at bumping up the number of work items added to the loop doesn't appear to make much difference. Our test needs to add work items from multiple threads created by the test itself.

Let's refactor first. We clean up the two tests that add work to the pool.

```
c9/9/ThreadPoolTest.cpp
TEST_GROUP(AThreadPool_AddRequest) {
   mutex m;
   ThreadPool pool;
   condition_variable wasExecuted;
   unsigned int count{0};
   void setup() override {
      pool.start();
   }

   void incrementCountAndNotify() {
      std::unique_lock<std::mutex> lock(m);
      ++count;
      wasExecuted.notify_all();
   }

   void waitForCountAndFailOnTimeout(
         unsigned int expectedCount,
         const milliseconds& time=milliseconds(100)) {
      unique_lock<mutex> lock(m);
      CHECK_TRUE(wasExecuted.wait_for(lock, time,
            [&] { return expectedCount == count; }));
   }
};

TEST(AThreadPool_AddRequest, PullsWorkInAThread) {
   Work work{[&] { incrementCountAndNotify(); }};
   unsigned int NumberOfWorkItems{1};

   pool.add(work);
   waitForCountAndFailOnTimeout(NumberOfWorkItems);
}

TEST(AThreadPool_AddRequest, ExecutesAllWork) {
   Work work{[&] { incrementCountAndNotify(); }};
   unsigned int NumberOfWorkItems{3};

   for (unsigned int i{0}; i < NumberOfWorkItems; i++)
      pool.add(work);

   waitForCountAndFailOnTimeout(NumberOfWorkItems);
}
```

In the ThreadPool class, we extract code from the destructor to a separate method with an intention-revealing name.

```
c9/9/ThreadPool.h
virtual ~ThreadPool() {
➤    stop();
}
➤ void stop() {
➤    done_ = true;
➤    if (workThread_)
➤        workThread_->join();
➤ }
```

9.9 Creating Client Threads in the Test

Our hypothesis this time is that the spurious failures are caused by data contention around the work queue. The main thread adds to the work queue, the pullWork() function removes from the queue, and the worker often asks whether there's work available in the queue.

Our tests aren't simply failing; they are generating segmentation faults. Concurrent modification of the work queue is the likely suspect. As an attempt at remediation, we first write a test that consistently generates the same failure.

```
c9/10/ThreadPoolTest.cpp
TEST_GROUP(AThreadPool_AddRequest) {
    mutex m;
    ThreadPool pool;
    condition_variable wasExecuted;
    unsigned int count{0};

➤    vector<shared_ptr<thread>> threads;

    void setup() override {
        pool.start();
    }

➤    void teardown() override {
➤        for (auto& t: threads) t->join();
➤    }
➤    // ...
};
// ...
TEST(AThreadPool_AddRequest, HoldsUpUnderClientStress) {
    Work work{[&] { incrementCountAndNotify(); }};
    unsigned int NumberOfWorkItems{10};
    unsigned int NumberOfThreads{10};
```

```
    for (unsigned int i{0}; i < NumberOfThreads; i++)
      threads.push_back(
        make_shared<thread>([&] {
          for (unsigned int j{0}; j < NumberOfWorkItems; j++)
            pool.add(work);
        }));
    waitForCountAndFailOnTimeout(NumberOfThreads * NumberOfWorkItems);
}
```

Our test creates an arbitrary number of work request threads via a for loop. It stores each thread in a vector so that the test can properly join to each upon completion. You can find this cleanup code in the test group's teardown() function.

With NumberOfThreads and NumberOfWorkItems set to one each, we see the same intermittent failure. We experiment with a few combinations until we discover that ten threads sending ten requests each consistently generates a seg fault. Yay!

We add lock guards to each of hasWork(), add(), and pullWork(). These guards use a mutex object (lockObject_) to prevent concurrent access to code in the scope following the lock guard.

```
c9/11/ThreadPool.h
#include <string>
#include <deque>
#include <thread>
#include <memory>
#include <atomic>
#include <mutex>

#include "Work.h"

class ThreadPool {
public:
  // ...
  bool hasWork() {
    std::lock_guard<std::mutex> block(mutex_);
    return !workQueue_.empty();
  }

  void add(Work work) {
    std::lock_guard<std::mutex> block(mutex_);
    workQueue_.push_front(work);
  }

  Work pullWork() {
    std::lock_guard<std::mutex> block(mutex_);
```

```
        auto work = workQueue_.back();
        workQueue_.pop_back();
        return work;
    }
    // ...
    std::atomic<bool> done_{false};
    std::deque<Work> workQueue_;
    std::shared_ptr<std::thread> workThread_;
    std::mutex mutex_;
};
```

The tests pass with no problems. We bump the number of threads up to 200, and things still look good.

9.10 Creating Multiple Threads in the ThreadPool

Is that it? Can we ever know whether we've addressed all concurrency holes? To find the remaining problems, one analysis tactic is to think about any "gaps" we have—where we make an assumption about a fact that might no longer be true because of the actions of other obstreperous threads.

The worker() function seems to remain the only code with any such potential. In worker(), we loop until there is work; each time through the loop establishes and immediately releases a lock within hasWork(). Once there is work, the loop exits, and control falls through to the statement pullWork().execute(). What if, during this short span, another thread has grabbed work?

Our ThreadPool currently manages only a single thread, meaning that the worker() function pulls and executes work one by one, with no such chance for a concurrency problem. Let's get our ThreadPool class to live up to its name and provide support for a pool of threads, not just one.

c9/12/ThreadPoolTest.cpp
```
TEST(AThreadPoolWithMultipleThreads, DispatchesWorkToMultipleThreads) {
    unsigned int numberOfThreads{2};
    pool.start(numberOfThreads);
    Work work{[&] {
        addThreadIfUnique(this_thread::get_id());
        incrementCountAndNotify();
    }};
    unsigned int NumberOfWorkItems{500};

    for (unsigned int i{0}; i < NumberOfWorkItems; i++)
        pool.add(work);

    waitForCountAndFailOnTimeout(NumberOfWorkItems);
    LONGS_EQUAL(numberOfThreads, numberOfThreadsProcessed());
}
```

The test DispatchesWorkToMultipleThreads demonstrates that client code can now start a specified number of threads. To verify that the ThreadPool indeed processes work in separate threads, we first update our work callback to add a thread if its ID is unique. Our assertion compares the thread count specified to the number of unique threads processed.

(Unfortunately, this test has the potential to fail on the rare occasion that one of the threads processes all of the work items. The exercise of eliminating this potential for sporadic failure is left to the reader.)

Changing ThreadPool to support spawning a specified number of threads requires little more than managing a vector of thread objects.

```
c9/12/ThreadPool.h
#include <string>
#include <deque>
#include <thread>
#include <memory>
#include <atomic>
#include <mutex>
#include <vector>

#include "Work.h"

class ThreadPool {
public:
   // ...
   void stop() {
      done_ = true;
      for (auto& thread: threads_) thread.join();
   }

   void start(unsigned int numberOfThreads=1) {
      for (unsigned int i{0u}; i < numberOfThreads; i++)
         threads_.push_back(std::thread(&ThreadPool::worker, this));
   }
   // ...
private:
   // ...
   std::atomic<bool> done_{false};
   std::deque<Work> workQueue_;
   std::shared_ptr<std::thread> workThread_;
   std::mutex mutex_;
   std::vector<std::thread> threads_;
};
```

Our test fails consistently. Given our suspicion around the worker() function, we add a line of code to handle the case where work is no longer available (in other words, where another thread picked it up).

```
c9/12/ThreadPool.h
Work pullWork() {
    std::lock_guard<std::mutex> block(mutex_);

➤   if (workQueue_.empty()) return Work{};

    auto work = workQueue_.back();
    workQueue_.pop_back();
    return work;
}
```

Tests pass again, so things are looking up. We know that our fix directly addressed the concurrency issue at hand.

The reactionary response to concurrency challenges is to throw synchronization at the problem. The end result can be much slower than it needs to be. In contrast, a test-driven approach helps ensure that you synchronize only elements that need it.

9.11 Back to the GeoServer

Now that we've designed and implemented a ThreadPool, let's take advantage of it. The first step is to change usersInBox() to take a listener, or callback, as an argument. We update its code to return User objects to the client via the callback so that they can be asynchronously gathered.

The listener implementation in our test simply tracks users passed to its updated() callback.

```
c9/13/GeoServerTest.cpp
TEST(AGeoServer_UsersInBox, AnswersUsersInSpecifiedRange) {
➤   class GeoServerUserTrackingListener: public GeoServerListener {
➤   public:
➤       void updated(const User& user) { Users.push_back(user); }
➤       vector<User> Users;
➤   } trackingListener;

    server.updateLocation(
        bUser, Location{aUserLocation.go(Width / 2 - TenMeters, East)});

➤   server.usersInBox(aUser, Width, Height, &trackingListener);

➤   CHECK_EQUAL(vector<string> { bUser }, UserNames(trackingListener.Users));
}
```

```
c9/13/GeoServer.h
class GeoServerListener {
public:
    virtual void updated(const User& user)=0;
};
```

```
class GeoServer {
public:
    // ...
    std::vector<User> usersInBox(
        const std::string& user, double widthInMeters, double heightInMeters,
        GeoServerListener* listener=nullptr) const;
    // ...
};
```

c9/13/GeoServer.cpp
```
vector<User> GeoServer::usersInBox(
        const string& user, double widthInMeters, double heightInMeters,
        GeoServerListener* listener) const {
    auto location = locations_.find(user)->second;
    Area box { location, widthInMeters, heightInMeters };

    vector<User> users;
    for (auto& each: locations_)
        if (isDifferentUserInBounds(each, user, box)) {
            users.push_back(User{each.first, each.second});
            if (listener)
                listener->updated(User{each.first, each.second});
        }
    return users;
}
```

As always, we seek incremental change, leaving in place the logic that directly returns a vector of users. This allows us to prove our idea before wasting a lot of time applying a similar implementation to other tests.

We update AnswersOnlyUsersWithinSpecifiedRange, as well as the slow, ignored test HandlesLargeNumbersOfUsers. We factor the common declaration of the GeoServerUserTrackingListener class into the test group. We remove any code that supports the old interest of returning the vector of users directly. Finally, we change usersInBox() to assume the existence of a valid GeoServerListener pointer. Refer to code/c9/14 in the source distribution for the cleaned-up code.

The GeoServer tests AnswersUsersInSpecifiedRange and AnswersOnlyUsersWithinSpecifiedRange must still work. But if we use a ThreadPool, we'll need to introduce waits in our tests, like the ones we coded in ThreadPoolTest. Instead, we choose to introduce a test double that reduces the ThreadPool to a single-threaded implementation of the add() function.

c9/15/GeoServerTest.cpp
```
TEST_GROUP(AGeoServer_UsersInBox) {
    GeoServer server;
    // ...
    class SingleThreadedPool: public ThreadPool {
```

```
    public:
        virtual void add(Work work) override { work.execute(); }
    };
    shared_ptr<ThreadPool> pool;
    void setup() override {
        pool = make_shared<SingleThreadedPool>();
        server.useThreadPool(pool);
        // ...
    }
    // ...
};
TEST(AGeoServer_UsersInBox, AnswersUsersInSpecifiedRange) {
    pool->start(0);
    server.updateLocation(
        bUser, Location{aUserLocation.go(Width / 2 - TenMeters, East)});
    server.usersInBox(aUser, Width, Height, &trackingListener);
    CHECK_EQUAL(vector<string> { bUser }, UserNames(trackingListener.Users));
}
```

We make ThreadPool's add() function virtual in order to allow the override.

Our test explicitly shows the code to start the pool, since it portrays a design choice—that it's the client's responsibility to start the pool. (This important piece of protocol is best described in a discrete test that *you* get to write.)

c9/15/GeoServer.h
```
class GeoServer {
public:
    // ...
    void useThreadPool(std::shared_ptr<ThreadPool> pool);
    // ...
};
```

c9/15/GeoServer.cpp
```
void GeoServer::usersInBox(
        const string& user, double widthInMeters, double heightInMeters,
        GeoServerListener* listener) const {
    auto location = locations_.find(user)->second;
    Area box { location, widthInMeters, heightInMeters };
    for (auto& each: locations_) {
        Work work{[&] {
            if (isDifferentUserInBounds(each, user, box))
                listener->updated(User{each.first, each.second});
        }};
➤       pool_->add(work);
    }
}

➤ void GeoServer::useThreadPool(std::shared_ptr<ThreadPool> pool) {
➤     pool_ = pool;
➤ }
```

Do we need to write a test that interacts with a multithreaded pool? For purposes of test-driving or plain ol' unit testing, *no!* We've demonstrated that a ThreadPool can take on work and dispatch it to different threads. We've demonstrated that the GeoServer logic to determine the users within a rectangle works correctly. And we've demonstrated that the GeoServer logic sends the work to the ThreadPool.

Any further test would be of another sort, and thus we write it only if we need it. Since our interest in using threading was to determine whether we could get immediate response from usersInBox() and have locations returned asynchronously, we *do* want a test.

We add a new test, similar to HandlesLargeNumbersOfUsers, but one that kicks off usersInBox() in a separate thread and uses the main thread to wait for all callbacks. We'll want this test in our slow suite.

```cpp
c9/17/GeoServerTest.cpp
TEST_GROUP_BASE(AGeoServer_ScaleTests, GeoServerUsersInBoxTests) {
   class GeoServerCountingListener: public GeoServerListener {
   public:
      void updated(const User& user) override {
         unique_lock<std::mutex> lock(mutex_);
         Count++;
         wasExecuted_.notify_all();
      }

      void waitForCountAndFailOnTimeout(unsigned int expectedCount,
            const milliseconds& time=milliseconds(10000)) {
         unique_lock<mutex> lock(mutex_);
         CHECK_TRUE(wasExecuted_.wait_for(lock, time, [&]
                  { return expectedCount == Count; }));
      }
      condition_variable wasExecuted_;
      unsigned int Count{0};
      mutex mutex_;
   };
   GeoServerCountingListener countingListener;
   shared_ptr<thread> t;

   void setup() override {
      pool = make_shared<ThreadPool>();
      GeoServerUsersInBoxTests::setup();
   }

   void teardown() override {
      t->join();
   }
};
```

```
TEST(AGeoServer_ScaleTests, HandlesLargeNumbersOfUsers) {
    pool->start(4);
    const unsigned int lots{5000};
    addUsersAt(lots, Location{aUserLocation.go(TenMeters, West)}});

    t = make_shared<thread>(
            [&] { server.usersInBox(aUser, Width, Height, &countingListener); });

    countingListener.waitForCountAndFailOnTimeout(lots);
}
```

(Given that there's a lot of common setup between the prior tests for usersInBox(), the test code you see here is representative of a heavily refactored solution. There's also considerable duplication between the wait/notify concepts implemented in GeoServerCountingListener and those used in ThreadPoolTest code. We'd want to refactor into a construct usable by any thread-oriented test.)

9.12 Teardown

Building multithreaded code is perhaps the most difficult task in software development. Few of us regularly write code that must support concurrency, which makes it that much harder. Using TDD, your approach to multithreaded code moves in the direction of scientific method and away from mystic art. Instead of hoping that your reasoning around concurrent execution is correct and instead of throwing locks and synchronization at any problems, you use TDD as a tool to validate or disprove your hypotheses about where the concurrency issues truly lie.

We've covered all the major topics in test-driven development. You've learned how to test-drive, you've learned how to test after when necessary, and you've learned how to tackle the specific problem of multithreading. Next up, you'll delve into a number of odds-and-ends topics about TDD.

## CHAPTER 10

Additional TDD Concepts and Discussions

10.1 Setup

Not everything always fits into a neat little package. In prior chapters, you learned the core of TDD: the TDD cycle, basic TDD concepts, construction guidelines, how to create and use test doubles, design considerations, how to code quality tests, and how to tackle legacy challenges. You also learned how to test-drive multithreaded code. From the coding stance, that's pretty much it...except for a few odds and ends.

In this chapter, you'll learn about the things that didn't fit elsewhere, including the following:

- *TDD and performance*: This is a bit of soothing around performance concerns to help you sleep at night when practicing TDD.

- *Integration and acceptance tests*: What other kinds of tests do you need, and how do they differ from unit tests?

- *The Transformation Priority Premise (TPP)*: This is a formalized approach for determining what you should code as the next test.

- *Triangulation*: This is a technique to drive generalizations into code (covered as part of the TPP section, though a topic in its own right).

- *Writing assertions first*: This is an alternate approach to crafting a test.

10.2 TDD and Performance

Acceptable performance is an important requirement in any system. It's also likely that many of you are programming in C++ expressly because of its potential for high performance. Throughout the book I've dismissed concerns about performance and directed you to read this section, but that's not because performance isn't important. It is.

Most of what falls under the umbrella of performance testing is neither TDD nor unit testing. This section presents a test-focused strategy for performance optimization and then discusses how unit-level testing can help you execute that strategy. It also discusses how design and performance relate, emphasizing that you should seek optimal design before you attempt to address performance concerns.

Performance considerations are generally nonfunctional requirements. The system needs to respond within half a second to user interaction under a load of up to 10,000 concurrent users. The system needs to process a batch within a four-hour overnight window. And so on. These are integration-level concerns (see Section 10.3, *Unit Tests, Integration Tests, and Acceptance Tests*, on page 278) that require an integrated and deployed system. You can't test these concerns with tests that focus on isolated pieces of logic.

From a (unit-level) test-driven standpoint, you will almost never have the knowledge up front to be able to say, for example, "This function must respond in five microseconds or less." Determining that need would require that you know how the performance characteristics of the function relate to an end-to-end behavioral need. Even if you could derive a specific micro-level performance specification, you'd find it difficult to determine a consistent measurement that would support all your platforms (development, integration, production, and so on) equally well, given variant machine characteristics.

A Performance Optimization Test Strategy

The general strategy for performance optimization is as follows:

- Using a test framework, build and execute driver code that baselines the existing performance of your system for the underperforming case.

- Ensure you have tests that demonstrate the proper behavior of the feature functionality—it's fairly easy to break things when optimizing a system.

- Change the driver code into a test that specifies the current performance baseline. This *baseline test* should fail if an attempted optimization degrades performance.

- Add a second *goal test* to execute the same functionality that passes only if the desired new performance is met. (This might be a second assertion in the baseline test.)

- Determine the performance bottleneck.

- Attempt to optimize code in the area of the bottleneck. You should be able to discern whether an algorithmic-level optimization is possible. (For example, replace an $O(n^2)$ algorithm with one that's $O(n \log n)$). If so, start there. Otherwise, start with optimizations that retain high-quality design and expressiveness. Often, suboptimal use of C++ can be a culprit (for example, how you pass arguments, use assignment, construct new objects, and make misguided attempts to do better than STL containers and/or Boost).

- Ensure your unit and acceptance tests still pass.

- Run the baseline test; if it fails (in other words, if the new performance is worse), discard the modifications and try again.

- Run the goal test; if it passes, ship it!

- Otherwise, you might be able to solve the performance challenge by identifying the next-biggest bottleneck, attempting to improve its performance, and so on. However, it's also possible that your optimization attempt was an inappropriate choice. Preferably, take note of the relative amount of improved performance, and shelve the code changes. Seek another optimization and repeat, checking each time to determine whether the optimizations will add up to the performance goal.

  If you do incrementally incorporate an optimization, ensure you update the criteria in the baseline test.

Here are some extremely important themes as you attempt to optimize:

- Run the performance tests on a machine with the same characteristics as the production target. Results from tests run elsewhere may not accurately depict the impact of optimizations in production, making such optimizations potentially a waste of time or worse.

- Don't assume anything. Your notions as to what should be optimized are often wrong. Always measure before and after.

- Get the design right first, and only then introduce optimizations. Introduce optimizations that sacrifice on maintainable design and readability only if you absolutely must. Get the design right first!

Relative Unit-Level Performance Tests

Unit-level performance tests can help you along the way, but you can't use them to determine whether you've met the performance goal. Instead, you'll use them as tools to help you probe at pieces of the puzzle.

In this section, you'll learn a simple technique for obtaining the average execution time of a tested function. The time will only have meaning as it relates to optimization attempts against that same function.

In the rare case where you are able to define a unit-level need up front, you can test-drive that need using the Relative Unit-Level Performance Tests (RUPTs, I'll call them). Otherwise, you'll be in the realm of Test-After Development (TAD).

The steps for a RUPT are much as you would expect.

1. Create a loop that executes the behavior you want to time repeatedly, perhaps 50,000 times. Looping through should eliminate any aberrations due to startup overhead or clock cycles. You'll want to make sure the compiler does not optimize away any of the behavior you want to time.

2. Just prior to the loop, capture the current time in a variable called start.

3. Just after the code that executes the behavior, capture the current time in stop. Your relative measurement is the elapsed time of stop - start.

4. Run the RUPT and note the elapsed time. Seek an elapsed time of a few seconds, and alter the number of loop iterations if needed.

5. Increase the number of iterations by an order of magnitude. Run the test and ensure that the elapsed time similarly increases. If not, your RUPT cannot accurately characterize your optimization attempt. Determine the reason and fix it.

6. Run the RUPT a few more times. If the elapsed times vary wildly, you do not have a valid RUPT. Determine the reason and fix it. Otherwise, note the average.

7. Attempt to optimize the code.

8. Run the RUPT several times and note the average.

9. If the improvement was considerable, run your performance and goal baselines. Otherwise, discard the change.

The RUPTs are probes that you should discard or relegate to a slush pile of meaningless code that you might plunder later. By no means should they appear in your production unit test suite.

Seeking to Optimize GeoServer Code

Let's work through a short example of creating a RUPT.

```
c9/24/GeoServerTest.cpp
TEST(AGeoServer_Performance, LocationOf) {
    const unsigned int lots{50000};
    addUsersAt(lots, Location{aUserLocation.go(TenMeters, West)});

    TestTimer t;
    for (unsigned int i{0}; i < lots; i++)
        server.locationOf(userName(i));
}
```

The TestTimer class is a simple class that spits out a performance measurement on the console once it goes out of scope. Refer to the following section (*The TestTimer Class*, on page 275) for its implementation.

Here's the code we're testing. Both locationOf() and isTracking() execute a find call. Is this an unacceptable performance sink?

```
c9/24/GeoServer.cpp
bool GeoServer::isTracking(const string& user) const {
    return find(user) != locations_.end();
}

Location GeoServer::locationOf(const string& user) const {
    if (!isTracking(user)) return Location{}; // TODO performance cost?

    return find(user)->second;
}
```

We set the number of iterations to 50,000 and run the test a few times. We note an average time (50ms on my machine).

We bump the number of iterations up to 500,000 and run the tests another few times, again noting the average. We expect to see the average correspondingly increase roughly by an order of magnitude, and it does. The average of three runs clocks in at 574ms. If it hadn't increased, we would have needed to figure out how to prevent the C++ compiler from cleverly optimizing the operations executed in the loop. (Under gcc, you can add an assembler instruction: asm("");.)

We change the code to eliminate the second call to the find() function.

```
c9/25/GeoServer.cpp
Location GeoServer::locationOf(const string& user) const {
    // optimized
    auto it = find(user);
    if (it == locations_.end()) return Location{};
    return it->second;
}
```

Yes, a comment is prudent (you might provide a bit more explanation, though). Programmers in a good TDD shop should always be seeking to improve the quality of the code. Without a comment to indicate why you coded it that way, a good programmer is likely to clean up a messier, performance-optimized chunk of code. And since you don't typically run performance-related acceptance tests continually, it may be difficult to discern the code change that caused a goal performance test to fail.

We rerun the performance tests and note a new average of 488ms, which is 86ms faster than before. The math says that introducing the redundant call to find() incurs a cost of almost 18 percent performance degradation per request. It sounds substantial and may well be, but remember that we're running half a million requests. Per request, we're talking 0.17 *micro*seconds difference.

These are facts about the changes in behavior from a performance perspective. While they provide only relative, isolated meaning value, they're not suppositions. We know that our attempt at code optimization was successful—that it improved the execution time of this small unit of code. That's more than we knew before. It's also more than most developers know after they attempt to optimize a solution.

The question becomes, is it useful? At this point, we would run our baseline and goal performance tests and determine whether the optimization is necessary. If not, it serves only to make the code more difficult, and we happily discard it.

The cost of retaining the optimization appears minimal. The locationOf() function increases by only a line of code, to three simple lines. Many useful optimizations create code that's considerably harder to decipher and maintain.

Yet there's another potential optimization route that would be easy to apply, given that we have a clean design. In a GeoServer that tracks tens or hundreds of thousands of users, a user cache might make a lot more sense. During any given time period, the server will likely be asked the locations of a much smaller subset of users, and many requests will duplicate a prior request. Currently, the lookups into the location_ map all funnel through the accessor function find(). We could change the code in find() to use a cache. Client code would retain its current, expressive design. In contrast, introducing a cache in a class where code always directly accesses member variables can represent a prolonged effort.

A clean design helps with performance optimization in a couple ways. First, it's easier to pinpoint performance problems using a profiler when you have small functions. Second, small classes and functions increase your potential to consider creative optimizations. They also increase the ease of making the changes once you've identified the problem. In contrast, imagine a 500-line function that hides a performance bottleneck. It will take you longer both to determine the problem and to resolve it. (And a 500-line function will almost never have sufficient tests to give you the confidence to make appropriate optimization changes.)

The TestTimer Class

The TestTimer class is a hastily coded, simple tool that you can place at any appropriate point in your test. It prints the elapsed time when it goes out of scope, as well as explanatory text passed to the constructor. Using the no-arg constructor results in the name of the current test being printed.

c9/25/TestTimer.h
```
#ifndef TestTimer_h
#define TestTimer_h

#include <string>
#include <chrono>

struct TestTimer {
    TestTimer();
    TestTimer(const std::string& text);
    virtual ~TestTimer();

    std::chrono::time_point<std::chrono::system_clock> Start;
    std::chrono::time_point<std::chrono::system_clock> Stop;
    std::chrono::microseconds Elapsed;
    std::string Text;
};

#endif
```

c9/25/TestTimer.cpp
```
#include "TestTimer.h"
#include "CppUTest/Utest.h"
#include <iostream>

using namespace std;

TestTimer::TestTimer()
    : TestTimer(UtestShell::getCurrent()->getName().asCharString()) {
}

TestTimer::TestTimer(const string& text)
    : Start{chrono::system_clock::now()}
    , Text{text} {}
```

```
TestTimer::~TestTimer() {
    Stop = chrono::system_clock::now();
    Elapsed = chrono::duration_cast<chrono::microseconds>(Stop - Start);
    cout << endl <<
        Text << " elapsed time = " << Elapsed.count() * 0.001 << "ms" << endl;
}
```

You can and should enhance the timer class to suit your needs. You might want to make it thread-safe (it is not). You might prefer using a different platform-specific timing API, or your system might provide a separate implementation for C++11's high-resolution clock. You might be able to measure using a smaller duration (nanoseconds!), or perhaps you need to use larger durations. Or you might choose to simply insert the three or four lines required directly into your tests, though that seems like unnecessary effort.

Performance and Small Functions

C++ programmers burn billions of anxiety calories annually over the performance cost of a member function call. For that reason, many programmers resist the notion of creating small functions and classes. "I don't want to extract that code into a separate function; it might represent a performance problem." Yet compilers today are very smart beasts, able to optimize code in many cases better than you ever could by hand.

Rather than base your resistance to small functions on old wives' tales, consider real data.

c9/26/GeoServer.cpp
```
Location GeoServer::locationOf(const string& user) const {
    // optimized
    auto it = locations_.find(user);
    if (it == locations_.end()) return Location{};
    return it->second;
}
```

Before manually inlining the find() function, the average execution time was 488ms. After inlining, the average execution time was 476ms, a statistically insignificant difference across a half-million executions.

Was the find() function inlined by the compiler in the first place? If we force the issue and tell gcc to not inline the function, as follows, there is no substantial difference in execution time (474ms):

c9/27/GeoServer.h
```
std::unordered_map<std::string, Location>::const_iterator
    find(const std::string& user)
    const
    __attribute__((noinline));
```

One other interesting aspect of small functions is that C++ compilers are more likely able to inline them in the first place. With larger functions, you actually decrease the compiler's chances to optimize code.

The reality is that not extracting code to smaller methods represents poor design, and it does virtually nothing to improve the performance of your application. Performance experts already know this.

And don't trust me, I could well be an old wife. Trust your own measurements.

Recommendations

Many thoughts on performance optimization are based on folklore and the experience of others. Don't trust the experiences of others. Then again, since most everyone is saying the same thing, it's probably worth listening to what all consistently say. And I'll add my experiences to the mix.

My Experiences with Optimization

As a programmer, I've been involved in a number of optimization attempts. As a consultant, I've worked with several programmers for whom optimization was their primary job (one on a system needing to consistently process 20,000+ transactions per second). In both realms, I've experienced and witnessed successes that stemmed from a disciplined approach similar to the previous recommendations. I've also seen a spectacular failure as one company hired high-priced consultants to desperately attempt to fix a live, production-scaling challenge by stabbing haphazardly at optimization attempts.

A few key elements appear to provide the best defense against performance challenges.

- A solid architecture, where the word *architecture* means the layout of all those things that will be very difficult to change once the system is in place. Specifically, where are the communication points between components (distributed across clients and servers), and how does the architecture support scaling without requiring code changes (in other words, by beefing up hardware)?

- A solid but flexible design with clean code, complete with tests that provide the flexibility to make confident, dramatic changes when needed.

- Performance goal tests from day one that specify future scaling expectations. If you expect to deploy your application initially to a dozen users and then ultimately to a hundred, you want to know as soon as possible when new code puts the scaling target at risk.

As far as code-level optimization goes, I have yet to see evidence, or hear it from a performance expert, that refutes the classic advice of getting the design right before attempting optimization and then optimizing only if absolutely necessary.

I've witnessed many wrong-headed optimization attempts. In some cases, they were based on misguided or downright false folklore (sometimes even based on another language!). In other cases, the performance recommendations were once true, but later compiler and runtime improvements rendered them obsolete.

Some code-level optimizations do fall in the category of "free." For example, passing by reference in C++ is usually more efficient than passing by value, and it costs nothing in expressiveness. Where such optimizations do not degrade readability or ease of maintenance, go for 'em. Otherwise, save the optimization attempts for later, much later.

10.3 Unit Tests, Integration Tests, and Acceptance Tests

TDD is a programmer practice to help you incrementally drive the design of code. You've learned how to use it to verify small bits of C++ logic by writing unit tests, which in turn allows you to continually shape the design of the code at will.

For the purposes of this book, *unit* means a small piece of isolated logic that affects some systematic behavior. The word *isolated* in the definition suggests you can execute the logic independently. This requires decoupling the logic from dependencies on things such as service calls, APIs, databases, and the file system. (Technically, independent code should also be decoupled from any other code, but a pragmatic approach suggests that it's not necessary for all code to be purely isolated.) As emphasized elsewhere in this book (for example, Section 4.3, *Fast Tests, Slow Tests, Filters, and Suites*, on page 86), the important aspect of unit tests for purposes of doing TDD is that they're darn fast.

By definition, unit tests are inadequate. Since they verify small isolated pieces of code, they can't demonstrate the correctness of an end-to-end deployed-and-configured solution. In addition to unit tests, your system requires tests that will provide high confidence that you are shipping a high-quality product. Depending on the shop, these tests include what might be called system tests, customer tests, acceptance tests, load tests, performance test, usability tests, functional tests, and scalability tests, to name a few (some of these are more or less the same thing). All of these tests verify against an integrated software product and are thus *integration tests*.

Who defines the integration tests varies depending on the circumstance. Typically, they are defined by people in one or more of three roles: tester, programmer, and customer.

Per the Agile community, customer tests are any tests defined to demonstrate that the software meets business needs. In an Agile process, these tests are defined before development in order to provide a specification of sorts to the development team—a close analog to the TDD process. Agile proponents will often refer to customer tests defined up front as *acceptance tests* (ATs). If the development team builds software that gets all the test to pass, the customer agrees to accept the delivery of the software.

How Do TDD and Acceptance Testing Relate?

Driving the development of a system by defining ATs up front is quite similar to driving the development of bits of logic using TDD. In fact, many teams employing the use of ATs in this manner refer to the process as *Acceptance Test–Driven Development* (ATDD).

You can read volumes about how acceptance tests might fit into your development process, what kind of tools are used, what the tests should look like, and so on. If you understand TDD, though, you already have most of the mentality needed to understand what ATDD is all about and how to succeed in its practice.

The important distinction between TDD and ATDD is who defines the tests (and therefore who consumes the tests). With TDD, programmers are responsible for defining unit tests in a programmatic language. As such, there's no expectation that anyone but programmers will read or otherwise consume the unit tests. (That doesn't mean you can slouch on their readability, however!)

With ATDD, customers (which might include people like product owners or business analysts) are responsible for defining ATs based on business needs. They rarely do this in a vacuum. Insights and information from everyone else on the team, including testers and programmers, are required to build robust acceptance tests. Everyone consumes tests created using ATDD.

You will find a number of books on ATDD, including *Specification by Example [Adz11]* and *ATDD By Example [Gä12]*. When searching, you may also find relevant information using the search phrase *specification by example*.

Programmer-Defined Integration Tests

As a programmer, you always have the option to create programmer-facing integration tests. A few well-chosen integration tests can be invaluable, and your shop might even require them. You might include tests that exercise your data access layer directly to get more immediate information and more direct failure messages about discrepancies between the code and the data store's definition. Or, you might use a series of smoke tests to quickly determine whether a deployment isn't configured properly.

However, integration tests are difficult to maintain. Since they deal with software deployed to a configured environment that must interact with the wild world of external services and data stores, integration tests are brittle. Keeping the tests up-to-date and running across all your deployment environments is a sizable challenge.

You're best off if you code only as many integration tests as you absolutely need, and no more. As a strategy, either seek to position an integration test as a customer test (that your customer is willing to take on) or remove its dependencies and use it as a unit test that demonstrates code-level logic.

If your team has already produced a number of tests using a unit testing tool like Google Test, you may find that many of them are really integration tests pretending to be unit tests. These tests attempt to verify bits of code logic but have many unfortunate dependencies that relegate them to the realm of slow and brittle integration tests.

Find the time to triage your integration tests. For each, determine one of the following four actions:

- Clean up the integration test and sell it to the business as an AT.
- Convert it to a fast unit test by removing its dependencies.
- Retain it as a rare nonacceptance integration test.
- Delete it.

Immediately remove any remaining integration tests from the fast unit test suite.

Overlap Between TDD and ATDD

One of the bigger sources of anxiety for a team practicing both ATDD and TDD is that some of the tests will inevitably appear to overlap, particularly if everything gets properly test-driven. Most acceptance tests usually represent functional interests and will demonstrate how the system works from the perspective of an actor interacting with the system. When doing TDD, you'll test-drive this user interface layer also. Is this duplicate effort?

Indeed, the tests at the interface layer will appear similar. However, remember that the audiences and goals for each set of tests are different. No one else will ever read your programmer tests. The acceptance tests, in contrast, are designed to be read by anyone.

The tests that a customer defines will provide broad coverage against a piece of end-to-end functionality. Since they will typically run quite slowly, such tests cannot hope to have high levels of coverage against the countless possible combinations and permutations. You can code TDD-produced unit tests, however, to rapidly slam through a much larger number of combinations and permutations.

From a design stance, the amount of overlap should be low. In a well-designed system, the interface layer is thin and largely a delegator to business domain classes (and there should be many more non-interface-layer classes than interface-layer classes). Thus, most of your unit tests against the interface layer need to simply prove that work was delegated appropriately.

From a pure testing standpoint, the benefit of having both unit tests and acceptance tests provides you with an extra layer of protection. Inevitably, your unit tests will miss covering an important scenario. Having a layer of tests above unit level that are defined by a different set of brains will provide you with an invaluable safety net. You'll write some tests to represent scenarios the business didn't think about, and vice versa. (But don't forget that nets are comprised of lots of gaping holes.)

Defects represent an incorrect or missing unit test. You correct defects by following a test-driven approach. First write a test that demonstrates the existence of the defect by failing. Then write the code that gets the unit test (and any corresponding acceptance tests) to pass.

10.4 The Transformation Priority Premise

Throughout the book, I've suggested that the next test you write is the one that grows your system by the smallest increment. If you strictly adhere to the TDD cycle, seeking to always demonstrate test failure before you move on, you will learn what it means to take too large a step. (See Section 3.5, *Getting Green on Red*, on page 60.) Following the last rule of simple design—minimize the total number of classes and methods (see Section 6.2, *Simple Design*, on page 141)—will also help by teaching you to avoid overdesigning your system and putting more code in place than need be. The third rule of TDD (Section 3.4, *The Three Rules of TDD*, on page 59) also tells you to put no more code in place than necessary to pass your tests.

Small steps are important, because larger steps will waste more time as your system grows. Create an overblown solution that far exceeds what a test demands, and you'll likely need to overhaul a good chunk of code a few tests down the road.

Success with TDD requires the ability to grow a system by small increments. You will shorten your path to mastery by having the will to back up and try a different route when necessary. (You'll need a good version control tool to support changing course.)

Another tool for determining your next test is Robert C. Martin's *Transformation Priority Premise (TPP)*, which proposes a priority list of transformations. Each transformation represents an alteration of code from specific to slightly more generic. Using the TPP, you choose a test that drives the highest-priority transformation against your existing code. The premise is that following the TPP allows you to grow your system using the smallest possible increments. Use the TPP, and you'll avoid the test-driven weeds.

You can find the original list of priorities at http://web.archive.org/web/20130113152824/http://cleancoder.posterous.com/the-transformation-priority-premise. The priority list isn't foolproof; it's a premise, after all. Other subsequent blog posts have proposed slightly tweaked priority lists.

Meet the Transforms

The TPP likely sounds a bit complex to you. Working through an example is worth 1,024 words. We'll step through the Soundex example from *Test-Driven Development: A First Example* using the *transform priority list* (TPL) in its original posting order.

({}→nil)	Replace no code with code that employs nil.
(nil→constant)	Replace nil with a constant.
(constant→constant+)	Replace a simple constant with a more complex constant.
(constant→scalar)	Replace a constant with a variable or argument.
(statement→statements)	Add unconditional statements.
(unconditional→if)	Split the execution path.
(scalar→array)	Replace a variable/argument with an array.
(array→container)	Replace an array with a more complex container.
(statement→recursion)	Replace a statement with a recursive call.
(if→while)	Replace a conditional with a loop.
(expression→function)	Replace an expression with a function.
(variable→assignment)	Replace the value of a variable.

(Source: http://en.wikipedia.org/wiki/Transformation_Priority_Premise.)

Given that we've already worked through Soundex, we'll focus our discussion on the code transformations and leave other chatter about the code to a minimum. Our first test differs slightly; we'll handle padding the zeros immediately.

tpp/1/SoundexTest.cpp
```cpp
TEST(SoundexEncoding, AppendsZerosToWordForOneLetterWord) {
    Soundex soundex;
    auto encoded = soundex.encode("A");

    CHECK_EQUAL("A000", encoded);
}
```

The failure to compile the test represents our first need for a transformation —from no code into code returning nil, the simplest possible transformation, topmost on the TPL. Passing the compile "test" requires an implementation for encode() that returns a nil value...but leaves us with a failing unit test.

```
tpp/1/Soundex.h
class Soundex {
public:
   std::string encode(const std::string& word) const {
      return nullptr;
   }
};
```

We fix the failing unit test by transforming nil into a constant, the second transform on the list.

```
tpp/2/Soundex.h
class Soundex {
public:
   std::string encode(const std::string& word) const {
➤     return "A000";
   }
};
```

Triangulation

The last time we built Soundex, we drove out the hard-coded constant "A" as part of the refactoring step. We introduced a variable in order to eliminate the duplication of the string literal from test to production code. We also decided that eliminating the *specific* hard-coded value in production code would make it consistent with the *general* goal stated by the test name (RetainsSoleLetterOfOneLetterWord). In doing so, we were following the spirit of the TPP: to incrementally generalize the code. Each transform on the TPL represents a move from specific to slightly more generic.

This time around, we will drive out the hard-coding by using a technique known as *triangulation*, first described in *Test Driven Development: By Example [Bec02]*. Triangulation involves approaching the same behavior from a different angle, by adding a second test case.

```
tpp/3/SoundexTest.cpp
TEST(SoundexEncoding, AppendsZerosToWordForOneLetterWord) {
   CHECK_EQUAL("A000", soundex.encode("A"));
➤  CHECK_EQUAL("B000", soundex.encode("B"));
}
```

We could make the failing test pass by introducing an if statement: if the first letter of the word is *A*, return "A100"; otherwise, return "B100". Introducing that code would represent the transform *(unconditional→if)*. We choose the higher-priority transform *(constant→scalar)*.

```
tpp/3/Soundex.h
class Soundex {
public:
    std::string encode(const std::string& word) const {
        return word + "000";
    }
};
```

Scanning the Test List

Where next? We want to grow the code using the highest-priority transformation possible. Let's take a look at the list of remaining tests:

```
PadsWithZerosToEnsureThreeDigits
ReplacesConsonantsWithAppropriateDigits
ReplacesMultipleConsonantsWithDigits
LimitsLengthToFourCharacters
IgnoresVowelLikeLetters
IgnoresNonAlphabetics
CombinesDuplicateEncodings
UppercasesFirstLetter
IgnoresCaseWhenEncodingConsonants
CombinesDuplicateCodesWhen2ndLetterDuplicates1st
DoesNotCombineDuplicateEncodingsSeparatedByVowels
```

We currently have an unconditional statement consisting of an expression using a constant and a scalar. That shrinks the relevant portion of the TPL a bit, since we need not worry about transforms from {}, nil, array, and if.

Any code requiring the ability to take a substring, string length, or even uppercase a letter would require introducing a function call (perhaps; approaches not requiring functions might work if we're creative in our thinking). For now we'll avoid tests that seem to require these functions and seek instead something of higher priority.

It looks as if most tests that don't require a function call are likely to require a conditional. Hard-coding specific constants only gets us so far before we require code that can make a decision. Let's tackle a bit of encoding.

```
tpp/4/SoundexTest.cpp
TEST(SoundexEncoding, ReplacesConsonantsWithAppropriateDigits) {
    CHECK_EQUAL("A100", soundex.encode("Ab"));
}
```

We generalize our code using the *(unconditional→if)* transformation.

```
tpp/4/Soundex.h
class Soundex {
public:
    std::string encode(const std::string& word) const {
➤       std::string code("");
➤       code += word[0];
➤       if (word[1])
➤           code += "100";
➤       else
➤           code += "000";
➤       return code;
    }
};
```

When using the TPP, relax a little and avoid prematurely tightening up the code. You must still eliminate duplication and retain expressiveness, but leave simple if statements and while loops alone for a while. You may find that avoiding more complex forms (ternary operators and for loops, for example) makes it easier to spot better opportunities for good refactoring.

Our solution is a bit rote, which is not a problem. It's not very clear and exhibits a bit of duplication. That's a problem. We refactor.

```
tpp/5/Soundex.h
class Soundex {
public:
    std::string encode(const std::string& word) const {
        std::string code("");
➤       code += head(word) + encodeTail(word);
➤       return zeroPad(code);
    }

➤   char head(const std::string& word) const {
➤       return word[0];
➤   }

➤   std::string encodeTail(const std::string& word) const {
➤       if (word[1] == 0) return "";
➤       return "1";
➤   }

➤   std::string zeroPad(const std::string& code) const {
➤       if (code[1] != 0)
➤           return code + "00";
➤       return code + "000";
➤   }
};
```

The code in zeroPad() still kind of stinks, doesn't it? We make a second refactoring pass.

```
tpp/6/Soundex.h
std::string zeroPad(const std::string& code) const {
    return code + (hasEncodedCharacters(code) ? "00" : "000");
}

bool hasEncodedCharacters(const std::string& code) const {
    return code[1] != 0;
}
```

What did I just say about fancy constructs like the ternary operator? It seemed to make sense here for eliminating a bit of code duplication. If it causes us any headaches, we'll back up and eliminate it.

We add a second assert to drive in encoding for a second consonant. In terms of an implementation, we could introduce a second if statement, but that would only introduce a duplicative construct and not generalize the code. We seek the next highest transform that applies: *(scalar→array)*.

```
tpp/7/SoundexTest.cpp
TEST(SoundexEncoding, ReplacesConsonantsWithAppropriateDigits) {
    CHECK_EQUAL("A100", soundex.encode("Ab"));
    CHECK_EQUAL("A200", soundex.encode("Ac"));
}
```

```
tpp/7/Soundex.h
class Soundex {
public:
    Soundex() {
        codes_['b'] = "1";
        codes_['c'] = "2";
    }
    // ...
    std::string encodeTail(const std::string& word) const {
        if (word[1] == 0) return "";
        return codes_[static_cast<size_t>(word[1])];
    }
    // ...
private:
    std::string codes_[128];
};
```

We complete the consonant list and do a little bit of refactoring for expressiveness.

```
tpp/8/Soundex.h
class Soundex {
public:
    Soundex() {
        initializeCodeMap();
    }
```

```cpp
void initializeCodeMap() {
    codes_['b'] = codes_['f'] = codes_['p'] = codes_ ['v'] = "1";
    codes_['c'] = codes_['g'] = codes_['j'] = codes_ ['k'] =
        codes_['q'] = codes_['s'] = codes_['x'] = codes_['z'] = "2";
    codes_['d'] = codes_['t'] = "3";
    codes_['l'] = "4";
    codes_['m'] = codes_['n'] = "5";
    codes_['r'] = "6";
}
// ...

std::string encodeTail(const std::string& word) const {
    if (word[1] == 0) return "";
    return codeFor(word[1]);
}

std::string codeFor(char c) const {
    return codes_[static_cast<size_t>(c)];
}

// ...
};
```

We scan the list of remaining tests again. Most still appear to require introducing a function call. Higher than a function call in priority, though, are two transformations that support looping, one via a while loop and the other via recursion. One test—ReplacesMultipleConsonantsWithDigits—appears to demand a looping solution.

Later versions of the TPL contain some priority variations. We're using the original version, which promotes transformations to a recursive solution over transformations to looping solutions. The emphasis has been a topic of debate. In a functional language, such as Erlang or Clojure, you want a recursive solution. In C++, the choice is up to you. You may want to compare the performance of a recursive solution to its iterative counterpart.

We'll stick with the original TPL ordering and find out where that takes us.

Growing out the code with the TPP has resulted in a solution where each step of the way so far has been a small, incremental change. We haven't required any major overhauls to existing code. Introducing a recursive solution is no different.

tpp/9/SoundexTest.cpp
```cpp
TEST(SoundexEncoding, ReplacesMultipleConsonantsWithDigits) {
    CHECK_EQUAL("A234", soundex.encode("Acdl"));
}
```

```
tpp/9/Soundex.h
std::string encode(const std::string& word) const {
    std::string code("");
➤   code += head(word);
➤   encodeTail(word, code);
    return zeroPad(code);
}
// ...
➤ void encodeTail(const std::string& word, std::string& code) const {
    if (word[1] == 0) return;
➤   code += codeFor(word[1]);
➤   encodeTail(tail(word), code);
}
➤ std::string tail(const std::string& word) const {
➤   return word.substr(1);
➤ }
```

There are a couple problems. First, it doesn't work. We need to adjust the number of zeros that get padded to the encoding. Second, hey! That's a function call to substr(), and we chose an increment that introduced recursion because it was higher than one requiring a function call.

The TPP, a premise and work in progress, isn't a panacea that will solve all your coding challenges. It's also not a hard set of rules. The goal of the TPL is to help you seek the next smallest increment. In our case, the recursive solution demonstrated itself to be a good incremental step, and that's what's important. That we had to introduce a function call to implement the solution seems an acceptable bending of the priority rules. (Recursive solutions dealing with collections—a string is but a collection of characters—typically require a function that extracts the tail of the collection. It's often the best approach.)

Fixing the padding problem can be done in a few ways. One is to initialize either a counter or a string representing the zeros to be padded and then decrement it each time an encoded character gets appended in encodeTail(). However, that requires an assignment statement, which is lower on the priority list. Simpler, and higher on the TPL, is to update the zeroPad() function to take into account the length of the code.

```
tpp/10/Soundex.h
const static size_t MaxCodeLength{4};
std::string zeroPad(const std::string& code) const {
➤   return code + std::string(MaxCodeLength - code.length(), '0');
}
```

We realize that encodeTail() can be "backed up" to operate on the first (0th) element of the word if we call it with the tail of the word (instead of with the complete word). We make the change, which allows us to make a small additional refactoring to increase the expressiveness of the code.

```
tpp/11/Soundex.h
std::string encode(const std::string& word) const {
    std::string code(1, head(word));
    encode(tail(word), code);
    return zeroPad(code);
}
void encode(const std::string& word, std::string& code) const {
    if (word.empty()) return;
    code += codeFor(head(word));
    encode(tail(word), code);
}
const static size_t MaxCodeLength{4};
std::string zeroPad(const std::string& code) const {
    return code + std::string(MaxCodeLength - code.length(), '0');
}
```

We love having the tests to allow us to make sure our change works!

Our core algorithm is tight and clear. As with the last time we built Soundex, the encode() function clearly states the policy for encoding a word. Let's see whether we can knock out the rest of the tests. We choose IgnoresVowelLikeLetters. It seems like it would require introduction of only an if statement.

```
tpp/12/SoundexTest.cpp
TEST(SoundexEncoding, IgnoresVowelLikeLetters) {
    CHECK_EQUAL("B234", soundex.encode("BAaEeIiOoUuHhYycdl"));
}
```

The test passes with no code changes! As always, we want to think about why (see Section 3.5, *Getting Green on Red*, on page 60), but it's of less concern now. If we're strictly adhering to the TPP, the premise is that it's guiding us to incorporate the smallest possible increments. Tests that pass prematurely are thus unlikely to represent building too much code.

The test passes because the codes_ lookup array returns null for any elements not contained. Appending null results in no change to the code. Moving on, we discover that IgnoresNonAlphabetics passes for the same reason.

We introduce CombinesDuplicateEncodings.

```
tpp/13/SoundexTest.cpp
TEST(SoundexEncoding, CombinesDuplicateEncodings) {
    CHECK_EQUAL(soundex.codeFor('f'), soundex.codeFor('b'));
    CHECK_EQUAL(soundex.codeFor('g'), soundex.codeFor('c'));
    CHECK_EQUAL(soundex.codeFor('t'), soundex.codeFor('d'));
    CHECK_EQUAL("A123", soundex.encode("Abfcgdt"));
}
```

Our test run dies with an std::length_error. A quick look at the backtrace (using gdb under Linux) indicates that the problem is in the zeroPad() function. If the code ends up being more than three characters, zeroPad() attempts to construct a string with a negative number of '0' characters.

Does that mean we should switch our focus to LimitsLengthToFourCharacters? The TPP suggests no, since it requires introducing a length() function call, while CombinesDuplicateEncodings should require only a conditional statement. However, the exception means we are not seeing a direct failure of our test, since the code can't run to completion. We decide to seek a failing test first and make a note to return and try the alternate route if we get into trouble. We disable the test and tackle LimitsLengthToFourCharacters instead.

tpp/14/SoundexTest.cpp
```
TEST(SoundexEncoding, LimitsLengthToFourCharacters) {
    CHECK_EQUAL(4u, soundex.encode("Dcdlb").length());
}
```

A small change incorporating *(expression→function)* passes the test.

tpp/14/Soundex.h
```
  void encode(const std::string& word, std::string& code) const {
➤     if (word.empty() || isFull(code)) return;
      code += codeFor(head(word));
      encode(tail(word), code);
  }
➤ bool isFull(std::string& code) const {
➤     return code.length() == MaxCodeLength;
➤ }
```

We reintroduce CombinesDuplicateEncodings. It runs cleanly and fails as expected. A solution involves passing the head of the word to the recursive encode() function as a basis for comparison to the current digit to be added. We try it with a name hastily chosen to avoid conflict with the head() function name.

tpp/15/Soundex.h
```
  std::string encode(const std::string& word) const {
      std::string code(1, head(word));
➤     encode(tail(word), code, head(word));
      return zeroPad(code);
  }
  void encode(const std::string& word, std::string& code,
➤         char H) const {
      if (word.empty() || isFull(code)) return;
➤     std::string digit = codeFor(head(word));
➤     if (digit != codeFor(H))
➤         code += codeFor(head(word));
➤     encode(tail(word), code, head(word));
  }
```

Our solution demands refactoring. Since we use both head and tail parts of the word to be encoded in encode(), we simplify its signature by passing in the entire word. We also choose a nonconflicting name and add a helper function to clarify what's going on. (Every line in encode() changed, so none of its lines is highlighted, nor is the new function isSameEncodingAsLast().)

```
tpp/16/Soundex.h
std::string encode(const std::string& word) const {
    std::string code(1, head(word));
    encode(word, code);
    return zeroPad(code);
}

void encode(const std::string& word, std::string& code) const {
    auto tailToEncode = tail(word);
    if (tailToEncode.empty() || isFull(code)) return;

    auto digit = codeFor(head(tailToEncode));
    if (isSameEncodingAsLast(digit, word))
        code += digit;
    encode(tailToEncode, code);
}

bool isSameEncodingAsLast(
        const std::string& digit,
        const std::string& word) const {
    return digit != codeFor(head(word));
}
```

A similar test, CombinesDuplicateCodesWhen2ndLetterDuplicates1st, should require roughly the same transformation. (We specify the assertion's expected value as starting with a lowercase letter, since we haven't yet tackled the concern of uppercasing the first letter in a Soundex encoding.)

```
tpp/17/SoundexTest.cpp
TEST(SoundexEncoding, CombinesDuplicateCodesWhen2ndLetterDuplicates1st) {
    CHECK_EQUAL("b230", soundex.encode("bbcd"));
}
```

The test passes because we already pass the entire encoding to the recursive encode() function. Another similar test passes, too.

```
tpp/18/SoundexTest.cpp
TEST(SoundexEncoding, DoesNotCombineDuplicateEncodingsSeparatedByVowels) {
    CHECK_EQUAL("J110", soundex.encode("Jbob"));
}
```

We're a little nervous about all these tests passing, so we think of another scenario to allay our concerns. It passes. Sheesh.

```
tpp/18/SoundexTest.cpp
TEST(SoundexEncoding, CombinesMultipleDuplicateEncodings) {
    CHECK_EQUAL("J100", soundex.encode("Jbbb"));
}
```

(There is one more possible alternate scenario, based on the fact that *H* and *W* might be treated differently, depending upon who you talk to. Since we ignored this potential difference last time we built Soundex, we'll keep things simple and ignore it again.)

We tackle uppercasing the first letter, which also requires we update the expectation in CombinesDuplicateCodesWhen2ndLetterDuplicates1st.

```
tpp/19/SoundexTest.cpp
TEST(SoundexEncoding, CombinesDuplicateCodesWhen2ndLetterDuplicates1st) {
    CHECK_EQUAL("B230", soundex.encode("bbcd"));
}

TEST(SoundexEncoding, UppercasesFirstLetter) {
    CHECK_EQUAL("A", soundex.encode("abcd").substr(0, 1));
}
```

The transformation, though simple, involves a function call. (We could code the logic of ::toupper() ourselves, but I don't think that's what the TPP wants us to do.) You've seen our implementation of upper(), so it's not shown here.

```
tpp/19/Soundex.h
std::string encode(const std::string& word) const {
➤    std::string code(1, toupper(head(word)));
    encode(word, code);
    return zeroPad(code);
}
```

Hmm. The last test prods a thought. What if the first letter is already uppercased in the input and the second letter is the same but in lowercase?

```
tpp/20/SoundexTest.cpp
TEST(SoundexEncoding, IgnoresCaseWhenEncodingConsonants) {
    CHECK_EQUAL(soundex.encode("BCDL"), soundex.encode("bcdl"));
}
```

Aha! Failure, and a quick resolution.

```
tpp/20/Soundex.h
std::string codeFor(char c) const {
➤    return codes_[static_cast<size_t>(lower(c))];
}
```

Are we done? We didn't add PadsWithZerosToEnsureThreeDigits. It does pass immediately, but we choose to add it for documentation purposes.

```
tpp/21/SoundexTest.cpp
TEST(ASoundexEncoding, PadsWithZerosToEnsureThreeDigits) {
    CHECK_EQUAL("I000", soundex.encode("I"));
}
```

The second time around is always a bit easier, but our success this time is due more to using the TPP than with our knowledge of the problem. We made a few judgment calls along the way and might not have even followed the TPP to the letter, but our end result speaks for itself.

Here's the core algorithm from our TPP-test-driven solution:

```
tpp/21/Soundex.h
std::string encode(const std::string& word) const {
    std::string code(1, toupper(head(word)));
    encode(word, code);
    return zeroPad(code);
}

void encode(const std::string& word, std::string& code) const {
    auto tailToEncode = tail(word);
    if (tailToEncode.empty() || isFull(code)) return;

    auto digit = codeFor(head(tailToEncode));
    if (isSameEncodingAsLast(digit, word))
        code += digit;

    encode(tailToEncode, code);
}
```

And here's the core algorithm from our non-TPP-test-driven solution:

```
c2/40/Soundex.h
std::string encode(const std::string& word) const {
    return stringutil::zeroPad(
        stringutil::upperFront(stringutil::head(word)) +
            stringutil::tail(encodedDigits(word)),
        MaxCodeLength);
}

std::string encodedDigits(const std::string& word) const {
    std::string encoding;
    encodeHead(encoding, word);
    encodeTail(encoding, word);
    return encoding;
}

void encodeHead(std::string& encoding, const std::string& word) const {
    encoding += encodedDigit(word.front());
}
```

```cpp
void encodeTail(std::string& encoding, const std::string& word) const {
    for (auto i = 1u; i < word.length(); i++)
        if (!isComplete(encoding))
            encodeLetter(encoding, word[i], word[i - 1]);
}
void encodeLetter(std::string& encoding, char letter, char lastLetter) const {
    auto digit = encodedDigit(letter);
    if (digit != NotADigit &&
            (digit != lastDigit(encoding) || charutil::isVowel(lastLetter)))
        encoding += digit;
}
```

I know which version I'd like to maintain. Not only did the TPP generate the simpler algorithm, it required less effort along the way.

The Transformation Priority Premise remains a premise, albeit a darn good one. The more I apply it, the happier I am with the outcome. But it's an advanced topic, one that is likely more palatable given a solid basis of understanding of how TDD plays out without it.

The TPP also demands a bit more up-front thought for each pass through the TDD cycle. You must think about a few things.

- What implementation of the current test has a higher priority? Are there more-creative approaches that you could dream up?

- Does another test have a higher priority than the one that seems to be begging to go next?

- Just what *are* the other tests in the mix? Maintaining a test list (*Test Lists*, on page 17) becomes almost essential to employing the TPP.

TDD without the disciplined add-on of the TPP works well enough, as you've seen throughout this book. But adopt the TPP, and you'll do more than survive—you'll thrive.

10.5 Writing Assertions First

As you interact more with other TDD practitioners, you'll find there seem to be as many ways to approach TDD as there are practitioners. Consider yourself fortunate if you manage to avoid vociferous debates about the One True Way. For example, you'll find developers who heavily promote One Assert per Test and others who think it's an overblown goal. You'll find practitioners who insist that the test's name be in an exact format and many others who don't worry about the name at all.

Is there a right or a wrong? Most of the time, you'll find proponents on both sides of each argument offering solid rationale behind their preference.

Throughout this book, you'll have noted my style, and no doubt there are things you find more appealing than others. My recommendation is to try the things you find alien or disagree with before dismissing them out of hand. You just might uncover a pleasant surprise. I long ago balked at One Assert per Test (see Section 7.3, *One Assert per Test*, on page 178) and now find value 99 percent of the time in adhering to it.

Ultimately, beyond following the TDD cycle and producing high-quality code, everything else is a matter of style and preference. Remember, however, that it's your duty as a professional to seek better ways of doing things. Regardless of how you feel about my style or yours, I hope we don't find each other working the same way two years from now.

Assert-Act-Arrange?

The order of steps in TDD's red-green-refactor cycle isn't negotiable, but the order in which you code individual statements within a test is. Many developers work top-down. They start by coding the *Arrange* portion of the test, move on to the *Act* statement, and finally *Assert* the results. There's nothing wrong with that approach (it happens to be the way I usually work), but a potentially better approach is to write the assertion first.

By now, you're used to designing test code against yet-to-be-written production code. The notion of writing an assert against nonexistent test code shouldn't be too shocking. But why would you want to?

Writing the assertion first makes you think about the *goal* of the behavior you're adding. It further forces you to describe what it means for the goal to have been achieved. If this is a struggle, perhaps you don't have enough information yet to continue writing the test.

More importantly, writing assertions first will grow your use of programming by intention, which should result in clearer tests. Your assertions will be declarations of intent. In contrast, if you've already written *Arrange* and *Act*, your assertion is more likely to be an implementation-specific detail.

Examples First, or Second at Least

Let's run through a quick example. We need a test for the GeoServer that returns an empty location when a user is no longer tracked.

`c9/18/GeoServerTest.cpp`
```
TEST(AGeoServer, AnswersUnknownLocationWhenUserNoLongerTracked) {
    CHECK_TRUE(locationIsUnknown(aUser));
}
```

We know what the outcome need be, so we express it, though we don't yet know how to implement the code that will verify that outcome. In the test group, we define a function that supplies default, failing behavior.

```
c9/18/GeoServerTest.cpp
TEST_GROUP(AGeoServer) {
    // ...
    bool locationIsUnknown(const string& user) {
        return false;
    }
};
```

After verifying that the test fails, we move on to defining the action.

```
c9/19/GeoServerTest.cpp
TEST(AGeoServer, AnswersUnknownLocationWhenUserNoLongerTracked) {
    server.stopTracking(aUser);

    CHECK_TRUE(locationIsUnknown(aUser));
}
```

Letting the name of our test be our guide, we provide an *arrangement*.

```
c9/20/GeoServerTest.cpp
TEST(AGeoServer, AnswersUnknownLocationWhenUserNoLongerTracked) {
    server.track(aUser);

    server.stopTracking(aUser);

    CHECK_TRUE(locationIsUnknown(aUser));
}
```

And finally, letting failure be our guide, we provide an implementation for the intention-revealing function locationIsUnknown().

```
c9/20/GeoServerTest.cpp
TEST_GROUP(AGeoServer) {
    // ...

    bool locationIsUnknown(const string& user) {
        auto location = server.locationOf(user);

        return location.latitude() == numeric_limits<double>::infinity();
    }
};
```

"Well, that's ugly," says someone on our team. We add the capability to ask whether a location is the "unknown" location to the Location class itself and change the implementation of locationIsUnknown().

```
c9/21/GeoServerTest.cpp
TEST_GROUP(AGeoServer) {
  // ...
  bool locationIsUnknown(const string& user) {
    return server.locationOf(user).isUnknown();
  }
};
```

We immediately recognize that the helper no longer pulls its weight, so we eliminate it entirely.

```
c9/22/GeoServerTest.cpp
TEST(AGeoServer, AnswersUnknownLocationWhenUserNoLongerTracked) {
  server.track(aUser);

  server.stopTracking(aUser);

  CHECK_TRUE(server.locationOf(aUser).isUnknown());
}
```

Oh! What was the point? Perhaps we could have designed the Location class that way from the get-go and written the single-line assertion immediately.

Maybe, maybe not. What's important is that the assertion ends up being a simple declaration, not how it got that way. Often you'll require a few dense, detailed code statements to verify a test. Even if you didn't start by declaring an intent for your assertion, you'll want to ensure you extract those few dense lines to an explanatory helper function.

Assertions requiring more than a single-line declaration create additional work for the test reader.

```
c9/23/GeoServerTest.cpp
TEST(AGeoServer, AnswersUnknownLocationWhenUserNoLongerTracked) {
  server.track(aUser);

  server.stopTracking(aUser);

  // slow reading. Fix this.
  auto location = server.locationOf(aUser);
  CHECK_EQUAL(numeric_limits<double>::infinity(), location.latitude());
}
```

Not only does the reader need to step through two lines of assertion, they need to determine the dependency between them (the expected argument portion of the CHECK statement references the location returned by the prior line). The reader must also mentally piece these two lines together into a single concept (that the location for the user is unknown).

10.6 Teardown

You learned about a few loose-end TDD topics in this chapter. As far as TDD is concerned, that's it!

No, just kidding, that's *not* it. This book provides enough for you to start digging deep into TDD practice, but a wealth of TDD discoveries awaits you. Test-drivers around the world are experimenting with the TPP and seeing how far they can go with it. Behavior-driven developers everywhere (Google *BDD*) are seeking to further bridge the gap between the business and development teams. Acceptance test-drivers are trying to better understand the boundaries between TDD and ATDD.

The nuts and bolts of TDD are easy in contrast to the real challenge: how do you succeed with TDD in a software development team? Once you're test-infected, you'll want other developers to understand your enthusiasm. And you'll want to improve your practice of the craft. In the next chapter, you'll learn some strategies and tactics for growing and sustaining TDD.

## CHAPTER 11

Growing and Sustaining TDD

11.1 Setup

You've learned the who, what, how, why, and when of TDD. If you continue to practice TDD regularly to the point where you're convinced of its benefits, you'll someday become *test-infected*[1]—you'll insist on using it as your primary programming tool. You'll quickly realize, however, that not everyone feels that way. Even if you're part of a team that's supposed to be test-driving your code, you'll find varying levels of adherence and support. You'll also encounter resistance and apathy, often based on lack of information. And even if your team is able to surmount the initial hurdle of getting everyone on board, you'll find it a challenge to keep things from degrading over time—much like your codebase. Sustaining TDD is not easy.

This chapter provides you with an assortment of ideas to help you sustain your ability to practice TDD. You'll learn about the following:

- How to respond to inquiries about and challenges to TDD
- Overviews of studies demonstrating benefits attained by using TDD
- How to avoid the "bad test death spiral"
- How to employ pair programming to sustain and review TDD efforts
- How to use katas and dojos to better your practice of TDD
- How to avoid abuse of code coverage metrics
- How continuous integration is an essential foundation for TDD
- Questions to help you derive standards for TDD practice
- Where to go for more information about community TDD practice

---

1. See "Test Infected: Programmers Love Writing Tests," http://junit.sourceforge.net/doc/testinfected/testing.htm.

11.2 Explaining TDD to Nontechies

You may be test-infected, but your enthusiasm won't be enough to win over converts, particularly those who aren't programmers by trade. This section provides you with two tools to support your conversations with noninfected people. First, a fabricated conversation will prepare you for typical questions by providing some brief but strong elevator-pitch answers. Second, a list of studies on the effectiveness of TDD will provide you with ammunition to help convince those who need research before they're willing to listen.

TD what?

Q.: What's TDD?

A.: It's a software development technique used by programmers to incrementally design their system.

Q.: What does it look like?

A.: Programmers break their work down into small chunks, or units. For each small chunk, they write a small test that provides an example of how that code should behave. They then write a small chunk of code that makes the test pass. Once they get the test passing, they make sure they clean up any design or coding deficiencies that they just introduced in the small chunk of code.

Q.: So they're just writing unit tests?

A.: They are using a unit test framework to help specify how every small bit of added code should behave. So yes, they're writing unit tests, but the tests also double as documentation on what the system does.

Q.: So they're just writing unit tests.

A.: They are using unit tests as a way of incrementally designing the system. The tests get written first.

Q.: I'm not seeing how this is any different from unit testing. So what if you write the tests first?

A.: You get different results. Writing tests after doesn't change anything. They might help the programmer find a few problems, but unit testing alone don't otherwise compel programmers to change the design and quality of the codebase.

Q.: But TDD does change the design and quality?

A.: A few studies (see Research on TDD, on page 303) demonstrate that there are fewer defects when applying TDD. Further, doing TDD allows programmers to continually change the code and design for the better.

Q.: How does TDD allow programmers to change the code any more than they did before?

A.:   *Every small chunk of code a programmer adds to the system comes into existence only once a test exists to demonstrate its behavior. That means all of the code in the system gets tested. Having tests for everything means that a programmer can make constant small changes as needed to keep the code clean. Without sufficient tests, the old adage of "If it ain't broke, don't fix it" is reality.*

Q.:   *So what? Can't we save time by not worrying about how clean the code is?*

A.:   *Some studies show that 80 percent of software efforts are expended on maintaining (not fixing) the software.[2] In a codebase growing to a large size over time, things that might have taken a couple hours to accomplish can bloat to taking several days. Even a simple question—"What does the software do in this case?"—can require a several-hour foray into a complex codebase on the part of the programmer.*

Q.:   *Doesn't that say something about the quality of programmers? Can't they just write clean code in the first place?*

A.:   *Think of programming like writing. Even good writers continually rework their sentences and paragraphs to improve understanding. And they still get presented with numerous problems by editors who review their work. It's enough of a challenge to write code that simply provides expected behaviors, so step 1 is to put the correct code in place. Step 2 is to improve the code by making sure it's part of a maintainable design.*

Q.:   *I'm still not understanding why you couldn't achieve the same results with just writing a few unit tests after the code gets completed.*

A.:   *For human reasons, it doesn't happen. First, once most programmers write the code, they think they're done with the "real" work. They have high confidence in their capability to write the correct code and are often satisfied by a simple manual test or two. So, they have little interest in writing additional unit tests to prove what they already know. They also feel they crafted the code well enough and less frequently take advantage of the tests to clean up their code. Programmers, in general, do as little as needed to get past what they view as management mandates. Second, time schedule pressures often dominate. Anything done after the fact—after the code gets built—gets short shrift.*

Q.:   *Shouldn't we allow programmers to use their own professional judgment about what code should be tested? Isn't some code so simple that it doesn't really need that level of testing? Aren't they wasting time by this rigid insistence on testing everything?*

A.:   *Most systems don't really have all that much code that's so simple it can't break, so there's not much testing effort to be saved here. I'm also no longer surprised by how many defects programmers uncover in areas of the system that look innocuous and perfect. Defects are very costly in many ways, and having*

---

2.   http://en.wikipedia.org/wiki/Software_maintenance

fewer by virtue of practicing TDD provides great savings. You'll also waste far less time on the seemingly simple challenge of figuring out how the existing system behaves.

Every programmer who's gone back and tried to write unit tests against a large, existing codebase reports that it's very difficult. The primary reason is that the codebase wasn't structured with testing in mind, and as a result it's much harder to hook tests into the system. The typical programmer punts when faced with such challenges.

Q.: I've heard some programmers say that you really only need 70 percent of your system unit-tested and that you can cover the rest with functional tests.

A.: Are you comfortable with 30 percent of your system not being covered with tests that provide fast feedback? If there are defects in that near-third of your system, you'll find out about them much later. If you need to rework that portion of the system to accommodate new features, it will be a considerably slower effort. You'll either need to add unit tests (which is harder with existing code) or use slower functional tests to make sure you don't break things.

Q.: Having fast tests for all logic makes sense. But don't you end up with a lot more code, in the form of tests, that you have to maintain?

A.: No. Most systems are probably double the size they need to be, if not more. Part of that is a by-product of the inability to safely remove redundant chunks of code as programmers add them. Anecdotal evidence suggests that yes, the amount of unit testing code might be equivalent, or even a little larger than, a production codebase. But a codebase created entirely by following TDD will likely be half the size. So, it comes out in the wash, plus you get all of the other side benefits of TDD.

Q.: I've heard that TDD doesn't really catch a lot of bugs. Doesn't this suggest that it's all a waste of time?

A.: TDD prevents you from integrating defects into the system in the first place. You always write a test, you always get it to pass, and if it doesn't pass, you fix it before committing the code. It seems like a better approach than checking in code and finding out only much later that it doesn't work or breaks something else.

Q.: You're making TDD sound like it's a silver bullet.

A.: TDD is a great tool, but it is only one tool in what needs to be a good-sized toolbox. TDD is insufficient. Proving that small units of code work in isolation doesn't prove that you can string them together in order to produce a desired functional need. You need also acceptance tests, which might also include performance tests, load tests, other forms of integration tests, and perhaps some level of exploratory testing.

Research on TDD

There have been a number of research studies on the effectiveness and cost of TDD. The following table summarizes results from George Dinwiddie's wiki page at StudiesOfTestDrivenDevelopment:[3]

Author/Year	Key Findings
Nagappan, N. et al, 2008	TDD reduced defect density 40 percent to 90 percent, at a cost of a 15 percent to 35 percent increase in *initial* development time.
Braithwaite, K., 2008[4]	This suggests there is an inverse relationship between TDD and code complexity.
Sanchez, J.C., et. al., 2007	TDD produced defect density below industry standards. TDD may decrease the degree to which code complexity increases as software ages.
Bhat, T., 2006	There was a significant increase in the quality of code produced using TDD, with an initial cost increase of at least 15 percent.
Siniaalto, M. 2006	TDD generated substantial productivity improvements in some cases and decreased productivity (but improved quality) in two of thirteen cases.
Erdogmus, H. 2005	Students who wrote more tests tended to be more productive. Minimum quality increases linearly with the number of programmer tests.
George, B. et al., 2003	TDD developers produce higher-quality code (passing 18 percent more functional tests) and take 16 percent more time for development. Programmers who write tests after produced insufficient tests.

One study alone might not be very convincing, but a half dozen showing similar results makes a strong case for these two claims:

- TDD results in higher-quality code.
- TDD increases the initial cost of development.

What's missing are studies based on the following hypotheses:

- TDD decreases long-term costs.
- The tests created by TDD reduce the time required to answer questions about system behavior.

3.   http://biblio.gdinwiddie.com/biblio/StudiesOfTestDrivenDevelopment
4.   "Measuring the Effective of TDD on Design," http://s3-eu-west-1.amazonaws.com/presentations2012/5_presentation.pdf

Most folks who continue to practice TDD don't do so based on the results of studies. They do so instead because they have found remarkable personal benefit in the practice, and most will tell you stories about how TDD has made a difference in their development careers.

11.3 The Bad Test Death Spiral, aka the SCUMmy Cycle

Sometimes teams embark on TDD and experience some good results for a while. Then things start sliding toward oblivion, speeding up quickly and ultimately ending up with the decision to abandon TDD. What causes this "bad test death spiral," and how do you prevent it?

The problem isn't unique to TDD. There's also the "bad agile death spiral" in which the short iterations of pseudo-Agile appear to produce good results for a while. A year or eighteen months in, however, the team is flabbergasted at the mess on their hands. The net result is that Agile gets abandoned and blamed for the waste.

Ben Rady and Rod Coffin described the *SCUMmy cycle* in their Agile2009 conference presentation, "Continuous Testing Evolved."[5] Their acronym SCUM describes the kinds of bad tests that generate the degradation: Slow, Confusing, Unreliable, Missing. Here's one possible path along the downward spiral (I've seen this path firsthand a few times in shops):

1. *The team writes mostly integration-style tests.* These tests tightly couple to volatile or slow dependencies, such as the database or other external APIs. While this results in slower tests, initially it doesn't add up to much real pain, because the team is still able to run a few hundred tests in a minute or two. (Think "frog in slowly boiling water.")

2. *The growing body of tests begins to pass the pain threshold.* Now there are enough tests to take several minutes to run.

3. *Developers run the test suite less frequently or run subsets of the tests.* The team also discovers that the tests are more difficult. They are typically longer, with more required setup, and thus require increased effort to understand and analyze when there's a problem. Other problems creep in, with tests failing intermittently because of volatile conditions outside the control of the unit tests. Developers begin to discover that the tests are often false alarms, indicating a problem not with the production system but instead with the test design.

---

5.   http://agile2009.agilealliance.org/files/session_pdfs/ContinuousTestingEvolved.pdf

4. *Developers delete tests.* The knee-jerk reaction to difficult tests is to start disabling or even deleting them. Developers find that deleting is much easier than spending an hour fixing a poorly designed test.

5. *Defects begin to increase.* The tests that remain likely don't cover enough detailed bits of logic and now offer only little value in preventing defects. (They never offered much in the way of documentation value either.)

6. *The team, or management, questions the value of TDD.* The team tries to plod on, but it's fairly obvious that the investment was a waste.

7. *The team abandons TDD.* Management makes a note of the highly visible fiasco.

What's a team to do? If the path to TDD is doomed, why even start?

Ideally, you've learned in this book that TDD requires you to constrain the scope of each test so that it tests a small piece of isolated logic. Systems built in this manner are unlikely to experience the bad test death spiral. Still, a quality system doesn't magically emerge from doing TDD. You and your team must actively seek to squash poor design in both the tests and the code. Doing that also requires the team to understand what good tests and code look like.

The following progression counters each step in the spiral. If you're actively monitoring what's going on, chances are you can prevent the spiral from progressing further downward.

1. *The team writes mostly integration-style tests.* Learn how to write unit tests. Reread this book, attend training, hire a coach, hold dojos, review more, read more, and so on. You'll also want to increase your knowledge of good design and code constructs.

2. *The growing body of tests begins to pass the pain threshold.* Split into slow and fast suites. Establish what it means for a test to be fast (5ms or less on a dev machine?). Require the team to acknowledge when they are adding another test to the slow suite. Learn what it takes to restructure a test (and the corresponding code) so that it's fast. Establish a habit of incrementally but regularly trying to transform a slow test into a fast test.

3. *Developers run the test suite less frequently or run subsets of the tests.* Fail the fast suite execution when a test exceeds the slow threshold. (I succeeded in modifying Google Test to this end for a recent customer.) This reinforces the importance of fast tests to the development team.

4. *Developers delete tests.* Monitor coverage. While establishing a coverage metric goal is of questionable value (see Section 11.6, *Using the Code*

Coverage Metric Effectively, on page 313), you do want to prefer increasing or at least stable coverage numbers. Unfortunately, replacing a bad test with equivalent coverage by good unit tests can require a bit of effort. But until the proper habits are in place, you're better off incrementally taking the time to do the right thing than giving up.

5. *Defects begin to increase.* Always write a test first in response to a defect. Defects are opportunities to recognize the deficiencies in TDD practice. For each defect, insist that an appropriate failing unit test gets written before the problem is fixed.

6. *The team, or management, questions the value of TDD.* Commit to quality. Insist that the practices of TDD, as well as other practices such as acceptance testing, refactoring, and pairing, are primarily about delivering quality software in the long haul and are not just about minimizing defects. Ensure that it's clear how and why these practices relate to quality, and ensure that the team employs the practices in a way that helps realize the goal of quality. Lack of concern over quality will devastate your system—the "bad quality death spiral" is even more unforgiving.

7. *The team abandons TDD.* Don't wait 'til it's too late! Management rarely tolerates second attempts at what they think is the same path to failure.

As with anything, you can practice TDD inappropriately and fail. But it's possible to succeed and to succeed wildly; otherwise, I wouldn't have bothered writing this book. Blaming the technique for insistence on doing it poorly isn't cool.

11.4 Pair Programming

The tests and code you write represent costly investments. In an ideal world, you would assume that all developers have the training needed, and more importantly the desire, to effectively write quality code. Yet a glance at just about any existing system suggests otherwise.

In this book, I've tried to make the case that most systems are a mess because programmers don't have a mechanism (such as TDD) to actively ensure the code doesn't degrade. But other reasons abound.

- *Lack of education*: Too many developers don't understand core design principles and constructs for coding well. Some think they already know enough and aren't willing to accept that there's more to learn.

- *Lack of concern*: Too many developers don't care that they are producing difficult code. Or they justify it because the system is already rife with bad code.

- *Time pressure*: How many times have you heard "Just ship it—we don't have time to worry about quality?"

- *Lack of review*: All it takes is one rogue developer to inflict serious damage on a codebase. Sometimes this developer comes in the form of a high-priced, short-term consultant. And sometimes the creator of the crummy code disappears before you uncover it, leaving you with an incoherent, unmaintainable mess.

- *Lack of collaboration*: In a team of more than one developer or in a codebase of any reasonable size, styles and quality quickly diverge. Understanding code written by another developer can be difficult without their explanation, and other developers may code solutions to problems that are already solved. Individuals may produce less-than-optimal solutions when they don't seek the wisdom of others.

The Rules of Pairing

The technique of pair programming purports to help by providing an active mechanism for continual review, collaboration, and peer pressure. Here's a summary of how pair programming works:

- Two programmers actively co-develop a solution.

- The programmers typically sit side by side (though other configurations, including remote pairing, are possible).

- At any given time, each is in one of two roles: *driving*, which means actively coding the solution using the keyboard, and *navigating*, which means providing review and strategic guidance. Pairing is *not* one person doing and the other simply sitting back and watching.

- The programmers in a pair swap roles frequently during a pairing session, potentially every time a test fails or passes.

- Pairing sessions are short-lived, with pairs reforming as often as every ninety minutes. A primary goal of rotating pairs in this manner is to increase knowledge, and accordingly reduce risk, across the team.

Much like TDD, studies of pair programming[6] show increased quality and an increase in the *initial* cost of development. The aphorism "two heads are better than one" should come to mind. The increase in cost is not double, as you might at first think. The higher quality brought about by the active review is one reason. Peer pressure and increased levels of communication, coordination, and education might also explain the lower cost. Other benefits abound, such as reduced risk and increased flexibility.[7]

Pair Programming and TDD

TDD supported with pair programming is a natural fit. Learning TDD is made dramatically easier with a support system in place. Developers are more likely to revert to old, non-TDD habits without a bit of peer pressure from their teammates. Sitting with an experienced TDDer can more than halve the time needed to ingrain the habit of TDD. Swapping pairs can help ensure that tests are written first and with care.

The cycle of TDD also provides natural role-switching points throughout a session. Many programmers practice ping-pong pairing. The first programmer codes enough of a test to demonstrate failure and then relinquishes the keyboard to the second programmer. The second programmer writes the production code that makes the test pass and then writes the next portion of the test (or the next test). Pairs might also alternate roles as they work through various iterations of refactoring the code once a test passes.

Pairs will from time to time debate the direction of the tests, particularly as they learn about each other's preferred styles. The general rule of thumb is to debate no more than five minutes before one of the pair grabs the keyboard and demonstrates what they mean. Usually the direction the tests take will win out the discussion.

Pair Rotating

As indicated earlier, pairing sessions should be short-lived. The natural tendency, though, is to allow the pairing session to last as long as it takes to complete a task, or perhaps an entire feature.

Indeed, swapping pairs incurs the overhead of *context switching*. If you're the new party to a pairing session (the *newcomer*), you must first discard your

---

6. See Dybå, T. et. al. "Are Two Heads Better Than One? On the Effectiveness of Pair Programming," at http://dl.acm.org/citation.cfm?id=1309094, which summarizes a number of pair programming studies.
7. See http://pragprog.com/magazines/2011-07/pair-programming-benefits for many other potential benefits.

often deep thoughts about the last problem you were solving. (I'll refer to the programmer you're joining as the *old hand.*) For most folks, this is no big deal, and a break of five or ten minutes does the trick. But you then face the steeper challenge of coming up to speed on a new problem. Depending on its difficulty, that might take a few minutes, but it also might require detailed, time-consuming explanation from the old hand.

With TDD in play, the focus changes. Instead of a detailed explanation from the old hand, you focus on the current failing test. (If there isn't one, you watch and listen as the old hand puts one in place.) Your goal is to read the name of the test and ensure it makes sense. You can then read the test's steps to help complete your understanding of the current coding task.

Worrying only about a single test, particularly a well-written, laser-beam-focused unit test, can make it much easier for you to begin contributing. You don't need to know all the details. Instead of providing a lengthy discussion of the details up front, the old hand incrementally guides you along.

The more a team practices swapping midtask, the easier it gets, particularly in a small team. But why not simply prevent swapping until the task is complete?

Remember that a key goal of pairing is review. Two heads are usually better than one, but it's still possible for a pair to go down an unproductive avenue. This is even more likely as a pair digs deeply into a solution, at which point many find it easy to convince themselves that they have the only right answer. A third party, someone not invested in the pair's deep, shared train of thought, can prevent bad solutions by interjecting with their untainted perspective.

Additionally, increasing swapping increases the likelihood that the newcomer is familiar with the particular area of code. With regular swapping on a modest-sized system, everyone ultimately gets their hands on all parts of the system.

Increased code quality can be another key benefit of swapping—if the team seeks and insists on it. Higher code quality can help further reduce context-switching overhead by reducing the time the newcomer requires to understand it. Code that isn't clear must be reworked. Pairs should quickly learn that it will save time to continually refactor for clarity, especially with respect to the tests.

Pair swapping represents a trade-off between increased initial effort and long-term payoffs, much like pair programming itself, TDD, and many other aspects of agile software development. Context switching will indeed cause you immediate pain, which you can learn to abate over time. But a team full of siloed developers, with little review and no shared knowledge, will create pain that will only continue to increase over time.

11.5 Katas and Dojos

In addition to continually seeking new knowledge, successful professionals practice their craft on a regular basis. Musicians use scales as warm-up exercises, cosmetic surgeons practice on cadavers, athletes run drills and scrimmages, speakers warm up in front of a mirror, and martial arts practitioners practice *katas*—choreographed patterns of movement.

During such practice sessions, practitioners repeat common and basic elements that they learned at the outset of their careers. These drills help ingrain basic skills. Practitioners also use them to warm up for a performance or challenge. In the midst of a challenge, a skilled performer seeks to let their "muscle memory" kick in as much as possible to handle basic movements. That can help improve their ability to think and better react to their environment.

Further, mastery of basic movements is an essential foundation for growth and exploration. More sophisticated and effective forms are often creative variants to basic forms. Advanced professionals may sometimes even find that they can throw out basic rules. Their deep knowledge of basic forms allows them to recognize and accept the costs of discarding them.

Many developers have applied the martial arts concept of katas to TDD. The concept is much the same: test-drive the solution to a brief programming challenge. Repeat until you are able to demonstrate an ideal path to the solution by eliminating wasteful steps. Dave Thomas supplies a number of sample problems at his site (http://codekata.pragprog.com).

Applying Katas to TDD

Does it make sense to practice test-driving code? To build software, you work with an ample number of tools at any given time. Your hands interact with a keyboard to produce code. You interact with an editor who provides numerous ways to accomplish tasks. You work with a language and set of libraries (including a test framework) that similarly provide countless ways to produce solutions. Finally, you think about many things. And while each bit of thinking through a solution might seem to represent a unique, nonrepeatable process, there are many repetitive themes (patterns) in software development.

The more you practice these elements, the better you will become at each. The longest pole in the tent is no doubt the thinking part, but it's still possible to get better at thinking through solving programming problems.

Where to get started? Find a kata that appeals to you, perhaps one you've seen demonstrated before. For a first kata, prefer something small, a challenge that you might be able to complete in an hour. Note the time and then test-drive a solution. If you get stuck, be willing to backtrack a bit. Finally, record the time you took to derive the solution.

If you became hopelessly mired, discard your attempt completely and try again, seeking help if need be. (You'll know if you need to choose another first kata.)

Review your solution, and think about the steps you took to derive it. Run the kata again, preferably immediately (or within a reasonable period of time so that you don't forget everything you just learned). Don't memorize, but instead think about a better sequencing of steps to follow. Compare the time you took to the first time.

Repeat the kata from time to time, perhaps one to three times per week. Seek out tweaks and other refinements. For example, explore a better API or language construct, and seek to eliminate some typing by using a better editor shortcut. At some point, you'll be close to an ideal solution, with the ability to derive it via a minimal set of steps and mistakes. It's now a tool in your warm-up bag!

To improve your test-driven problem-solving ability, you'll want to grow the number of katas in your bag. Solving different types of problems can teach you different techniques and help you get better at coming up with important insights.

Code Kata: Roman Numeral Converter contains a simple starting point, the Roman numeral exercise, in which you test-drive an algorithm to convert an Arabic number to its Roman numeral equivalent. You might also try other exercises from this book, such as the Soundex example, as your first kata. Table 1, *Kata Resources*, on page 312 describes many useful kata resources.

Dojos

Katas are typically a solo pursuit (although they also work well with a pair). They're something you can pick up at any time and bang away at for five minutes or fifty minutes. But you can also take your attempts at TDD mastery to the next level by performing katas as a team in a *dojo*. Like Japanese

Site/List Name	URL	Description
CodeKata	http://codekata.prag-prog.com	Dave Thomas's original kata site
Craftmanship Kata-logue	http://craftsman-ship.sv.cmu.edu/katas	Rates and sources various katas
Coders Dojo	http://codersdojo.org	Also allows you to try and share katas (in Ruby)
Software Craftman-ship Code Kata	http://katas.softwarecrafts-manship.org	Contains videos of various katas
TDD Problems	https://sites.google.com/site/tddproblems/	Designed primarily for demon-strating TDD, but you can also use these problems as katas
cyber-dojo	http://www.cyber-dojo.com	An online dojo that allows you to code and test in the browser

Table 1—Kata Resources

martial arts dojos, a TDD dojo is a group training session with some level of ceremony and structure.

For a typical dojo, allot sixty to ninety minutes in a room where you can project a single screen to everyone. To warm up the team to the notion of dojos, your first dojo might involve a single presenter or pair who demonstrates their path through a solution for a kata that they've already done before. The presenter's job is to ensure everyone understands their programming choices before they move on to the next step.

For subsequent dojos, *randori*-style is more entertaining and engaging. Various structures for randori dojos exist; here's one as described by the Coding Dojo wiki (at http://codingdojo.org):

- A starter pair tackles the problem chosen by the entire group at the outset of the dojo.

- The pair switches roles frequently between driver and navigator, perhaps using ping-pong pairing.

- The pair has a time limit, somewhere from five to fifteen minutes, to advance the solution. They are expected to describe what they are doing as they go.

- One member of the pair (typically the driver) swaps out of the pair once the time limit hits and is replaced by an audience member. All attendees are expected to swap into the pair at least once during the dojo.

- The audience may offer suggestions as appropriate.

You might choose a sensei to offer advice by asking questions (but not providing answers) and to otherwise help facilitate the dojo.

If the kata runs any more than a half-hour or so, take a five-minute break midway through. Finish with a brief retrospective: discuss what went well with the session, and decide what you will do differently for the next.

Randori dojos provide opportunities for everyone on the team to get involved. You might revert to presentation style when there's a new problem that the team wants to tackle or when someone wants to demonstrate an end-to-end solution that they find more effective.

Dojos are about collaboration and sharing. Your team will have a better understanding of how others on the team approach problem solving, and you'll pick up lots of new ideas along the way.

11.6 Using the Code Coverage Metric Effectively

Code coverage—the percentage of lines of code exercised by your unit tests—is the new "lines of code" metric, sure to be abused by lazy managers. The naive interpretation of the metric is that 100 percent means you have comprehensive coverage, and 0 percent indicates that you haven't even tried. You can find a number of code coverage tools for C++; most are not free. COVTOOL (http://covtool.sourceforge.net) is one open source test coverage tool.

A good coverage tool will also annotate your source, showing you specifically which lines of code get executed when you run your tests. The real value in measuring coverage lies here: knowing which lines of code aren't covered can help you determine where you need to add tests.

If you always follow the simple TDD cycle to drive your code, your coverage metric will approach 100 percent. (It might not ever be 100 percent because of some limitations in the tools and their ability to discern how certain code elements are used. That's OK.) But you already knew that—if you only write code in the presence of a failing test and you never write more code than necessary to pass the test, you have 100 percent coverage by definition. I personally don't usually bother with code coverage tools for this reason. Still, if you're struggling with always following the habit of writing a test first or if you tend to write more code than needed to pass a test, a coverage tool can provide you with valuable feedback.

A system-wide, average coverage number less than 90 percent tells you the codebase wasn't (fully or at all) developed using TDD, and nothing more. A coverage number of 90 percent or more similarly tells you little—it *usually* indicates that the codebase was built using TDD, but it's also possible to write integration tests that blast through a large amount of code. More typically, the coverage across a non-test-driven system is considerably less (and in my experience, rarely more than 70 percent). It's hard to cover every last branch with integration tests, and it's also hard to write comprehensive unit tests after you've already written the code.

It's also possible to do TDD, write focused unit tests, attain coverage levels in the 90+ percentile range, and create tests that are difficult to maintain. In other words, high numbers may look good but might not tell the whole story.

Never set coverage numbers as goals. Managers who insist on high coverage numbers get what they ask for—high coverage numbers and little else useful.

11.7 Continuous Integration

How many times in your career have you heard the phrase "It worked on *my* machine?" Or perhaps you have uttered it yourself? Until your code is integrated with the rest of the production code and passes all tests running on an approved machine (one with an environment similar to production), you don't really know that it works. (You still don't *really* know that it works, of course, until it's sitting in front of the customer.)

The job of a *continuous integration* (CI) server is to monitor your source repository and kick off a consistent build process when a commit occurs. Once the build completes, the CI server notifies any interested parties and retains build output for future reference.

Your build script should compile, link, deploy, run unit tests, run any other tests, and do anything else you deem necessary to demonstrate that you could ship your system—at least to the next level. Some high-capability teams have enough confidence in the build that they have evolved one level to the notion of continuous delivery—with each successful build, software is deployed to production.

Your CI build might take a while to run, and that's OK. The nice part about having a CI server is that you can continue to work, and you'll know once it finds out about any problems. Be careful, though. Don't allow the tool to let you get complacent about your overall build time. A slowly but surely increasing build process will soon become a problem. Getting feedback several times throughout the day is essential.

In a TDD shop, a CI server is a foundational tool. It makes no sense to proceed without one. The tests (including any nonunit tests) represent your best indicator of the health of your overall system. When you commit, you want to know that your code adds to the value of the system and doesn't break anything in the latest, integrated version of the codebase.

Make sure your team is in agreement about all the processes surrounding the CI server (see the next section on standards). You should know what's expected of you when you commit, and you should know what should happen in the event that the CI server reports a build failure.

Numerous CI servers exist. Well-known tools include Jenkins, buildbot, CruiseControl, and TeamCity. You'll want to choose one that meshes well with your environment and your build scripts. You'll find some good discussion on appropriate CI tools at StackOverflow.[8]

11.8 Deriving Team Standards for TDD

You'll want to make sure your team approaches TDD with a few simple standards. Don't let these standards be a barrier to getting started, however. Like everything else in Agile and TDD, the goal is to put a little into place and then continue to refine things as you go forward.

Here are a few of the key things you'll want to agree upon:

* Unit testing tool (Google Test, CppUTest, or CppUnit, for example). Over time, you might migrate to a better tool if one emerges. At that point, it's OK to do so incrementally. For now, though, find a unit testing tool that suits your team best and stick with it until you have good reason not to.

* Other tools, including mock frameworks and code coverage tools.

* Integration standards. Team members should agree what level of testing occurs before integrating code to the source control system. Ideally, developers should run all unit tests, as long as it isn't a barrier to frequent integration (because of existing legacy system problems). You should never permit the check-in of failing tests.

* Test run standards. How slow can tests be? Can tests spew output onto the console (ideally not)?

---

8. See http://stackoverflow.com/questions/145586/what-continuous-integration-tool-is-best-for-a-c-project.

- Failure process. When the build breaks, what should happen, and who needs to be involved?

- Disabled/commented-out tests. Generally, you'll want to insist that these don't get checked in. If a compelling reason exists, the committer should be required to provide an explanatory comment.

- Test naming forms. DoesSomethingWhenSomeContextExists isn't a bad place to start, though you might want to avoid being dogmatic about the form. Conciseness and readability are important factors.

- Test structure. Are you following AAA? How are fixtures named? Where do tests physically go (both from a packaging and file organization standpoint)?

- Assertion form. Hamcrest or not? Are assertion comments OK?

Spend an hour in a meeting debating standards for your codebase, capture it in a short list of bullets, shake hands, and move on. Revisit the standard if you start to recognize conflict in the code. Standards are nice to have, but never let them be a barrier to moving forward.

11.9 Keeping Up with the Community

TDD is a continuing exploration. New and better ideas continually arise about how to best practice TDD. I've personally sought to regularly incorporate new ideas about TDD over the dozen-plus years I've practiced it. My tests and code from 2000 disappoint me, and my tests and code from yesterday disappoint me too. That's OK, since the cycle of TDD itself is built on the notion of continual improvement.

This section provides you with a few ideas on how to find out what's new and interesting in the rest of the TDD world.

Reading Tests

Learning how to read code is a worthwhile skill. And an even better way to read code is to first look at the tests that describe it.

Open source projects provide an easy way to learn more about how others practice TDD. You'll find a wide variety of styles out there, and you'll no doubt already recognize some bad practices in the tests you read.

Don't limit yourself to looking only at C++ tests. The core principles of TDD apply equally well to all languages.

Blogs and Forums

Be part of the discussion! The following table describes several active forums and blogs where TDD is discussed often or always:

Site/List Name	URL	Who/What
Test-Driven Development Yahoo! Group	http://tech.groups.yahoo.com/group/testdrivendevelopment/	Email-based discussion forum
Extreme Programming Yahoo! Group	http://tech.groups.yahoo.com/group/extremeprogramming/	Email-based discussion forum
LinkedIn Test-Driven Development Group	http://www.linkedin.com/groups/Test-Driven-Development-155678	Web-based discussion forum
Agile Otter Blog	http://agileotter.blogspot.com/	Tim Ottinger, coauthor of *Agile in a Flash* (*Agile in a Flash: Speed-Learning Agile Software Development* [LO11])
James Grenning's Blog	http://www.renaissancesoftware.net/blog/	The author of *Test-Driven Development in Embedded C* (*Embedded Test Driven Development Cycle* [Gre07])
Michael Feathers	http://michaelfeathers.typepad.com/michael_feathers_blog/	The author of *Working Effectively with Legacy Code* (*Working Effectively with Legacy Code* [Fea04])
Uncle Bob	http://blog.8thlight.com/uncle-bob/archive.html	The author of *Clean Code* (*Clean Code: A Handbook of Agile Software Craftsmanship* [Mar08])
Coding Is Like Cooking	http://emily-bache.blogspot.com/	Emily Bache, author of *The Coding Dojo Handbook* (*The Coding Dojo Handbook* [Bac12])
Sustainable Test-Driven Development	http://www.sustainabletdd.com/	Authors Scott Bain and Amir Kolsky
Jeff's Blog	http://langrsoft.com/jeff/	Yours truly

11.10 Teardown

Congratulations! You've learned a wide array of information about Test-Driven Development and how it can benefit you and your team. In this chapter, you learned a few ideas about how to keep the fire burning, both personally and within your team.

TDD is a simple cycle of specify, build, and improve. This book has provided you with a specification for how to practice TDD. You must build out your knowledge of TDD through continuing application and practice. Most importantly, you owe it to yourself and your team to continue to improve upon what this book has helped you learn.

Comparing Unit Testing Tools

A1.1 Setup

The examples you've seen in this book use Google Test/Google Mock and CppUTest. You might already be using a different unit testing tool, or your environment might demand consideration of a different tool. In this chapter, you'll get a quick overview regarding the features to consider for an appropriate unit testing tool for TDD.

A1.2 TDD Unit Testing Tool Features

Just about any tool you consider will work for Test-Driven Development. Some tools make it easier, however, and some contain features that make TDD into more of a chore. Many tools contain additional fancy bells and whistles that you'll probably never need when doing TDD. Some tools have different design considerations, such as a minimal footprint, and as a result may include features that clash with the goals of TDD.

I consider the following features to be "must haves" for doing TDD:

Discrete test names	The tool should support the ability to identify tests uniquely, preferably using a combination of a scoping/ grouping name and a test name. At least one tool supports test names only as an afterthought, by default providing only numbers for a test.
Ease of adding new tests	Tests should automatically register so that they are executed by default. The tool should not require the programmer to separately register a defined test. Older tools such as CppUnit require programmers to explicitly register new tests with a suite.

Fixture support	The tool should provide the ability to define fixtures that provide setup/teardown hooks, as well as the ability to group common test helper functions.
Isolated tests	The tool should support the ability to easily ensure that each unit test can run with no dependency on the outcome of any other unit test.
Equality assertions	The tool should provide the ability to compare two quantities and produce clear, expressive failure messages.
Test suites	The tool should support the ability to easily execute arbitrary groups of unit tests.
Mocking support	The tool either should directly provide support to simplify the effort to define and use mocks or should support working in conjunction with a third-party mocking tool.

The following features may enhance your test-driving experience but aren't essential:

Hamcrest	The tool should provide an enhanced assertion facility that supports matchers (and the ability to define custom matchers). Sustaining TDD requires highly readable tests, and Hamcrest can aid in this goal.
Customizable output	The test tool should provide the ability to easily customize test-run output. By default, the tool should provide a simplified summary view showing only test failure detail.
Exception assertions	The tool should provide a direct means of asserting that an exception was thrown.
Test execution statistics	The tool should provide summary statistics on the test run and should provide times for each individual test execution.
Memory leak testing	The tool should support the configurable feature of failing if memory was allocated during execution of an individual test but not released.
Robustness	The tool should provide the option to complete an entire test run even when unexpected exceptions are thrown or the application causes a crash. (This feature is more useful when running tests in a CI build server than it is when test-driving.)

The following features may sound nice but are irrelevant for the purposes of practicing TDD:

Parameterized tests	You might find a rare case where having the ability to slam a bunch of data against a single test is useful. It is not, however, a test-driven practice, and it's reasonably easy to code on your own if necessary.
Dependencies	For integration tests, it can be highly useful to be able to force an order of execution. Creating tests that are dependent upon the result of others, however, has nothing to do with TDD.

A1.3 Notes on Google Mock

Google Mock provides built-in support for mocks, provides a good Hamcrest library, and appears to be widely used.

Google Mock provides inadequate support for test suites. While Google Mock does provide the ability to execute a subset of tests using a command-line filter, it provides no direct support for permanently defining suites. (You could circumvent this deficiency by redirecting input from a series of files.)

The default test run output from Google Mock provides information on all tests, unfortunately. In a large suite, the volume of output describing successfully executed tests will make it difficult to find information on failed tests without command-line manipulation.

To counter this problem, you can create a custom test event listener in a matter of minutes that produces simplified output for a Google Test execution. See https://code.google.com/p/googletest/wiki/AdvancedGuide#Extending_Google_Test_by_Handling_Test_Events for further details.

A1.4 Notes on CppUTest

CppUTest provides most of the features essential to a TDD-focused unit testing tool. Its ability to run a subset of a test is provided through a command-line switch, similar to that of Google Test's filter capability (but not quite as robust).

A significant bonus feature in CppUTest is its memory leak detection facility, which can potentially be configured to run with other unit testing tools.

A1.5 Other Unit Testing Frameworks

You might consider one of the following unit test frameworks:

Boost.Test	http://www.boost.org/doc/libs/1_53_0/libs/test/doc/html/index.html
CppUnit	http://cppunit.sourceforge.net/doc/1.11.6/cppunit_cookbook.html
CppUnitLite	http://c2.com/cgi/wiki?CppUnitLite
CUTE	http://cute-test.com/
CxxTest	http://cxxtest.com/
Unit++	http://unitpp.sourceforge.net/

A1.6 Teardown

The landscape of C++ unit testing tools continues to change. Rather than summarize the existing tools at the time of publication, the goal of this appendix is to help you define the criteria by which you choose your team's unit testing tool. You can find a number of sites that provide a comparison of the available tools. One detailed article that compares a few of the tools is http://gamesfromwithin.com/exploring-the-c-unit-testing-framework-jungle, but note that it is from 2010 and discusses neither CppUTest nor Google Test.

Your choice for an appropriate C++ unit testing tool is unlikely to be dead wrong. Your tool will probably change for the better over time, and even if it doesn't, you'll usually have the opportunity to customize it. Pick one and go with it.

Code Kata: Roman Numeral Converter

A2.1 Setup

In Section 11.5, *Katas and Dojos*, on page 310, you learned about using katas to help you ingrain fundamental TDD concepts, particularly its incremental approach to growing a solution. This appendix supplies you with one possible kata to practice on your own. Test by test, you'll drive the implementation of a Roman numeral converter.

A2.2 Let's Go!

What are we building?

Story: Roman Numeral Converter
We need a function that takes an Arabic number and returns its Roman numeral equivalent (as a string).

One, Two, Three, ...

Getting the first test to pass will take us a few minutes, since there's a good amount of setup work to do (getting the build script in place, adding header includes, and so on). There are also decisions to be made: What are we going to name our test method? What should the interface to our function look like?

We choose to make our conversion a free function. Here's the first, failing test:

```
roman/1/RomanConverterTest.cpp
TEST(RomanConverter, CanConvertPositiveDigits) {
   EXPECT_THAT(convert(1), Eq("I"));
}
```

One of the goals for a kata is to minimize our movements. While I'm not enamored with free functions, they're a fine place to start when we have a purely functional need. When done, we can scope the function as a static class member if needed.

To make things even simpler, we'll keep the test and convert() implementations in the same file for now. Here's the entire file, including the code to make our first test pass:

```
roman/2/RomanConverterTest.cpp
#include "gmock/gmock.h"

using namespace ::testing;
using namespace std;

string convert(unsigned int arabic)
{
   return "I";
}

TEST(RomanConverter, CanConvertPositiveDigits) {
   EXPECT_THAT(convert(1), Eq("I"));
}
```

Moving right along, converting two seems the next most sensible place to go.

```
roman/3/RomanConverterTest.cpp
TEST(RomanConverter, CanConvertPositiveDigits) {
   EXPECT_THAT(convert(1), Eq("I"));
   EXPECT_THAT(convert(2), Eq("II"));
}
```

You might have noticed that we're using EXPECT_THAT as opposed to my preferred use of ASSERT_THAT. To remind you of the distinction, if an EXPECT_THAT assertion fails, Google Test keeps executing the current test. If an ASSERT_THAT assertion fails, Google Test halts the current test's execution.

Normally, you want one scenario—a single test case—per test function. With a single case, it usually makes little sense to continue executing the test if an assertion fails—the rest of the test is generally invalid.

With respect to the Roman converter, however, there's little sense to creating new test methods, given that the externally recognized behavior ("convert a number") remains unchanged for each new case. Were we to have separate test methods for our two cases so far, our names would be tedious and would add little value: Convert1, Convert2.

Since we have one test function with lots of discrete cases, using EXPECT_THAT makes more sense. If one assertion fails, we still want to know what other cases pass or fail.

To get our second assertion to pass, we treat the new conversion of two like a special case by introducing an if statement. So far, that's all we know. We have two special cases—one and two—and our code mirrors that knowledge.

roman/3/RomanConverterTest.cpp
```cpp
string convert(unsigned int arabic)
{
   if (arabic == 2)
      return "II";
   return "I";
}
```

Here's a third assertion:

roman/4/RomanConverterTest.cpp
```cpp
EXPECT_THAT(convert(3), Eq("III"));
```

Now we sense a pattern and can take advantage of it with a simple loop.

roman/4/RomanConverterTest.cpp
```cpp
string convert(unsigned int arabic)
{
   string roman{""};
   while (arabic-- > 0)
      roman += "I";
   return roman;
}
```

Simple, simple. We don't worry about optimization yet; hence, concatenating to a string is good enough for now, and a for seems unnecessary.

Ten Sir!

One, two, three...ready for four? Not necessarily. TDD doesn't have any rules that force us to construct tests in a certain order. Instead, we always want to apply a bit of thought to what our next test should be.

Four in Roman—IV—is a subtraction of sorts, one (I) less than five (V). We haven't even hit five (V) yet, so perhaps it makes sense to hold off on four until we at least tackle five. Regarding V, it seems like a simple special case. Perhaps we should think about what is similar to what we already have going. One, two, three results in the progression I, II, III. Let's look at another similar progression, that of X, XX, XXX.

roman/5/RomanConverterTest.cpp
```cpp
EXPECT_THAT(convert(10), Eq("X"));
```

Ten is another special case, best dispatched with an if statement.

```
roman/5/RomanConverterTest.cpp
string convert(unsigned int arabic)
{
   string roman{""};
   if (arabic == 10)
      return "X";
   while (arabic-- > 0)
      roman += "I";
   return roman;
}
```

Eleven promises to be a little more interesting.

```
roman/6/RomanConverterTest.cpp
EXPECT_THAT(convert(11), Eq("XI"));
```

```
roman/6/RomanConverterTest.cpp
string convert(unsigned int arabic)
{
   string roman{""};
   if (arabic >= 10)
   {
      roman += "X";
      arabic -= 10;
   }
   while (arabic-- > 0)
      roman += "I";
   return roman;
}
```

If our converter is passed a number greater than ten, we append an X, subtract 10 from the number, and drop through to the same while loop. We figure that assertions for twelve and thirteen should pass automatically.

```
roman/6/RomanConverterTest.cpp
EXPECT_THAT(convert(12), Eq("XII"));
EXPECT_THAT(convert(13), Eq("XIII"));
```

Both assertions indeed pass. A new assertion for twenty fails.

```
roman/7/RomanConverterTest.cpp
EXPECT_THAT(convert(20), Eq("XX"));
```

Getting it to pass is as simple as changing the keyword if to while.

```
roman/7/RomanConverterTest.cpp
string convert(unsigned int arabic)
{
   string roman{""};
   while (arabic >= 10)
   {
      roman += "X";
```

```
        arabic -= 10;
    }
    while (arabic-- > 0)
        roman += "I";
    return roman;
}
```

Duplicating Almost-Duplication to Eliminate It

We have an implementation with what appears to be near-duplicate code.
The while loops are similar. Faced with "almost duplication," our next step is
to make things look as much alike as possible.

roman/8/RomanConverterTest.cpp
```
string convert(unsigned int arabic)
{
    string roman{""};
    while (arabic >= 10)
    {
        roman += "X";
        arabic -= 10;
    }
    while (arabic >= 1)
    {
        roman += "I";
        arabic -= 1;
    }
    return roman;
}
```

After refactoring, we have two loops with the same logic, varying only in data. We
could extract a common function to eliminate the duplication, but it seems a less-
than-stellar choice since two separate elements are changing (the Arabic total
and the Roman string). Let's instead extract a conversion table:

roman/9/RomanConverterTest.cpp
```
string convert(unsigned int arabic)
{
    const auto arabicToRomanConversions = {
        make_pair(10u, "X"),
        make_pair(1u, "I") };
    string roman{""};
    for (auto arabicToRoman: arabicToRomanConversions)
        while (arabic >= arabicToRoman.first)
        {
            roman += arabicToRoman.second;
            arabic -= arabicToRoman.first;
        }
    return roman;
}
```

The duplicate loops collapse into a generalized loop that in turn is part of an iteration over the conversion pairs.

Finishing Up

Our algorithm paraphrased goes like this: for each pair representing an Arabic-to-Roman digit mapping, subtract the Arabic value and then append the corresponding Roman value until the remaining total is less than the Arabic digit. (We could use a different data structure, as long as we ensure that the conversion mappings get iterated in order, descending from largest to smallest.)

A bit of thought suggests that the algorithm should work for any digit mapping, as long as we add it to the table. Let's try five, which we previously considered a special case.

roman/10/RomanConverterTest.cpp
```
EXPECT_THAT(convert(5), Eq("V"));
```

Getting the test to pass requires only adding an entry to the conversion table.

roman/10/RomanConverterTest.cpp
```
const auto arabicToRomanConversions = {
    make_pair(10u, "X"),
    make_pair(5u, "V"),
    make_pair(1u, "I") };
```

We're now writing tests mostly for confidence purposes (see *Testing for Confidence*, on page 69), since we're doing little other than adding data to a table, but that's OK. Let's add a few more confidence measures. What about fifty, one hundred, and combinations thereof?

roman/11/RomanConverterTest.cpp
```
EXPECT_THAT(convert(50), Eq("L"));
EXPECT_THAT(convert(80), Eq("LXXX"));
EXPECT_THAT(convert(100), Eq("C"));
EXPECT_THAT(convert(288), Eq("CCLXXXVIII"));
```

We find they all easily pass, too, with requisite additions to the conversion table.

roman/11/RomanConverterTest.cpp
```
const auto arabicToRomanConversions = {
    make_pair(100u, "C"),
    make_pair(50u, "L"),
    make_pair(10u, "X"),
    make_pair(5u, "V"),
    make_pair(1u, "I") };
```

Finally, we're again faced with the challenge we've been avoiding. What about four?

roman/12/RomanConverterTest.cpp
```
EXPECT_THAT(convert(4), Eq("IV"));
```

We could try supporting four by introducing a bit of subtraction logic. But doing so seems like it would involve some rather convoluted contortions and conditionals in our code. Hmm.

Remember, TDD isn't a mindless exercise (see *Thinking and TDD*, on page 58). At each step, you need to think about many things, including what the next step should be. So far, seeking the tests that drive in simpler implementations has worked well for us, as has seeking tests that look to represent similar patterns. And we improved our ability to follow this simple-and-simpler trajectory through the tests by ensuring our code was appropriately refactored at each step.

From time to time, you'll also need a few critical insights in order to best succeed. Sometimes they come easily, sometimes they don't. The more you program and the more you seek to experiment with things, the more often the bulbs will light in your head. A fantastic aspect of TDD is that it affords such experimentations. Try something clever, and you'll know in a few minutes whether it works. If not, revert and try something else.

What if we consider the Roman representation of four as a single digit, despite that it requires two of our alphabet's characters (IV)? Imagine, for example, that the Romans used a single special character to represent it. At that point, it's simply another entry in the conversion table.

roman/12/RomanConverterTest.cpp
```
const auto arabicToRomanConversions = {
    make_pair(100u, "C"),
    make_pair(50u, "L"),
    make_pair(10u, "X"),
    make_pair(5u, "V"),
    make_pair(4u, "IV"),
    make_pair(1u, "I") };
```

The algorithm remains untouched. We can finish up with a couple final assertions that verify our algorithm supports all the other subtraction-oriented numbers, including 9, 40, 90, 400, and 900, as well as the other couple digits we haven't yet added (500 and 1,000). For these assertions, I entered *convert n to roman* (where *n* is the number to convert) as a Google search and used the answer it returned as my assertion expectation.

roman/13/RomanConverterTest.cpp

```cpp
#include "gmock/gmock.h"

#include <vector>
#include <string>

using namespace ::testing;
using namespace std;

string convert(unsigned int arabic)
{
    const auto arabicToRomanConversions = {
        make_pair(1000u, "M"),
        make_pair(900u, "CM"),
        make_pair(500u, "D"),
        make_pair(400u, "CD"),
        make_pair(100u, "C"),
        make_pair(90u, "XC"),
        make_pair(50u, "L"),
        make_pair(40u, "XL"),
        make_pair(10u, "X"),
        make_pair(9u, "IX"),
        make_pair(5u, "V"),
        make_pair(4u, "IV"),
        make_pair(1u, "I") };

    string roman{""};
    for (auto arabicToRoman: arabicToRomanConversions)
        while (arabic >= arabicToRoman.first)
        {
            roman += arabicToRoman.second;
            arabic -= arabicToRoman.first;
        }
    return roman;
}

TEST(RomanConverter, CanConvertPositiveDigits) {
    EXPECT_THAT(convert(1), Eq("I"));
    EXPECT_THAT(convert(2), Eq("II"));
    EXPECT_THAT(convert(3), Eq("III"));
    EXPECT_THAT(convert(4), Eq("IV"));
    EXPECT_THAT(convert(5), Eq("V"));
    EXPECT_THAT(convert(10), Eq("X"));
    EXPECT_THAT(convert(11), Eq("XI"));
    EXPECT_THAT(convert(12), Eq("XII"));
    EXPECT_THAT(convert(13), Eq("XIII"));
    EXPECT_THAT(convert(20), Eq("XX"));
    EXPECT_THAT(convert(50), Eq("L"));
    EXPECT_THAT(convert(80), Eq("LXXX"));
    EXPECT_THAT(convert(100), Eq("C"));
```

```
    EXPECT_THAT(convert(288), Eq("CCLXXXVIII"));
    EXPECT_THAT(convert(2999), Eq("MMCMXCIX"));
    EXPECT_THAT(convert(3447), Eq("MMMCDXLVII"));
    EXPECT_THAT(convert(1513), Eq("MDXIII"));
}
```

And...done (except for enforcing the constraint that the number must be from 1 to 4,000).

We ended up with a short, simple, and concise implementation for our algorithm. A bit of web searching will show you many other solutions that have far more complexity for no additional benefit. Following TDD and refactoring appropriately can often guide you toward an optimal solution.

A2.3 Practice Makes Perfect

If you haven't already, you should follow the exact steps detailed in this appendix to build the Roman numeral converter. Don't stop there, however. Implement the converter a second time, *without* referring to this book. Think about what the next step should be, build a test, find a simple way to implement it, and refactor your code. Then do it again—maybe not immediately, but perhaps the next day or a week later. Time yourself with each run through the kata, seeking to minimize the keystrokes and effort required to derive a complete solution. If you've been away from TDD or C++ for a while, use it as a warm-up exercise.

A2.4 Teardown

In this appendix, you saw another example of how you can use TDD to drive the incremental growth of an algorithm. Of course, things don't always go this smoothly. Every time you tackle a new problem, chances are you'll have false starts and will need to undo a bit of code and try again. Practicing short examples like the Roman numeral converter as a kata should help you become more comfortable with taking short, incremental steps toward a solution. For further details on katas, refer to Section 11.5, *Katas and Dojos*, on page 310.

Bibliography

[Adz11]   Gojko Adzic. *Specification by Example*. Manning Publications Co., Green-wich, CT, 2011.

[BE12]   Daniel Brolund and Ola Ellnestam. *Behead Your Legacy Beast: Refactor and Restructure Relentlessly with the Mikado Method*. Daniel Brolund, Ola Ellnestam, http://www.agical.com, 2012.

[Bac12]   Emily Bache. *The Coding Dojo Handbook*. LeanPub, https://leanpub.com, 2012.

[Bec00]   Kent Beck. *Extreme Programming Explained: Embrace Change*. Addison-Wesley Longman, Reading, MA, 2000.

[Bec02]   Kent Beck. *Test Driven Development: By Example*. Addison-Wesley, Reading, MA, 2002.

[EB14]   Ola Ellnestam and Daniel Brolund. *The Mikado Method*. Manning Publica-tions Co., Greenwich, CT, 2014.

[FBBO99]   Martin Fowler, Kent Beck, John Brant, William Opdyke, and Don Roberts. *Refactoring: Improving the Design of Existing Code*. Addison-Wesley, Reading, MA, 1999.

[FP09]   Steve Freeman and Nat Pryce. *Growing Object-Oriented Software, Guided by Tests*. Addison-Wesley Longman, Reading, MA, 2009.

[Fea04]   Michael Feathers. *Working Effectively with Legacy Code*. Prentice Hall, Englewood Cliffs, NJ, 2004.

[Gre07]   James W. Grenning. Embedded Test Driven Development Cycle. *Embedded Systems Conference*. Submissions, 2004, 2006, 2007.

[Gre10]   James W. Grenning. *Test Driven Development for Embedded C*. The Prag-matic Bookshelf, Raleigh, NC and Dallas, TX, 2010.

[Gä12]   Marcus Gärtner. *ATDD By Example*. Addison-Wesley Professional, Boston, MA, 2012.

[LO11]   Jeff Langr and Tim Ottinger. *Agile in a Flash: Speed-Learning Agile Software Development*. The Pragmatic Bookshelf, Raleigh, NC and Dallas, TX, 2011.

[Lan05]   Jeff Langr. *Agile Java: Crafting Code With Test-Driven Development*. Prentice Hall, Englewood Cliffs, NJ, 2005.

[Lan99]   Jeff Langr. *Essential Java Style: Patterns for Implementation*. Prentice Hall, Englewood Cliffs, NJ, 1999.

[MFC01]   Tim MacKinnon, Steve Freeman, and Philip Craig. Endo-Testing: Unit Testing with Mock Objects. *Extreme Programming Examined*. 1:287-302, 2001.

[Mar02]   Robert C. Martin. *Agile Software Development, Principles, Patterns, and Practices*. Prentice Hall, Englewood Cliffs, NJ, 2002.

[Mar08]   Robert C. Martin. *Clean Code: A Handbook of Agile Software Craftsmanship*. Prentice Hall, Englewood Cliffs, NJ, 2008.

[Mes07]   Gerard Meszaros. *xUnit Test Patterns*. Addison-Wesley, Reading, MA, 2007.

[OL11]   Tim Ottinger and Jeff Langr. *Agile in a Flash*. The Pragmatic Bookshelf, Raleigh, NC and Dallas, TX, 2011.

Index

The Joy of Math and Healthy Programming

Rediscover the joy and fascinating weirdness of pure mathematics, and learn how to take a healthier approach to programming.

Mathematics is beautiful—and it can be fun and exciting as well as practical. *Good Math* is your guide to some of the most intriguing topics from two thousand years of mathematics: from Egyptian fractions to Turing machines; from the real meaning of numbers to proof trees, group symmetry, and mechanical computation. If you've ever wondered what lay beyond the proofs you struggled to complete in high school geometry, or what limits the capabilities of the computer on your desk, this is the book for you.

Mark C. Chu-Carroll
(282 pages) ISBN: 9781937785338. $34
http://pragprog.com/book/mcmath

To keep doing what you love, you need to maintain your own systems, not just the ones you write code for. Regular exercise and proper nutrition help you learn, remember, concentrate, and be creative—skills critical to doing your job well. Learn how to change your work habits, master exercises that make working at a computer more comfortable, and develop a plan to keep fit, healthy, and sharp for years to come.

This book is intended only as an informative guide for those wishing to know more about health issues. In no way is this book intended to replace, countermand, or conflict with the advice given to you by your own healthcare provider including Physician, Nurse Practitioner, Physician Assistant, Registered Dietician, and other licensed professionals.

Joe Kutner
(254 pages) ISBN: 9781937785314. $36
http://pragprog.com/book/jkthp

Seven Databases, Seven Languages

There's so much new to learn with the latest crop of NoSQL databases. And instead of learning a language a year, how about seven?

Data is getting bigger and more complex by the day, and so are your choices in handling it. From traditional RDBMS to newer NoSQL approaches, *Seven Databases in Seven Weeks* takes you on a tour of some of the hottest open source databases today. In the tradition of Bruce A. Tate's *Seven Languages in Seven Weeks*, this book goes beyond your basic tutorial to explore the essential concepts at the core of each technology.

Eric Redmond and Jim R. Wilson
(354 pages) ISBN: 9781934356920. $35
http://pragprog.com/book/rwdata

You should learn a programming language every year, as recommended by *The Pragmatic Programmer*. But if one per year is good, how about *Seven Languages in Seven Weeks*? In this book you'll get a hands-on tour of Clojure, Haskell, Io, Prolog, Scala, Erlang, and Ruby. Whether or not your favorite language is on that list, you'll broaden your perspective of programming by examining these languages side-by-side. You'll learn something new from each, and best of all, you'll learn how to learn a language quickly.

Bruce A. Tate
(330 pages) ISBN: 9781934356593. $34.95
http://pragprog.com/book/btlang

The Pragmatic Bookshelf

The Pragmatic Bookshelf features books written by developers for developers. The titles continue the well-known Pragmatic Programmer style and continue to garner awards and rave reviews. As development gets more and more difficult, the Pragmatic Programmers will be there with more titles and products to help you stay on top of your game.

Visit Us Online

This Book's Home Page
http://pragprog.com/book/lotdd
Source code from this book, errata, and other resources. Come give us feedback, too!

Register for Updates
http://pragprog.com/updates
Be notified when updates and new books become available.

Join the Community
http://pragprog.com/community
Read our weblogs, join our online discussions, participate in our mailing list, interact with our wiki, and benefit from the experience of other Pragmatic Programmers.

New and Noteworthy
http://pragprog.com/news
Check out the latest pragmatic developments, new titles and other offerings.

Save on the eBook

Save on the eBook versions of this title. Owning the paper version of this book entitles you to purchase the electronic versions at a terrific discount.

PDFs are great for carrying around on your laptop—they are hyperlinked, have color, and are fully searchable. Most titles are also available for the iPhone and iPod touch, Amazon Kindle, and other popular e-book readers.

Buy now at *http://pragprog.com/coupon*

Contact Us

Online Orders:	*http://pragprog.com/catalog*
Customer Service:	*support@pragprog.com*
International Rights:	*translations@pragprog.com*
Academic Use:	*academic@pragprog.com*
Write for Us:	*http://pragprog.com/write-for-us*
Or Call:	+1 800-699-7764

CPSIA information can be obtained at www.ICGtesting.com
Printed in the USA
LVOW02s1945101013

356368LV00008B/13/P